CONVENIENT
CRITICISM

CONVENIENT CRITICISM

LOCAL MEDIA AND GOVERNANCE IN URBAN CHINA

Dan Chen

SUNY PRESS

Published by State University of New York Press, Albany

For information, contact State University of New York Press, Albany, NY
www.sunypress.edu

Library of Congress Cataloging-in-Publication Data

Name: Chen, Dan, author
Title: Convenient criticism : local media and governance in urban China / Dan Chen, author.
Description: Albany : State University of New York Press, [2020] | Includes bibliographical references and index.
Identifiers: ISBN 9781438480299 (hardcover) | ISBN 9781438480305 (pbk.) | ISBN 9781438480312 (ebook)
Further information is available at the Library of Congress.

10 9 8 7 6 5 4 3 2 1

To Those Who Persist

Contents

Illustrations

Tables

Figures

Acknowledgments

This book developed over many years from an instinctual curiosity to an intellectual product. I owe much gratitude to the many people without whom this pursuit would not have come to fruition. My interest in media politics began during my high school years of admiring the critical reporting by the most popular local news program at the time, *Zero Distance in Nanjing*, which woke my civic mind and political awareness. My curiosity for politics grew thanks to the structured and supportive environment provided by my parents. We lived through an era of profound transformation, allowing me to witness communal generosity, struggle, and reinvention, exemplified by my hometown community of working people. Their lived experiences shaped my initial instinct for intellectual pursuit and lent significance to my research. For this, I am deeply indebted to my parents and my community. Along the same line, I am also indebted to all the people who generously shared their good faith, effort, and time, which make up the foundations of this research. Their names have to be withheld, but this book honors their solicitude.

In building an academic career, I was fortunate to have generous mentors who lightened my path. More often than I realize, their scholarly passion and style influence my own. For this, I owe deep gratitude to John James Kennedy at the University of Kansas, Barrett L. McCormick at Marquette University, and other professors at these two institutions who provided guidance that paved the way for this book to take shape.

Extensive fieldwork depends on financial and institutional support. I am grateful for the generous funding provided by the Department of Political Science and the Center for Global and International Studies, University of Kansas; the China and Inner Asia Council of the Association for Asian Studies; the China Studies Centre, University of Sydney;

Elizabethtown College; and the University of Richmond for completing this book.

Being a China scholar affords me access to a community of invigorating and generous colleagues. I owe gratitude to Greg Distelhorst, Oya Dursun-Özkanca, Rongbin Han, Haifeng Huang, April Kelly-Woessner, Kyle C. Kopko, Olivier Krischer, Orion Lewis, Wenbin Li, Peter Lorentzen, Andrew MacDonald, E. Fletcher McClellan, Joyce Nip, Ying Qian, Maria Repnikova, Yaojiang Shi, Le Tan, Wenfang Tang, Jessica Teets, Luigi Tomba, Yuhua Wang, Jiebing Wu, Jinghong Zhang, Yingnan Zhou, participants at the International Studies Association 2018 conference, and participants at my talks given at the China Studies Centre, University of Sydney, in August 2019, and the School of Public Administration, Zhejiang University, in September 2019. They offered ideas, questions, suggestions, and, most importantly, spiritual support for completing this book.

This book would not be possible without my editor at SUNY Press, Michael Rinella, the readers, and the production team. I am grateful for their belief in the value of this book. The revision process benefited much from my engaged colleagues at the University of Richmond, whose camaraderie is deeply appreciated.

Finally, this book would not have reached its current form without the intellectual challenge, inspiration, and support from my life partner, Michael Rabin. I am grateful that my intellectual journey has been shaped by his passion and wisdom.

Introduction

On February 23, 2017, a popular news program airing on the Jiangsu provincial television city channel reported a news story about a misbehaving local official. According to an anonymous hotline call to the program in November 2016, a civil affairs department director surnamed Xu was repeatedly absent from his work at a street committee in the Gulou District of Nanjing, the capital city of Jiangsu. Reporters then started a three-month investigation. They disguised as ordinary citizens in need of government help on pension funds, an issue of Director Xu's responsibility. The excuse from Xu's coworkers was always, "Director Xu is in a meeting." Through meticulous investigation, reporters discovered that Xu had been playing mahjong at a nearby mahjong room extensively during work hours. In the next day's broadcast, on February 24, the news program aired a follow-up report, stating that the street committee had put Xu on an immediate leave and that the discipline commission of the Gulou District had placed him under investigation, as a result of this program's report disclosing Xu's misconduct. That same day, the street committee convened an organization-wide meeting to educate its officials about their duties and disciplines. Why would the Chinese authoritarian state, equipped with a sophisticated media control system, allow such critical reporting to correct official misconduct?

Over four decades of reform and opening, the media landscape in China has been transformed. Media criticism has become a steady component in the political life of government officials and ordinary citizens, despite the notoriously elaborate and effective censorship system. While the informational, supervisory, and propagandist values of media criticism for the party-state have been discussed in the literature, what remains puzzling is the prevalent yet varied levels of *local* critical reporting and the subsequent corrective action, as shown in the above example. Why would local officials correct misbehavior instead of lobbying their superiors to censor critical reports? What convenience does the supposedly inconvenient media criticism provide, and to whom? Finally, how has the media's role in politics evolved, and what does it mean for governance at the local level?

This book addresses these questions by focusing on local television news programs in China. Having emerged in the late 1990s, these programs pioneered in placing an unprecedented, though comparatively limited, amount of journalistic focus on inept policy implementation and inadequate public service provision at village, township, county, and district levels. Media scholars and practitioners refer to this type of television news as "livelihood news"[1] (民生新闻), indicating the remarkable departure in both style and content from traditional television news programs,[2] which inhabit a formal language to reinforce carefully rehearsed narratives on political ideology, government policy, and high-level leaders. Livelihood news programs, instead, use a colloquial language to enliven ordinary citizens' concerns and grievances. The pioneering livelihood news programs broadcast in Jiangsu, Anhui, Sichuan,[3] and elsewhere were an overnight success, during a time when a series of media reforms substantially elevated the importance of profitability for media outlets. Their enviable ratings propelled other television stations to follow suit. Now, every provincial and municipal television station in China has at least one livelihood news program, operating parallel to their traditional news programs. Having become a prominent voice among the few local media outlets dedicated to covering local affairs, livelihood news programs have grown to shape local narratives on politics and governance and to participate in the local governance process by correcting misbehaving street-level bureaucrats. Their sustained popularity and influence in the past two decades present the unique opportunity to further understand the role of local media in Chinese politics and governance.

Reassessing Media Criticism under Authoritarian Rule

In the literature on media politics in China, research into the opaque, fluid, yet exacting rules of media control captures important dynamics in the state-media relationship (Brady 2008; Han 2018; Hassid 2015; Lee 2000; King, Pan, and Roberts 2013, 2014, 2017; Repnikova 2017a;

Roberts 2018; Shirk 2011; Stockmann 2013; Tong 2011; Y. Zhao 1998, 2008; Zhou 2000). While our understanding of censorship and other suppressive measures against journalism is greatly extended, the prevalent existence of media criticism demands a different perspective to unravel how critical reporting, the common object of censorship, features in the authoritarian rule.

Existing studies that examine media criticism, defined as journalistic reports critical of government agencies, policies, or officials, primarily investigate the nationally known newspapers, such as *Southern Weekend*, *Dahe Daily*, and *Southern Metropolis Daily*, through which to illustrate the intricate and volatile dynamics of control, resistance, and maneuver between critical journalists and their censors. This type of shackled watchdog journalism has nonetheless led to consequential policy changes. Prominent examples include reports on the 2003 SARS epidemic that pressured government officials into action and reports on the death of Sun Zhigang in police custody in 2003 that led to the national reform of the extrajudicial detention system. The peak of investigative journalism in the mid-aughts was unprecedented in the seven-decade history of the People's Republic. However, if high impact characterizes investigative journalism during its golden years, then high volatility is its aftermath. The rapidly shrinking space for investigative reporting afterwards has led to a large-scale exodus of critical journalists, damaging the field of investigative journalism.[4] Furthermore, the dynamics of high impact and high volatility do not capture this other dimension in the state-media relationship that enables low-impact but sustainable critical reporting.

Expanding scholarly attention from the national level to local levels[5] and from print media to television[6]—the medium with the highest penetration rate[7] and a high level of credibility[8] in China—this book examines critical reports by local television livelihood news programs and reveals two fundamentally different reporting models, which I refer to as *organic criticism* and *orchestrated criticism*.

Organic criticism stems from a regular journalistic news production process where news leads are sourced from citizens, beat reporters, and others within the state-defined reporting boundaries. Orchestrated criticism, in contrast, is directed by local leaders who assign critical topics to journalists, directly or indirectly, so that the local media can help supervise the subordinate bureaucrats and advance the governance agendas. It is important to note that leader orchestration does not mean that produced critical reports are fake or fabricated; they are real news reports, though their topics are determined by local leaders. Essentially, local leaders participate in the news production process and to a certain degree play the role of program producer, influencing the selection of news topics.

While organic criticism is produced through a bottom-up channel, orchestrated criticism is produced in a top-down fashion. Despite the key differences in their news source and political nature, the two types of critical reporting are often mixed in the broadcast, sharing similar topics and often indistinguishable from the audience's perspective. Both feature citizen grievances and governance problems arising from rapid urbanization, and both follow the narrative that assigns blame to the negligence or incompetence of street-level bureaucrats. For example, air pollution, illegal construction, and food safety issues due to lackadaisical governmental oversight at the grassroots level are common topics in television livelihood news; street-level bureaucrats, who are responsible for the final stage of policy implementation, are the unfailing target of blame. The more serious critical reports expose petty corruption or negligence of duty by local officials, such as the news story about Director Xu. After the initial broadcast, both types of critical reports may lead to follow-up reports that highlight successful resolutions due to correction of misbehavior, ending a critical report with a positive outcome. Operationally, organic and orchestrated criticism can be differentiated through immersive fieldwork that enables investigation of the source and nature of media criticism, discussed further in the following chapters.

Given their topics and reporting narrative, television critical reports are not as impactful as the investigative reports published by influential newspapers that led to national policy changes; instead, television critical reports mostly address individual grievances and criticize street-level bureaucrats. With television being the most strictly controlled form of media in China (Shirk 2011, 11), television journalists are unable to liberally examine the policymaking process or to ably analyze governance problems. However, the seemingly low-impact outcome is nonetheless significant at the grassroots level, shown by the media's emerging role in facilitating public service provision and redressing citizen grievances (D. Chen 2017a). More important, the modest scope allows this type of low-impact critical reporting to be sustainable, avoiding the consequence of high volatility that typically follows high impact. Chapter 1 elaborates on how these two types of media criticism are produced and analyzes their connections and distinctions.

Existing Explanations of Media Criticism

So why is local television critical reporting allowed and what purpose does it serve? Scholars investigating media criticism in China argue that it provides distinctive values to the authoritarian regime—media criticism collects information on emerging problems and offers consultation for government officials (Huang, Boranbay-Akan, and Huang 2019; Repnikova 2017a; Shirk 2011, 5; Y. Zhao 2004, 181); it supervises local officials and holds them accountable for misconduct (Chan 2002; Cheong and Gong 2010; Lorentzen 2014; Shirk 2011, 5; Zhao and Sun 2007; Zhou and Cai 2020); it diverts citizen blame from the central leadership to the local governments (D. Chen 2017c; Cai 2008; Cai 2015, ch. 6; Yang et al. 2014). Together, these arguments point to the regime's need for information, bureaucratic control, and public opinion manipulation.

On the other hand, excessive media criticism poses a challenge to the authoritarian rule. Susan Shirk (2011, 17) points out that critical reporting is riskier than relying on confidential internal reporting within the bureaucracy to tackle the problem of local noncompliance. Once a problem is reported by the media, the stakes in resolving that problem become higher, because a lack of resolution would likely instigate a public fallout. Peter Lorentzen (2014) notes that media criticism can be effective at supervising local officials only after striking a delicate balance between media control and freedom. These arguments highlight the importance of addressing the limits of media criticism, in addition to understanding the utilities it provides to the authoritarian rule. Why are certain critical reports acceptable but not others? This research gap necessitates unpacking media criticism and studying the differences within. For example, Li Shao's (2018) recent research sheds light on the different types of criticism by finding that media censorship tends to tolerate criticism of government performance, especially in public goods provision, while strictly prohibiting criticism that challenges the political rule. Analyzing not only the content but also the source and impact of media criticism, this book differentiates television critical reports and explicates their utilities and limits by situating them in the process of local governance.

More important, the existing explanations, though helpful for understanding the utilities of media criticism, address this question primarily from the central leadership's perspective, thus being unable to offer a sufficient account of media criticism at the local level. In China's decentralized media control system, traditional media outlets, including newspapers and television stations, are owned and *directly* managed by local governments at matching administrative levels. For example, municipal television stations are directly managed by municipal governments in their day-to-day news production, though higher-level governments and the broader political context certainly also exert influence. Therefore, local governments are empowered to censor critical reports about themselves (Tong 2010), which eludes the existing explanations that focus on the interests of the central leadership and are largely detached from local politics. If media criticism helps the regime supervise local officials, then these local officials ought to have strong incentives to block critical reports by the local media that implicate themselves.

An illustrative example of the local power in media control is the central leadership's response to a journalistic practice called cross-regional supervision (异地监督), which was popular in the late 1990s and the early part of the following decade. Journalists developed this practice to dodge local media control by covering wrongdoing by local governments in neighboring localities (Liebman 2011). As this strategy became more popular, local leaders grew wary of cross-regional supervision. They successfully petitioned the central leadership to ban this practice in 2005 and closed this loophole in local media control (Shirk 2011; Tong and Sparks 2009; Y. Zhao 2008). Given this logic, why would local leaders allow media criticism in their own jurisdiction, where they have the power to control critical reporting?

Furthermore, the existing explanations have yet to offer a systematic account for the *variations* in topic, frequency, and rectifying consequences of critical reporting, which again requires a decentralized view on government authority. To be sure, recent studies in the area of online censorship have made great strides in identifying the logic behind controlling online critical information (e.g., Gueorguiev and Malesky 2019; King, Pan, and Roberts 2013, 2014, 2017). For example, some recent studies find that the variation in the rectifying effect of online media exposure of official misconduct can be attributed to the publicity of such exposure and whether the nature of the wrongdoing is a priority concern for the government (Cheong and Gong 2010; Huang, Boranbay-Akan, and Huang 2019; Zhou and Cai 2020). While these findings are illuminating, the variables of publicity and alignment with government priorities remain somewhat inexact. Furthermore, the underlying perspective still treats the government as a unitary entity without adequately considering the diverging interests of local leaders, which may be a natural result of the more centralized Internet censorship authority. To understand local critical reporting in television news, there needs to be a systematic examination of its regional and temporal variations from the local leadership's perspective.

Convenient Criticism

To gain a better understanding of media criticism at the local level, this book first revisits some established assumptions in the conceptual framework of authoritarian media control. Specifically, when media control is eased or lifted, the media can facilitate an open public discourse that would pave the way for political liberalization, playing an important role in regime transition (Diamond and Plattner 2012; Howard 2010; Lawson 2002; Randall 1993; Skidmore 1993); when media control persists or evolves with more sophistication, the media can consolidate authoritarian rule by effectively manipulating public opinion through censorship and propaganda (Brady 2008; Stockmann 2013; Y. Zhao 1998; White, Oates, and McAllister 2005). These assumptions on how media and politics interact, despite their theoretical utilities, do not fully capture the dynamics of limited yet sustainable local critical reporting in China. The derived view on journalists also does not fully describe the mission of Chinese television journalists. This book takes this framework as a starting point, challenging and building on it in three ways.

First, conceptualizing media control primarily as suppression of journalism obscures how the media can be used to advance authoritarian rule in other important ways. The suppression of journalism is undoubtedly important—its theoretical and empirical implications have generated seminal works in this field that articulate the increasingly sophisticated tactics of state control over the media and the consequence of public opinion manipulation and authoritarian consolidation (Hassid 2008; Stern and O'Brien 2012; Stockmann and Gallagher 2011; Stockmann 2013). However, the logic of media control as suppression, persuasive as it is, suggests that criticism is inconvenient to authoritarian rule, thus unable to fully explain why critical reporting on citizen grievances and other governance problems is allowed and sometimes even encouraged by local leaders. As a recent commentary points out, the centrality of the "repression-resistance" axis has led to "authoritarian determinism," rendering reductionism in the study of political communication in China

(Guan 2019). This research gap necessitates careful consideration of the political and governance context in which media criticism emerges.

Recent studies have started to move away from this binary perspective. Maria Repnikova (2017a) insightfully argues that the central state and critical journalists formed a fluid collaborative relationship based on their shared goal to improve governance. To further understand the political significance of the less critical, more pragmatic television journalists at the local level, this book reconceptualizes media control as a broad mechanism of political domination that limits journalism to any form of reporting deemed by the political authority as convenient, which can be either adulatory or critical. In this conceptualization, media control is embodied as not only suppressing media criticism but also expropriating it. As this book demonstrates, in the complex and dynamic realities of politicking, suppression is not the only way that media control is exercised. Strategically encouraging media criticism can increase local leaders' capacity of bureaucratic control and their advantage in career advancement. This is especially true for leaders who are savvy about leveraging informal politics outside of formal institutional powers, such as media criticism, to mitigate the principal-agent problem in the local bureaucracy where street-level implementation is lax or absent. Therefore, critical reporting in this context should be understood as a result of political control, rather than a lack of it.

When local leaders allow organic criticism, journalists select news leads about individual grievances or governance problems from citizen hotline calls and social media posts, report on these problems in the frame of bureaucratic ineptitude, and sometimes correct misbehaving street-level bureaucrats. Through this mechanism, local leaders can shift the burden of supervising street-level bureaucrats to local media outlets, rather than overseeing their subordinates in a centralized, active, and direct way. This logic is similar, though on a more limited scale, to Mathew McCubbins and Thomas Schwartz's (1984) "fire-alarm oversight" model that describes a decentralized way of legislative oversight over the executive branch in democratic politics, where legislatures rely on interest groups, the media, or constituents to "sound an alarm" and report problems in policy design or implementation.

When local leaders pursue orchestrated criticism, they direct local media outlets to cover specific governance issues, which are typically priorities on their governance agendas. Journalists producing these reports are empowered, with limited supervisory authority, to help local leaders achieve their governance goals. Orchestrated criticism follows a logic similar to "going public," a media strategy used by some presidents and members of Congress in the United States to overcome institutional weakness in achieving policy agendas (Cook 2005; Kernell 2007; Vinson 2017). Chinese local leaders' orchestration of critical reporting also attempts to achieve political and policy objectives by compensating for the institutional insufficiency in reducing laxity or noncompliance when street-level bureaucrats carry out administrative orders or implement policies. By resorting to critical reporting, local leaders employ the media power of publicity to stage veiled public humiliation of misbehaving street-level bureaucrats, who then immediately correct their misbehavior due to public disgrace and the worry over adverse career impact. However, unlike their American counterparts who may publicly criticize fellow politicians, local leaders in China orchestrate critical reporting behind the scene to disparage their subordinates. In this way, the media are leveraged to influence not only the public by shaping their opinions, but also the governing elites by inducing compliant behavior (Kedrowski 1996; Malecha and Reagan 2012; Vinson 2017).

Taken together, in allowing organic or orchestrated criticism, local leaders' career interests empower local media to participate in the governance process that is often plagued by laxity, noncompliance, and maneuver. For local leaders, critical reporting can enhance their bureaucratic control over subordinates, which then likely improves governance outcomes and their career prospects. Furthermore, this strategic use of media criticism advances the theory of media effects by expanding the media's role in authoritarian politics from manipulating public opinion to correcting elite behavior.[9]

Second, this book challenges the implication of a deeply antagonistic relationship between the authoritarian state and the media, emanating from conceptualizing media control exclusively as suppression. This view obfuscates the dimension of collaboration or concord between the state and the media. Recent works by Maria Repnikova (2017a) and Rongbin Han (2018), for example, respectively show that the central state and critical journalists actually share the common goal of governance improvement, and that the pro-government voices online, which often turn out to be more potent than the dissenting ones, command the cyberspace. The demanding, persistent political control over journalists and other media content providers does not necessarily diminish the mutually beneficial aspects of the state-media relationship.

It has been well established that the small elite segment of print journalists[10] who courageously resist state control disproportionally encounter political suppression. But typical Chinese journalists, including local television journalists, seek to build lasting bridges between the government and citizens. These journalists, referred to in this book as *pragmatic journalists*, mostly work for local print, broadcast, and radio outlets, and they reliably follow orders from their superiors within both their news organizations and the local governments.[11] Yet, they are not merely a mouthpiece for the regime. The commercial pressure to compete for viewers and the journalistic identity of "helping ordinary folks solve problems"—a commonly used livelihood news slogan with a populist flavor—drive pragmatic journalists to engage in limited critical reporting. Still, they are different from critical print journalists in that their primary goal for critical reporting is not to engender impactful policy change, but to produce immediate, incremental governance improvements that correct misbehaving street-level bureaucrats and redress citizen grievances. This journalistic intention complements local leaders' career interests that are typically pegged to competitive governance records.

In producing organic criticism, journalists continually learn and abide by the changing boundaries of critical reporting at the local level. With local leadership change occurring every few years, journalists steer their critical reporting along the shifting political currents, the signs of which are delivered through both formal ways of administrative orders and directives and informal ways of conversations, negotiations, and trial and error. When local leaders are perceived to appreciate media criticism, journalists employ several tried tactics to push for critical reporting, discussed in detail in chapter 2. For example, journalists can ride the wave of local governance initiatives or campaigns by focusing their critical reporting on relevant governance problems. On these topics, journalists have more space to criticize street-level bureaucrats for lackluster oversight. Journalists can also use the rhetorical frame of "rightful resistance" (O'Brien and Li 2006) by invoking relevant laws, regulations, policies, and speeches to justify their critical reporting. These reports, however, are typically followed up in subsequent news broadcasts highlighting the resultant governance improvement, ending a negative news story with a positive outcome that underscores government responsiveness.

In producing orchestrated criticism, journalists are empowered to supervise specific government bureaus and their bureaucrats responsible for policy implementation. Local leaders determine the topics and boundaries of criticism, sparing journalists the effort to negotiate for critical reporting. Here, the converging interests on governance improvement between local leaders and television journalists animate a concerted, mutually beneficial relationship in the pursuit of media criticism. If seen instead through a binary view of journalists as resistant or acquiescent, implied by conceptualizing media control only as suppression, television journalists' intricate role in local governance would be lost. This role allows pragmatic journalists' work, such as television livelihood news programs, to exert persistent, though incremental, impact on local governance, unlike the isolated breakthroughs of influential critical reporting that rarely repeat themselves.[12]

Third, this book dissects the changing boundaries of critical reporting, contributing new findings on the factors that regulate the patterns of critical reporting. It finds that local leaders' career interests and individual characteristics such as age and leadership style are among the powerful explanations. Media factors such as market competition and contextual factors such as national and local political events and local economic development also account for the variations. Given these variables, media criticism is convenient only when motivated political leaders know how to use it, suggesting a complex media strategy consisting of not only bolstering propaganda but also expropriating criticism. When local leaders perceive worthy benefits in recruiting the media as a loyal and eager partner to address governance problems, the resulting critical reporting aligns and advances the interests of three key actors in the local governance process—local leaders, local media, and aggrieved citizens—by criticizing and correcting street-level bureaucrats.

On a deeper level, convenient criticism captures the evolving ways in which the media are perceived and employed by the party-state. As early as 1902, Vladimir Lenin argued in *What Is to Be Done?* that "a newspaper is not only a collective propagandist and collective agitator but also a collective organizer." (Lenin 1963–70, 5:10–11) This media conception was put into practice when he declared in 1917 that "all bourgeois newspapers be shut down" in the former Soviet Union (Fu 1996, 144). Similarly, the Chinese party-state grasped control and monopolized institutions such as education, newspapers, magazines, television and radio broadcasting, and social science research, all of which "were regarded as tools of political indoctrination under the jurisdiction of the party's Department of Propaganda." (Fu 1996, 144) Therefore, journalism in its orthodox sense barely existed at the beginning of the People's Republic.

Persuasion, indoctrination, and mobilization were the main purposes of the media. Then, media reforms started in the 1980s as part of the fundamental policy shift of reform and opening; it consisted of deregulation, commercialization, and partial privatization (Stockmann 2013). As a result, the space for journalism has grown, not least indicated by the peak of investigative journalism in the mid-aughts, as discussed earlier. More significantly, the power of media criticism made savvy politicians realize that the political potential of the media expands beyond public opinion manipulation; the media can also enhance bureaucratic control over subordinates. As local leaders discover the effectiveness of media criticism at eliciting swift responses and actions to achieve governance goals, journalists are empowered within a limited scope to criticize and correct low-level government officials. The increasingly prevalent use of media criticism for intraparty purposes shows how far the state-media relationship has evolved since Lenin's conception of the communist media.

Media Capture at the Local Level

The theory of convenient criticism elucidates media supervision of a different kind; instead of the media independently supervising the state, as implied in the notion of the fourth estate and other idealized views of the media as an agent that speaks truth to power, the theory of convenient criticism shows that the state can capture media criticism, through either passively allowing it or proactively pursuing it. The goal is not to limit state power, but to improve governance so that relevant political interests are advanced. This mechanism of media politics sheds light on the innovative force in governance and politicking, released in the complex and elastic party-state system.

 The theory of convenient criticism also illuminates the locus of media capture and its intricacies. Local leaders' capture of the local media is not absolute, and they have to balance competing priorities. In China, within each municipal and provincial party-state, the propaganda department directly oversees the work of the local television station. The local propaganda department is under the direction of the local party secretary, who is in charge of all affairs in the local jurisdiction; simultaneously, it is also under the control of the central leadership via the propaganda system (宣传系统) that links the Central Propaganda Department to its local branches. As elaborated in chapter 2, such a line/piece (条/块)—

horizontal and vertical—crosshatching administrative structure allows local discretion while ensuring central control. An important implication is that local party secretaries may have to compete with directions from higher-level leadership delivered through the propaganda system while leveraging media criticism to increase their bureaucratic capacity and advance their governance agenda, given that the bandwidth of local media reporting is finite. Of course, local party secretaries are keenly aware of the importance of following through propaganda tasks from the higher level, especially during sensitive political times such as leadership transition, Party Congress meetings, and People's Congress meetings. Therefore, how to balance the locus of media capture so that it serves local leaders' career interests while accomplishing propaganda tasks from the higher-up is a telltale sign of local leaders' ability to maneuver media capture to their advantage. Furthermore, to achieve the delicate balance between critical reporting and its potential backlash of political instability adds another layer of complexity. The strategic use of media criticism is an outcome of as much political ambition as astuteness.

Indeed, because the state already captures the media through effective media control, media capture at the local level is more about who within the party-state dominates that capture.[13] In the Maoist era when the media were merely a mouthpiece of the party-state, media capture was more uniform across the country; the content of media reporting was highly synchronized. In the reform era, policy changes have led to rapid media commercialization, which, inadvertently, has showcased the vast possibilities brought about by the media power of publicity. It can facilitate accomplishment of governance goals, for example. As a result, the media, as they are perceived and utilized by the party-state, have diversified from an ideological weapon into a governance instrument. Local party secretaries who are ambitious and savvy enough to realize how the media can greatly aid their political careers have greater incentives to dominate the capture of the local media. By allowing or even encouraging limited critical reporting, local party secretaries control the narrative of media criticism and discipline misbehaving subordinates, the discursive and practical implications of which reinforce the image of a local government that is, though imperfect, responsive and capable. As discussed in detail in the following chapters, some local party secretaries' heavy involvement in the production of critical television reports clearly indicates a media capture that is intended not only to influence political discourse and public opinion, but also to improve governance and advance their political careers.

This book builds on the existing literature on media criticism. By focusing primarily on the central-level media outlets, existing studies have found that the central party-state allows media criticism to supervise and discipline local governments for compliance, as discussed earlier. The theory of convenient criticism lowers the level of inquiry from the central level to the local level, yet the findings here are more than just applying a similar mechanism of limited media supervision to the local level. Local party secretaries, the main determiner of local critical reporting, are driven by a set of career interests that are different from those of the central leadership. As discussed in chapter 3, even among local party secretaries, those at the provincial level have distinct career interests from those at the municipal level, which in part explains the varying patterns of critical reporting. Furthermore, even within a leader's tenure cycle, the incentive to pursue critical reporting changes; it is stronger at the beginning of the tenure cycle and it fades as one prepares for the next promotion. Although the mechanism of using the media to induce misbehavior correction is similar, the different immediate goals mean that the frequency, intensity, and substantive topics of critical reporting vary across region and time, discussed in detail in chapter 5.

Contributions to Understanding Authoritarianism

By situating local critical reporting in the local governance process, this book reveals the evolving roles that local leaders, local media, and citizens play in their respective pursuits of career advancement, profit and impact, and justice and prosperity. These findings have further implications for the study of authoritarianism.

Addressing Citizen Grievances

Addressing citizen grievances is key to maintaining "performance legitimacy" (Nathan 2009), a crucial factor in prolonging the authoritarian rule. Existing studies on authoritarian politics find that citizen grievances can be addressed by limited political openings, or quasi-democratic institutions, such as the formal institutions of elections, parliaments, and the rule of law (Brownlee 2007; Distelhorst 2017; Gallagher 2017; Gandhi 2008; Lust-Okar 2005; Magaloni 2006; Manion 2015; Truex 2016; Yuhua Wang 2014), and the informal measures that tolerate civil society groups (Hildebrandt 2013; Teets 2014; L. Tsai 2007) and local protests (X. Chen 2012; O'Brien and Li 2006). These limited political openings deflate challenges and epitomize authoritarian resilience.

Building on these theoretical insights, the theory of convenient criticism reveals another mechanism through which citizen grievances, typically framed in television reports as individual problems rather than mobilizable issues, can be addressed in an effective and sustainable way. Journalists help citizens articulate their grievances and strategize about acceptable but potent narratives of corrective critical reporting. In orchestrated criticism, citizen grievances in relevant issue areas receive immediate responses due to local leaders' calculated support. In organic criticism, street-level bureaucrats also tend to respond quickly due to fear of public humiliation and adverse career impact.

The channel of corrective critical reporting is similar to the local governments' own feedback systems aiming at absorbing citizen grievances, such as the letters and visits bureau (Dimitrov 2013, 2015; Luehrmann 2003) and the online complaint system (Cai and Zhou 2019; Distelhorst and Hou 2017). However, these governmental feedback systems may be difficult for average citizens to access, and they often fail to effectively respond due to insufficient rule of law (Hu, Wu, and Fei 2018) and distortion of information by the intermediate levels within the local governments (Lorentzen 2017, 478–79; O'Brien and Li 1999: 179; Pan and Chen 2018). Many citizens turned to the media precisely because governmental feedback systems turned out to be futile. Indeed, most petitions filed online or through the letters and visits bureaus received no response (Ling 2014; Chen, Pan, and Xu 2016), and many aggrieved citizens had to use the "troublemaking" tactic to elicit an effective response (X. Chen 2009, 2012). The limitations of the governmental feedback systems can, to a certain degree, be mitigated by media criticism, especially when the issues overlap with local leaders' governance agendas.

Limitations of the State-Society Framework

This book's focus on local media reveals the limitations of the state-society framework in studying authoritarian politics in China. The mutually beneficial relationship between local governments and local media and between local media and aggrieved citizens position pragmatic journalists somewhere in between the state and the society. Pragmatic journalists are different from the traditional civil society, such as nongovernmental organizations (NGOs), religious groups, and civil associations, because they work for media organizations owned and controlled by the state.[14] Meanwhile, after three decades of media reforms that catalyzed the remarkable evolution of journalistic norms and practices, pragmatic journalists' professional identities have aligned with the interests of ordinary citizens, which often contradict local governance outcomes.

Because the local media straddle the state and the society, they have established credibility among both. Citizens trust the local media due to their effectiveness at correcting misbehaving street-level bureaucrats and the observable progress on redressing grievances; local leaders trust the local media as an institution firmly under their control. Television journalists are known to obey political boundaries, different from their elite counterparts at print media outlets who have developed a reputation for muckraking. This quality has turned into an advantage for television journalists when they interact with local officials. Consequently, local television news programs are in a unique position to advance the interests of both the state and the society by disciplining street-level bureaucrats and addressing citizen grievances. This is fundamentally different from the role played by other civil society groups such as NGOs and religious groups that the authoritarian regime distrusts and constrains.

Other recent studies have also challenged the dualistic framework of state and society. As Yuen Yuen Ang (2018, 45–46) insightfully points out, "the presumed dichotomy between the state and society is a false one," and in China "there has always been an intermediate layer of actors between the state and society," such as the educated, landholding elites in ancient China and the civil service today. Local media also occupy an intermediate position where they have access to those in power through their official status while being rooted in local communities as a result of their commercial orientation and journalistic motivations. In his recent article, Philip C. C. Huang (2019) argues that a more important dimension to understanding China's governance system is the long-term interactions *between* state and society, which has given rise to "the third sphere" where much of governance occurs through administrative contracting. This view further explicates the logic of convenient criticism, where critical reporting becomes a governance instrument operated by the media power of publicity, rather than administrative authority or political power, to achieve immediate governance outcomes. In other words, critical reporting is "contracted" to improve governance. The news production process, as shown in this book, consists of frequent interactions among citizens, journalists, and local officials, bridging and integrating the traditionally conceptualized state and society.

Informal and Innovative Local Politics

Local leaders' innovative and strategic use of media criticism to increase bureaucratic control and improve governance reflects the importance of informal politics in mitigating the inadequacy of formal institutional powers (D. Chen 2016; Heilmann and Perry 2011). Leveraging the media power of publicity to discourage noncompliant behavior at the lower levels of bureaucracy is an unscripted strategy that accomplishes local leaders' political objectives. This innovative energy stems from the complex and elastic political system that rewards achieving desirable governance goals. Competence, including that achieved through innovative means, is often seen as an effective path toward career advancement.

The innovative energy in authoritarian media politics finds resonance in democracies. Bartholomew Sparrow (1999), Michael Schudson (2002), and Timothy Cook (2006) argue that the news media should be seen as a political institution exerting influence in the political process and affecting policy. More recently, Danielle Vinson (2017) finds that elected officials in the United States often "go public," also an unscripted strategy, to achieve their policy objectives when faced with gridlock or legislative opposition within formal political institutions. Beyond the United States, the edited volume *How Political Actors Use the Media* highlights the importance of studying not only how the media affect public opinion but also how political actors use the media in innovative ways to advance their goals in Western democracies (Van Aelst and Walgrave 2017). In a similar vein, local leaders in China use media criticism when their formal power in the bureaucratic structure is insufficient to fully discipline subordinates. Importantly, this use of media criticism is not institutionalized, accentuating the role of informal politics in understanding the fragmented yet responsive governing apparatus in China (Junyan Jiang 2018; K. Tsai 2006; L. Tsai 2007).

Indeed, the informality that characterizes Chinese politics has been studied extensively in the literature. Between the party-state and the population, Yao Li's (2018) recent study on the rising protests finds that informal rules structure the state-protester interactions and mitigate conflict, demonstrating regime resilience. Within the party-state, the notions of underinstitutionalization, flexibility, pragmatism, experimentation, and "guerrilla policy style" (Gallagher 2017; Heilmann and Perry 2011) all indicate "how flexibility and discretionary power are built into the governing institutions of autocracies" (Gallagher 2017, 47). In fact, informal politics in China can be traced back to the revolutionary era and the initial years of the People's Republic. As Sebastian Heilmann and Elizabeth Perry (2011, 3–4) eloquently put it,

> China's governance techniques are marked by a signature Maoist stamp that conceives of policy-making as a process of ceaseless change, tension management, continual experimentation, and ad-hoc adjustment. Such techniques reflect a mindset and method that contrast sharply with the more bureaucratic and legalistic approaches to policy-making that obtain in many other major polities.

The strategy of convenient criticism employed by political leaders at provincial and municipal levels adds additional tactics of informal politics into the repertoire of governing tools. The informality means that media criticism correcting street-level bureaucrats and improving governance is often ad hoc, subject to change based on a number of factors related to individual leaders and the governance context. As the following chapters show, such informality can turn into an advantage for ambitious and astute local leaders, but it can also stifle media criticism when favorable conditions are absent. Such uncertainty grows out of the complex maneuvers in local politics.

Fluid Yet Clear Media Control

Informal politics also accounts for media control at the local level. Although we already know much about the logic and tactics of media control, more needs to be learned about the actual practice of how media control is carried out on a daily basis and at the local level. As Vivienne Shue and Patricia Thornton (2017, 2) observed, scholars "have tended to concentrate too narrowly on governing *institutions* as opposed to governing *practices*" (italics in original). To be sure, existing studies have already highlighted the importance of fluidity, improvisation, and ambiguity in understanding Chinese state control over the media (e.g., Hassid 2008; Repnikova 2017a; Stern and Hassid 2012; Stern and O'Brien 2012), yet these useful characterizations have yet to offer a more exact depiction of the patterns of media control at the local level.

Observing the day-to-day news production process at provincial and municipal television stations, this book traces the mechanism of media control to local discretion, necessitated by the crosshatching bureaucratic structure and fragmented authoritarianism. Local discretion allows local leaders' career incentives, their leadership styles, and the governing context to shape their preferences regarding the boundaries of critical reporting, which shifts as the governance context changes and as the local leadership alters every few years. Meanwhile, pragmatic journalists diligently and continually learn the changing media preferences and adjust their reporting accordingly. Their competent understanding through both informal signals and formal rules from the incumbent local leadership enables them to quickly identify the shifting boundaries of critical reporting and stay in line. As a result, the varying levels of media criticism indicate effectiveness, rather than precariousness, of local media control. It is pragmatic journalists' studious and proficient understanding of the changing boundaries of critical reporting at the local level, rather than the lack of it (Hassid 2008; Stern and Hassid 2012; Stern and O'Brien 2012), that contributes to the effectiveness of media control and, by extension, the longevity of their model of livelihood news. Therefore, situating critical reporting into local governance allows this book to attribute the animating forces behind local media control to local leadership and the governance context.

Redefining Media Politics under Authoritarianism

Pragmatic journalists make up the majority of news workers in China. Unlike critical journalists working for nationally known newspapers and magazines, pragmatic journalists pursue a professional goal of incremental governance improvement and immediate grievance redress, which affords them a strong sense of social reputation and positive impact. In this process, however, while their journalism is invigorated by commercial and professional forces, it is ultimately defined by the party-state. In other words, their journalistic agency has been channeled by astute politicians, kept alive but confined to defined boundaries, to advance relevant political interests. Critical reporting allowed or orchestrated by local leaders and its rectifying effect make television journalists the recognizable hero in improving local governance, shown by the popularity of their programs and the appreciation spontaneously offered by citizens who received their help. The satisfaction of professional aspirations then propels television journalists to identify with this unique style of corrective critical reporting, reinforcing their pursuit of advocacy work for aggrieved citizens that is clearly demarcated and officially endorsed. As a result, selective and limited critical reporting that disciplines street-level bureaucrats and redresses citizen grievances becomes a professional ideal for pragmatic journalists. Because this model of news production has earned great appreciation from the general public, pragmatic journalists internalize it as a gold standard for impactful journalism. In the long term, the inflated sense of journalistic empowerment perpetuated in this model of news production enables the party-state to capture media criticism and reinforce its dominance.

This adroit manipulation of journalism is echoed in other authoritarian countries. In their recent study on the manipulation of economic news in Russia, Arturas Rozenas and Denis Stukal (2019) find that autocrats manipulate news not just through censorship. On economic affairs, for which citizens have reasonable benchmarks through their incomes, market prices, and other observables, the Russian state television strategically frames economic facts, rather than censoring them, in a way that blames external factors for bad news and attributes good news to domestic politicians. These recent developments in authoritarian media politics reveal that, the crude ways of media control, that is, suppression of journalism through propaganda and censorship, have grown into more sophisticated tactics of media manipulation. Convenient criticism, a form of limited critical reporting utilized by local leaders as a governance instrument in China, contributes to this growing repertoire of media manipulation that aims to mold journalism into an active and sustainable mechanism advancing authoritarian rule. Criticism, conventionally understood as inconvenient to autocrats, is now embraced and expropriated by the more sophisticated authoritarian regimes like China and Russia.

Nonlinear Implications for Authoritarian Durability

The findings in this book reveal new dynamics in the local state-media relationship in China. They do not yet, however, portend boon or doom in the political future of the party-state. Media criticism is a convenient tool only when used as such. When media criticism is used to rein in street-level bureaucrats and to mitigate the inadequacy in local leaders' institutional power, it increases the efficiency and quality of local governance. Additionally, correcting misbehaving government officials on television indicates governmental recognition of legitimate citizen grievances, reinforcing the hegemony of the current political system. As elaborated in the next chapter, iteration of this process reduces the need to resort to alternative channels to realize individual interests, fostering support for the status quo.

While the informality of media criticism can be a source of power, it can also undermine critical reporting. Local leaders have the power to encourage critical reporting, and they can also shut it down. Therefore, convenient criticism can stagnate or even lose its utility when political leaders limit or reject the media channel as a way of absorbing citizen feedback and increasing bureaucratic control.

Furthermore, the convenience of media criticism goes only as far as intended by local leaders; thus, the success and intensity of media-induced governance improvement vary across region and time. Specifically, critical reports that can pass the local political scrutiny typically reflect problems that the local government already has an interest in addressing, not the ones beyond its governance agenda. Therefore, the lack of in-depth reporting on real issues means that governance is improved by way of immediate, short-term results, rather than sustainable, long-term solutions.

Sources and Methods

This book utilizes a mixed-methods approach to illustrate and explain how local leaders use media criticism to improve governance, how journalists negotiate with street-level bureaucrats who they intend to criticize, and how aggrieved citizens find motivated allies in the complex and opaque governance process. The data were collected from three sources. First, I conducted ethnographic observation in two separate years—2013 and 2016—for a total of three months at a municipal television station in Jiangsu. This immersive fieldwork enabled me to trace the process of news production, which is necessary to parse the forces, incentives, and negotiations in the dynamic interactions between journalists and local officials. I use pseudonyms when referring to this program, its producer and journalists, and the party secretary in charge of the municipality.

Second, I supplemented the ethnographic observation with 47 semi-structured interviews of over 80 hours with reporters, editors, and producers at 20 television, print, and online media outlets and with media scholars. Some of the media scholars have had experiences working as mid-level television executives and interacting with local government officials in charge of media affairs. These interviews provide the necessary historical and political context and offer behind-the-scenes revelations that help develop and validate the arguments in this book. The interviews and ethnographic observation are complementary, enabling me to triangulate the evidence. The interviews were conducted intermittently from 2012 to 2018. I revisited eight interviewees to crosscheck my findings as this research project progressed. In 2013, one interviewee graciously granted me access to journalists working at a municipal television station in Jilin to conduct a survey. Though nonrepresentative of pragmatic journalists in China, this survey provides useful portrayals of journalists and their evolving professional identities. Details about ethnographic observation and interviews are provided in appendix A.

Third, I built an original dataset using content analysis and data from governmental documents and media sources. The content analysis coded news reports from five television livelihood news programs at provincial and municipal levels in Jiangsu and Shaanxi from November 2016 to December 2017.[15] This original dataset is analyzed to test the expectations developed from the fieldwork and to draw conclusions on the scope, impact, and variations of media criticism. Importantly, three fieldwork sites where interviews and ethnographic observation were conducted are three of the five livelihood news programs included in the dataset, providing additional information to crosscheck and interpret the quantitative data. Where possible, I also draw on other sources, including government documents, existing research, and news reports, to triangulate the findings. Details about data sources and the coding procedures are provided in appendix B.

As much as the research design tries to include a diverse and somewhat representative group of television livelihood news programs, practical constraints limit the dataset to five programs in two provinces. Though these programs are not representative of all local television livelihood news programs in China, they nonetheless provide reasonable variations on the key variables. More important, the quantitative findings are situated in and interpreted with qualitative findings from in-depth fieldwork at a variety of media outlets. The theoretical mechanism of convenient criticism is demonstrated by the qualitative cases and validated on a larger scale by the quantitative results. The findings in this book shed further light on authoritarian media politics, and the core argument on convenient criticism may provide a promising direction for future research.

Plan of the Book

The five chapters in this book follow an analytical order to present, explain, and illustrate the theory of media criticism. Chapter 1 presents the levels and variations of local critical reporting and outlines the theory by introducing the constitutive pieces of the conveniences afforded by media criticism to various involved actors. Situating media criticism in the local governance process, this chapter argues that critical reporting on bureaucratic ineptitude is convenient, first and foremost, to local leaders by advancing their political careers via increased bureaucratic control and immediate governance improvements; it is also convenient to the local media by advancing their commercial interests and to the journalists by fulfilling their professional aspirations for reputation and impact; finally, it is convenient to citizens by redressing their grievances. Ultimately, the iteration of media criticism correcting misbehaving bureaucrats and redressing citizen grievances reinforces the political hegemony. Besides advancing citizens' material interests, the narrative of media criticism, which blames street-level bureaucrats for governance problems and highlights subsequent governance improvement, strengthens the regime's political dominance by calibrating citizen expectations and maximizing the discursive power of correction.

Chapter 2 delves deeper into the day-to-day business of critical news production, contextualizing and expanding on chapter 1 by exploring how the political, market, and journalistic forces interact and fit together. It starts with a zoomed-out view that overlooks the national media landscape, analyzing how the crosshatching structure of the Chinese bureaucracy shapes media control at the local level. It then addresses how local leaders' political interests and career incentives are translated into the news production process via proficient journalistic learning. Tracing the process of news production at local television stations, two demonstrative in-depth cases are presented to illustrate how advocacy-minded journalists, through learning, adapting, and maneuvering, translate media preferences of local leaders into higher or lower levels of critical reporting.

Chapters 3 and 4 contextualize and elaborate on the bureaucratic, political, and journalistic conveniences, putting together pieces from the recent historical past to shed light on the current institutional structures that incentivize local leaders and local media to pursue critical reporting. Chapter 3 examines the historical legacy, the institutional factors that form local leaders' career interests, and the individual-level characteristic of leadership style that shapes media control at the local level, outlining the political opportunities as well as constraints for critical reporting. These opportunities and constraints, however, do not fully explain the form and content of criticism, which are shaped by the choices of journalists and the influence of the local governance environment. Chapter 4 outlines the origins of the immense commercial pressure faced by local television stations, before zeroing in on the formation of the unique populist-flavored advocacy journalism that absorbs citizen grievances and reflects governance problems arising from rapid urbanization.

After the theory of convenient criticism is presented and explained, chapter 5 illustrates the validity of this theory through a quantitative analysis substantiated by qualitative cases. It systematically tests the expectations regarding variations in media criticism from the previous chapters using an original dataset. The results show differing explanatory powers of factors in three broad categories—local leaders, local media, and the governance environment. Qualitative cases of two livelihood news programs in Xi'an and Nanjing illustrate the differing processes of how critical reports correct misbehavior and improve governance. Finally, the conclusion summarizes the main arguments and theoretical contributions of this book and discusses the limits of convenient criticism and implications for the authoritarian rule.

Chapter 1

Convenient Criticism

Media criticism is driven by complex motivations. Political actors with the power to shape or determine media criticism have diverse incentives and interests that evolve with the changing political context. Existing studies have found that, from the central government's perspective, media criticism can be conducive to the authoritarian rule by revealing and resolving emerging governance problems (Chan 2002; Huang, Boranbay-Akan, and Huang 2019; Nathan 2003; Repnikova 2017a; Shirk 2011; Stockmann 2013; Y. Zhao 1998, 2008; Zhou 2000). However, why local governments allow local media to scrutinize themselves remains a puzzle; furthermore, the variations in the level of critical reporting remains underexplored.[1] Addressing these questions requires a close examination of the state-media dynamics at the local level. Focusing on the incentives of local leaders and pragmatic journalists, the theory of convenient criticism postulates that, when local leaders throw calculated support behind critical reporting, pragmatic journalists are empowered to generate both profit and impact by scrutinizing street-level bureaucrats, addressing citizen grievances, and ultimately improving local governance. This concerted dimension of the local state-media relationship indicates that the supposedly opposite pull of the state and the market (Esarey 2005; Stockmann 2013; Y. Zhao 1998, 2008) has evolved into an array of political, commercial, and journalistic forces with growing common ground. The resulting alliance between local leaders and local media, albeit varied, allows critical reporting to provide benefits to both.

This book is certainly not the first to point out the media's role in governance improvement, but it reveals a specific mechanism in this rather broad role. Existing studies emphasize that media criticism can catalyze policy change (e.g., Qian and Bandurski 2011; Repnikova 2017a, ch. 6; Yang and Calhoun 2007), especially after natural and man-made disasters such as the SARS epidemic in 2003 and the Wenchuan earthquake in 2008. Instead of focusing on policy change, this book argues that media criticism improves governance by increasing bureaucratic control at the local level. Critical reporting in television news can correct misbehaving street-level bureaucrats, thereby redressing citizen grievances and generating immediate governance results. The mechanism of increasing bureaucratic control situates media criticism in the local governance process by addressing intragovernmental dynamics between local leaders and their subordinates; this is different from the mechanism of policy change that systematically addresses problems inflicting relationships between the government and citizens.

The mutually beneficial relationship between local leaders and local media in pursuing selective critical reporting is not an equal one. Local leaders determine the topics and intensity of critical reporting, though they do so by channeling pragmatic journalists' professional aspirations for positive social impact and their need to manage profit pressures. Therefore, journalistic agency survives but morphs into a normative space that acknowledges the rightful authority of the party-state, from which it draws capacity to correct official misbehavior. As a result, the formative role that politics plays in defining journalism leads to a unique form of journalistic agency that seems truncated from the outside but engenders vigor from the inside. Furthermore, because of its focus on grassroots-level citizen grievances rather than large-scale policy changes, media criticism in local television news has created a narrative that recognizes misconduct and injustice but also highlights rectification and improvement. This dexterous blend of discursive appeasement with tangible positive changes reinforces the hegemony of the party-state in the eyes of many aggrieved citizens.

In the following sections, this chapter explains how media criticism is convenient to—in the order of significance—local leaders, local media, and aggrieved citizens. Local leaders' need for immediate, career-advancing governance results nudges local media's critical reporting in the direction of bureaucratic ineptitude, which is then mitigated by the instant, corrective effect stemming from the public nature of media criticism. In this process, local media's commercial interests and journalistic aspirations benefit from their critical reporting that reflects citizens' interests and demands, but they also align with local governance agendas. Bureaucratic ineptitude is what citizens are typically exposed to and therefore is easily blamed as a source for proliferating governance problems. The acknowledgment of official wrongdoing combined with rectification ultimately reinforces government authority. To illustrate how these conclusions are reached, this chapter starts with a definition and differentiation of media criticism.

Defining and Categorizing Media Criticism

In the pre-reform era, media outlets in China were totally controlled by the state; the content of news was highly synchronized with the official mouthpiece. Critical reports on government officials were rare and mostly centered on cases that were already prosecuted or investigated by the political authority. In the reform era, the policy of supervision by public opinion (舆论监督), first officially referenced in 1987 by then president Zhao Ziyang,[2] made critical reporting possible. Since then, this policy was leveraged by journalists to engage in limited but real critical reporting on local officials, especially after the media reforms picked up pace in the 1990s. Under the continuing state control, critical reporting has strict yet fluid limits (Hassid 2008; Stern and Hassid 2012; Stern and O'Brien 2012). It is typically restricted to local officials' wrongdoing, including lackluster policy implementation and insufficient public goods provision; any criticism beyond bureaucratic ineptitude at the local level that implicates principles, ideologies, or the party-state would surely be censored.

Television Critical Reporting versus Print Investigative Journalism

The limited space for critical reporting shaped television journalists' strategy to focus on citizen grievances and grassroots-level officials. The resulting narrow scope of critical reporting in television livelihood news propelled some Chinese media scholars to lament that these reports were too "trivial" (Y. Chen 2013). However, the focus on "trivial" local affairs not only allows individual cases of grievance to be addressed, but also sustains critical reporting. The continued success of television livelihood news programs forms a contrast with the ebb and flow of investigative journalism practiced by elite print news outlets (Svensson 2017; Wang and Sparks 2019), revealing pragmatic journalists' distinctive qualities of keen political sensibility and willing compromise.

Despite sharing a similar interest in critical reporting, there are important distinctions between critical reporting produced by television livelihood news programs and investigative journalism typically practiced by journalists working for print media outlets. Certainly, all critical reporting in China needs to be qualified in that it arises out of a politically controlled media environment; but even within the realm of compromised critical reporting, there are distinctions in scale and depth. Investigative journalism in China, when at its peak in the mid-aughts, has led to policy changes and prosecution of corrupt officials. The Sun Zhigang case in 2003 led to the national reform of the extrajudicial detention system; journalist Luo Changping's exposé published in 2004 on corruption in Hunan led to the arrest and prosecution of a mayor and four other top government officials (Kuhn 2017). Such broad impact was rarely achieved by television critical reporting, which tends to lack in the scope of topics and the depth of investigation. This is in part due to the different journalistic preferences and also the stricter political control over television than other forms of media in China (Shirk 2011, 11).

In the past decade, however, the shrinking space for investigative journalism undermined the scope and depth of investigative reporting, affecting how much truth journalists can dig out and tell (Hernández 2019; Li and Sparks 2018; Tong 2011; Tong and Sparks 2009). As Ke Li and Colin Sparks (2018, 423) insightfully point out, "Even minor changes in the political climate . . . have a disproportionately dampening effect on investigative journalism." The career uncertainty, personal risk, and poor compensation make it difficult to recruit investigative reporters, at a time when a tightening political environment already drove groups of veteran investigative journalists out of this profession. A national survey of investigative journalists shows an extremely low morale and a high propensity to leave the profession (Zhang and Shen 2012).

In the mid-2010s, leading newspapers started to make changes to survive in an increasingly unwelcoming political environment. Based on their fieldwork, Ke Li and Colin Sparks (2018) find that the *Beijing News* adopted the strategy of "maturity," meaning that instead of merely reporting on social problems and other negative issues, their in-depth reporting also emphasizes possible solutions. This, on a certain level, is similar to television journalists' strategy to end a negative news story with a positive outcome when they use follow-up reports to highlight government responsiveness and governance improvement. On the other hand, the selection of topics also reflects the retreat of investigative journalism. The Global Investigative Journalism Network, an international association of journalism organizations, compiled a list of the best investigative stories from China in 2017, which mostly focused on stories of individuals, corporations, and industries, shunning stories that might implicate political authorities (Global Investigative Journalism Network 2018).

Nevertheless, investigative journalism in China, albeit crippled by political control, still exemplifies more investigative depth and a broader scope than a typical television livelihood news report, which lasts anywhere between two to five minutes in broadcast. For television livelihood news programs, their journalistic mission of helping ordinary citizens redress grievances or solve problems naturally leads to a focus on individual stories and an emphasis on immediate results. In-depth investigation into the root cause of a problem or a careful consideration of possible solutions does not fit the fast pace of television reports, which have been tailored to, but also have cultivated a relatively short span of, audience attention. During my fieldwork, journalists and producers from different municipal television stations told me of the same preference for reporting style, that is, "short, plain, and fast" (短、平、快). However, under the surface of seemingly unremarkable, limited critical reporting, diverging paths of critical news production have taken shape at local television stations.

Organic Criticism versus Orchestrated Criticism

Despite the common appearance of criticism, not all critical reports in television livelihood news are intended and produced in the same way. There lacks a conceptual distinction between what this book refers to as *organic criticism* and *orchestrated criticism*. While organic criticism is produced by pragmatic journalists through a regular journalistic process, orchestrated criticism is directed by local leaders, who empower pragmatic journalists to scrutinize incompetent or negligent street-level bureaucrats in priority governance issue areas. In producing orchestrated critical reports, journalists are assigned specific governance topics, rather than relying on sources from journalistic beats, hotline calls, or social media posts. It is important to note again here that orchestrated critical reports are not fabricated reports; they are real news stories, although the topic selection process is captured by the local leader who reproduces his or her governance agendas as journalistic reporting agendas. Therefore, the political motivation of orchestrated criticism is fundamentally different from that of organic criticism; orchestrated criticism represents a concentrated bureaucratic push to generate immediate governance results, while organic criticism reflects citizen grievances more generously.

Several features distinguish these two types of media criticism. First, the sources of news reports are different. Organic criticism relies on leads from citizens and journalists; orchestrated criticism is directed by local leaders, typically through the propaganda department of the local provincial or municipal party committee. Second, the different news sources determine the different review processes that select politically acceptable critical reports. Organic criticism is produced by news professionals. Program producers and channel directors at the television station are the first line of gatekeepers who select news stories and shape critical reporting, based on the honed political sensibilities required by their positions. Orchestrated criticism, on the other hand, is less reliant on television executives to discern the boundaries of critical reporting; local leaders' involvement spares journalists the effort to parse the tea leaves of shifting boundaries.

Third, the narrative of critical reporting varies more in organic criticism and less in orchestrated criticism. Orchestrated criticism typically follows this standard narrative: the initial report exposes a governance problem and pinpoints misbehaving street-level bureaucrats as responsible parties; then, a follow-up report featuring misbehavior correction and governance improvement airs in the next day or so, if not in the same report. Together, this narrative suggests unfailingly fast and effective rectification. Therefore, orchestrated criticism consists of a series of reports that ends a negative news story with a positive outcome, highlighting governance improvement. Organic criticism, in contrast, may or may not result in a positive change; for those reports that do resolve governance issues, the process varies greatly. For example, among the organic critical reports examined in chapter 5, some reports resulted in immediate misbehavior correction, while other reports were followed up three weeks later when a resolution finally took place. Some reports had a second or even a third follow-up report, indicating the nonlinear process of reaching a resolution. These variations suggest different levels of resistance in rectification among local bureaucrats, which is largely contingent upon the political backing of the critical report, the nature of the wrongdoing, and the political connections of the criticized bureaucrats.

Furthermore, organic criticism varies in its topic, investigative depth, and outcome. Some critical reports investigate governance problems outside of the local government's agenda, while others focus on issues that the local government currently concentrates on. Some reports expand from single cases to implicate systematic problems, while others focus on individual grievances. Some reports lead to misbehavior correction and governance improvement, while others result in little change.

In contrast, orchestrated criticism is produced within a defined scope. Local leaders' keenness for fast results empowers journalists to investigate and criticize street-level bureaucrats on predetermined topics, guaranteeing misbehavior correction. The stronger local leaders' support is, the more likely street-level bureaucrats will cooperate and right the wrong instantly. However, this assembly-line style production of critical reports tends to be superficial, with little in-depth discussion of governance issues and little consideration for long-term solutions. Consequently, similar problems reemerge, and the cycle of critical reporting and misbehavior correction repeats itself. Though organic criticism is also limited in these respects, in comparison it has relatively more space to explore long-term considerations. The conditional empowerment in orchestrated criticism is primarily intended to advance local leaders' short-term career interests, which is different from organic criticism that primarily means to help ordinary citizens. As such, orchestrated criticism is seen by some media scholars interviewed in this book as an insincere "political show" (政治秀). Indeed, the "show" element is exactly what local leaders look for. Their strategic use of media criticism is calculated to tackle defined problems, necessitating close control over this process that can only be achieved with a premeditated "show," as opposed to organic criticism, which is embedded with more uncertainty.

Some may argue that organic criticism can also be understood as orchestrated by local leaders through passive permission rather than active direction. This is true to the extent that all news reports in China can be seen as results of state control. Organic criticism and orchestrated criticism are certainly related, because they are produced in the same political environment; however, the common political limitations that they are subject to should not diminish their distinctions, including the news source, the production process, and the outcome of critical reporting. The differentiation between organic and orchestrated criticism is essential to revealing the evolving dynamics in the local state-media relationship.

Television Livelihood News Programs

This book focuses on critical reports produced by television news programs at provincial and municipal levels, where both organic criticism
and orchestrated criticism have flourished. The specific type of television
news examined in this book is referred to as "livelihood news" (民生新
闻). As a result of the media reforms in the 1980s, local television stations, previously fully state-funded, started to generate revenues through
advertising and other means to sustain their operation (Miao 2011). The
intensifying commercial pressure drove many television news producers
to seek innovative ways to report news, departing from the traditional
television news programs where most airtime was devoted to propaganda
highlighting and reiterating leader speeches and party principles. There
was very little focus on local issues concerning ordinary citizens and the
language was hollow and ideological. Against this backdrop, in the 1990s
pioneering television producers started to revolutionize local television
news broadcasts, transforming them into popular programs that cover
local issues of citizen interests using a colloquial language and a story-
telling style. More important, these programs ventured into the realm
of critical reporting. As the example of *Zero Distance in Nanjing* later in
this chapter demonstrates, being able to find a voice in covering real
and deserving issues in local affairs brought life to the previously dull
and feigned television news. It is thus unsurprising that the model of
livelihood news turned out to be an instant success, albeit at a surpris-
ingly massive scale in terms of profit and impact.

The departure from traditional television news also benefited from
the media reforms originating from the broader policy of reform and
opening. The model of livelihood news shifted the discursive focus from
political propaganda to ordinary citizens, dividing up the discursive space
between the government and the people and allocating a generous share
to the latter's everyday concerns. Slogans and policies from the top-down
are not the only voice in the public discourse anymore; ordinary citizens'
grievances are also recognized as legitimate and important, worthy of the
authority's attention.

This discursive power sharing, however, is specious; citizen grievances are carefully packaged as grassroots-level, solvable governance
issues by livelihood news programs. The news production process, still
tightly controlled by the local government, overwrites the more honest

investigation of citizen grievances, replacing it with a cookie-cutter narrative that conveniently blames the street-level bureaucrats, who are often portrayed as negligent and incompetent. This narrative suits local leaders' political interests to discipline subordinates and generate governance outcome. However, it is also convenient for aggrieved citizens, not only because their grievances received overdue attention, but also because this news production process can lead to immediate, though admittedly compromised, resolutions. The frequent protagonists in livelihood news reports—rural migrant workers, low-income urban workers, and scammed consumers—have grievances that can only be truly resolved with policy and institutional changes, which are beyond the reach of television news reports. Instead, framing these grievances as individual cases and pressing the policy implementers on the ground can often result in quick and successful resolutions, without requiring systematic changes and thus attainable in China's fragmented bureaucracy that often operates on informal maneuvers. Thus, this scaled-down narrative of critical reporting actually enables speedy resolution. Iteration of this problem-solving news production process allows the controlled narrative of critical reporting to prevail.

Furthermore, grievance redress, though individual rather than systematic, satisfies citizens whose immediate material interests are advanced through this news production process. Such satisfaction can be genuine, indicated by the deep historical roots of the centrality of livelihood in what politics is about in China. The idea that "people have a just claim to a decent livelihood and that a state's legitimacy depends upon satisfying this claim" goes far back in Chinese political thought, with origins in the teachings of Confucius and elaborations by Mencius (Perry 2008). The moral claim to subsistence characterizes protests and other popular challenges against the Chinese Communist Party (CCP) today. In studies of Chinese public opinion, the outcome-oriented perception of politics illuminates the "puzzle" that Chinese people simultaneously desire democracy and support the CCP (Dalton, Shin, and Jou 2007; Lu and Shi 2015; Shi and Lu 2010). Redressing material grievances through livelihood news, therefore, satisfies citizens' desire for and claim to subsistence, which in turn benefits livelihood news programs seen as effective at helping ordinary citizens.

Zero Distance in Nanjing is one of the earliest livelihood news programs, launched by the Jiangsu provincial television station city channel in 2002. Its journalistic mission was "three close"—"close to reality, close to livelihood, and close to people" (Zhang and Wang 2012, 4). This mission aptly summarizes the distinctive features of livelihood news that thrives in the discursive space carved out for ordinary citizens, contrasting the traditional, propaganda-centered television news in China. Shortly after the initial launch, its ratings shot up to 9.2% between January and April 2003 (Miao 2011, 103). In July 2004, the average rating was 8.3%, with the highest rating of the month being 17.7% (R. Wang 2011). For reference, provincial television news program ratings concentrated between 2% and 5% in 2015, according to the *2016 China TV Rating Yearbook*. The skyrocketing ratings had generated considerable profits for Jiangsu provincial television station. In 2004, the advertising revenue from *Zero Distance in Nanjing* was over US$13.14 million, whereas the advertising revenue of the entire city channel in 2001 was only US$3.38 million (Xie and Zhou 2005, 9). The instant success of *Zero Distance in Nanjing* captivated the national attention and other television stations quickly followed suit; now every local television station has at least one livelihood news program (Miao 2011, 103). Details that illustrate this revolutionary change at the pioneering Jiangsu provincial television station are provided in chapter 2.

Parallel to the brisk development of livelihood news programs, local television stations continue to operate their traditional news programs, which serve as the mouthpiece of the local party-state. On style and format, these programs mirror the *Evening News* (新闻联播) broadcast on China Central Television (CCTV), and they are evaluated primarily by the local party-state rather than audience ratings (X. Xu 2009). In contrast, whether a livelihood news program stays on the air is predominantly decided by audience ratings. This dual-track structure of television news programs—one with an official style primarily featuring propaganda and the other with a colloquial style reporting livelihood news—arguably serve local leaders better than a single track of either traditional or livelihood news. With the dual-track structure, local leaders can preserve a more sanitized version of local news, hedged against the political risk stemming from the critical reporting in livelihood news. Moreover, local leaders can wield two media tools—propaganda news for politics and livelihood news for governance. Focusing on media criticism, this book examines livelihood news programs and leaves propaganda news for future research.

Reporting Urban Governance Problems

The political and journalistic motivations for media criticism determine that the content of critical reporting in television livelihood news is largely derived from the context of problematic urban governance. Governance problem areas where citizen grievances concentrate typically constitute local leaders' governance agendas and local media's reporting priorities.

During the rapid urbanization in the past three decades, Chinese cities and newly urbanized areas have seen profound transformation (Tomba 2017), including rising levels of living standards and expanding opportunities for social mobility (Rocca 2017). However, they also suffer from a series of governance problems that beget widespread public discontent (Eggleston, Oi, and Wang 2017). As Carl Minzner (2018, 53–57) observes, the various problems afflicting urban China, including inhibitive housing prices, abuse of power by local police and officials, clashes between street vendors and city management officers, and the astonishing erosion of social trust, have alarmed scholars as well as some political leaders, who warn about these deep social tensions in their writings. In this context, media criticism can be useful at mitigating these problems through at least three mechanisms.

First, when governance problems arise due to bureaucratic ineptitude, media criticism can help discipline street-level bureaucrats to improve governance. The principal-agent problem is a common obstacle in achieving governance goals. The media power of publicity and the concern for adverse career impact propel street-level bureaucrats toward immediate rectification. This is the most common mechanism of convenient criticism.

Second, when governance problems emerge due to the inability of the legal and administrative infrastructure to keep pace with rapid socioeconomic changes, media criticism can crowdsource ideas and build broad-based support for long-term solutions. For example, bike-sharing services became popular overnight around the year 2016, creating problems such as illegal parking and street congestion. Many busy pedestrian lanes were occupied by shared bikes, causing extensive public complaints. How to deal with this unexpected problem is thorny for the local government, because relevant policies and regulations were nonexistent for this nascent business. Allowing media criticism on this issue not only shows a sincere attitude on the government's side to solve this problem, but also collects ideas to create a broadly supported policy to tackle this issue. Livelihood news programs in cities like Nanjing, Xi'an, and Shanghai devoted long segments to discuss how best to manage bike-sharing services in 2016, before the municipal governments in these cities rolled out their trial regulations.[3]

Third, media criticism can reveal emerging governance issues, reflecting problems that have yet to develop into large-scale, systematic symptoms. For example, after two decades of real estate boom and skyrocketing home prices, the central government used policy and regulatory tools, such as restricting consumer lending and limiting frequent reselling of homes, to rein in the real estate industry and prevent a housing bubble. Premier Li Keqiang even touted a property tax to curb rising home prices. However, despite the regulatory measures, real estate developers were quick to find new ways to sustain a high growth. According to a *Financial Times* report in April 2018, top real estate developers now sell schools and senior care centers bundled with homes in residential complexes to attract buyers (Feng 2018). However, back in May 2017, local livelihood news programs in Jiangsu and Shaanxi already covered a similar phenomenon. In these reports, real estate developers promised kindergartens and elementary schools affiliated with their residential complexes; yet after buyers paid down payments or full home prices, the developers failed to deliver promised schools, causing bitter grievances among the buyers. By absorbing these grievances, livelihood news programs were able to reflect this emerging problem, which in part results from the local government's incompetent oversight to prevent business fraud and contract violations.

Of course, not all governance problems are covered by livelihood news, due to the obvious political constraints. The mechanisms discussed in this section apply to grassroots problems in everyday life, which tend to be so specific that a superficial investigation into bureaucratic ineptitude seems more fitting than a systematic, in-depth look into the root cause, especially when a quick resolution is expected. Furthermore, journalists are mindful that coverage of critical topics does not jeopardize social order, as stability maintenance is a top priority for local leaders (Foley, Wallace, and Weiss 2018). In addition to the political constraints that limit the scope of critical reporting, livelihood news programs are also required to synchronize with the official rhetoric on major political and policy issues. Consequently, the governance problems that do make it to television screens tend to align closely with the local governance agenda. This alignment lubricates both the critical reporting process and the subsequent misbehavior correction and grievance redress.

Variations in Critical Reporting

Citizen grievances resulting from governance problems are among the most common topics in television livelihood news; however, the amount of critical reporting varies both cross sectionally and longitudinally. Based on a content analysis of five livelihood news programs in Jiangsu and Shaanxi from 2016 to 2017, this section presents the descriptive statistics showing the variations in critical reporting, setting up the dependent variables in this book. Then, the remainder of this chapter outlines the bureaucratic, political, and journalistic motives for critical reporting and its variations, ending with an in-depth discussion on the discursive and political implications of livelihood news.

The Livelihood News Programs

Basic information about the five provincial and municipal livelihood news programs and the local leader in each locality are summarized in table 1.1. As mentioned in the previous chapter, I use a pseudonym for the livelihood news program *ABC*, produced by a municipal television station in Jiangsu; this is the site where I conducted ethnographic observation. All together, these five programs are selected for three reasons. First, these programs are popular in the local media markets. Typically, each local television station has several competing livelihood news programs; the selected programs are among the highly rated in each local media market. Most of these programs were created in the early part of the 2000–2009 decade, representing the first-generation programs with continued influence. Second, these programs vary by region. While Jiangsu represents the coastal, eastern part of the country with higher levels of socioeconomic development, Shaanxi represents the in-land, northwestern part of the country with lower levels of socioeconomic development. Finally, these programs vary by their administrative levels. In both Jiangsu and Shaanxi, provincial-level news programs are selected along with municipal-level programs in the capital cities. In Jiangsu, the municipal-level news program *ABC* from a prefecture-level city is also selected to allow further variation in administrative levels.

Three programs are selected from Jiangsu. *Zero Distance*, the new version of *Zero Distance in Nanjing* (name change in 2009), was created in 2002 by the Jiangsu television station. It is a daily 60-minute program broadcast in early evening. It is widely considered by Chinese media scholars as the pioneering livelihood news program (Shaolei Wang 2006). It has cultivated famed anchors, such as Meng Fei (孟非) and Da Lin (大林), known for their sharp commentary often critical of bureaucratic ineptitude. *Live Broadcast Nanjing* was created in 2003 by Nanjing television station. It is a daily 70-minute program broadcast in early evening. ABC was created in 2001 by the municipal television station in a prefecture-level city in Jiangsu. It is a daily 40-minute program broadcast in prime time. According to my interviews, in the early aughts ABC's ratings were once as high as 15% in the local media market. All three programs are early livelihood news programs that remain influential.

Two programs are selected from Shaanxi. *Number One News* was created in 2010 by Shaanxi television station. Despite its younger age, this program has gained popularity during a time of fierce competition among livelihood news programs (Lan 2015). It is a daily 60-minute program broadcast in early evening. *Xi'an Zero Distance* was created in 2004 by Xi'an television station. It is a daily 60-minute program broadcast in early evening.

Coding

Content analysis captures the main topics covered by the livelihood news programs and their frequency. The coding unit is each news story. Videos of news reports from the five programs were obtained from their official websites and a total of 28,660 reports were analyzed and coded. Two student coders, whose native language is Mandarin, were trained to conduct the content analysis. The percent agreement was 90.2%. More details about the coding rules and process are provided in appendix B.

Scope

To show the amount of critical reporting and its impact, I measure the scope of livelihood news reports and the intensity of critical reporting. Scope refers to the breadth of topics covered by a news program; it is measured by how covered topics are distributed during a given time period, that is, the percentage of the reports in each topic category within a news program. Intensity refers to the frequency of critical reports, including those featuring official misbehavior correction and governance improvement.

Table 1.1. Television Livelihood News Programs

Program	Launch Year	Location	Broadcast Time	Administrative Level	Data Range	Departing Party Secretary (Tenure)	Current Party Secretary (Tenure)*
Zero Distance	2002	Jiangsu	18:40–19:30	Provincial	2016/11– 2017/12	Li Qiang (2016/06–2017/10)	Lou Qinjian (2017/10–2017/12)
Live Broadcast Nanjing	2003	Jiangsu	17:30–18:30	Deputy Provincial Municipal	2016/10– 2017/12	Wu Zhenglong (2016/09–2017/05)	Zhang Jinghua (2017/05–2017/12)
ABC	2001	Jiangsu	21:30–22:20	Municipal	2016/11– 2017/12	XYZ (2012/02–2017/12)	XYZ (2012/02–2017/12)
Number One News	2010	Shaanxi	17:50–18:30	Provincial	2016/11– 2017/12	Lou Qinjian (2016/03–2017/10)	Hu Heping (2017/10–2017/12)
Xi'an Zero Distance	2004	Shaanxi	18:00–19:00	Deputy Provincial Municipal	2016/11– 2017/12	Wei Minzhou (2012/06–2016/12)	Wang Yongkang** (2016/12–2017/12)

Notes:
*These Party secretaries are still in their positions at the time of this research. The cutoff time reflects the data range in this research rather than their actual tenures.
**As of March 2019, Wang Yongkang was appointed as a standing committee member of the CCP Heilongjiang provincial party committee and a vice provincial governor. His tenure as the party secretary of Xi'an lasted just over two years.

Figure 1.1 shows the scope of the livelihood news programs from November 2016 to December 2017. The height of the bar represents the reports in that category as a percentage of total reports. Note that the governance problem category was coded to include only the critical reports without correction; the governance improvement category was coded to include only critical reports that feature correction. Among these five programs, *Xi'an Zero Distance* and *Zero Distance* have the highest percentages of the governance problem and governance improvement categories; *Live Broadcast Nanjing* and *Number One News* are ranked in the middle, while *ABC* has the lowest percentages.

The governance achievement category is coded to include positive reports that praise government efforts at improving governance. Reports in this category may focus on successful implementation of local policies,

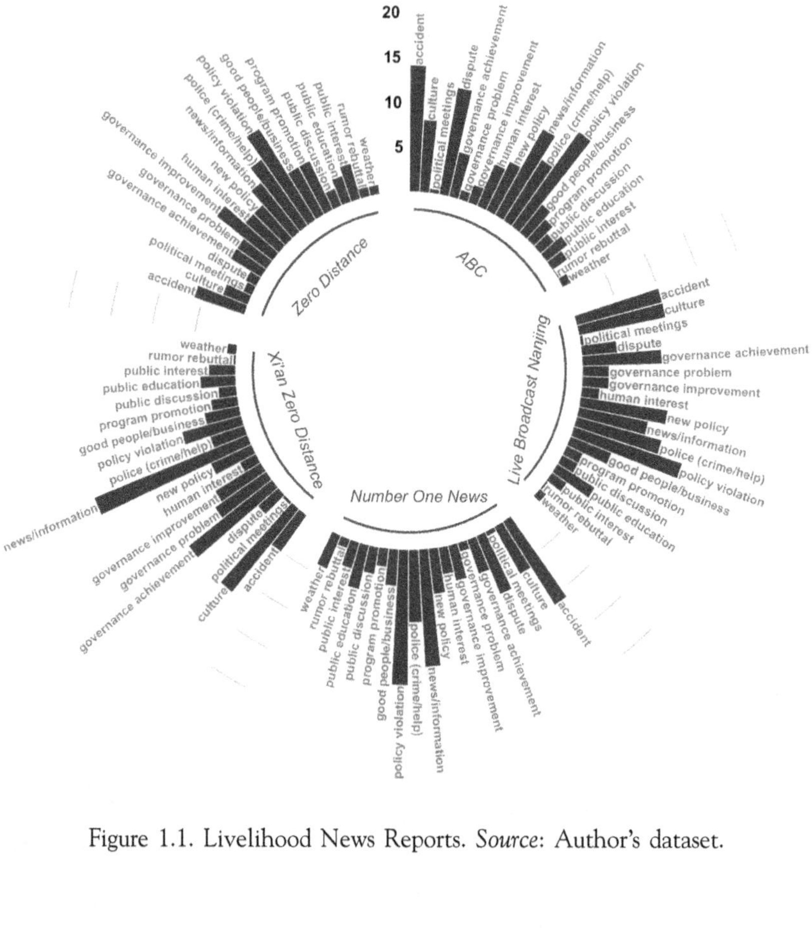

Figure 1.1. Livelihood News Reports. *Source*: Author's dataset.

completion of local initiatives, and citizens praising the local government. *Xi'an Zero Distance* and *Live Broadcast Nanjing* have the highest percentages of this category, despite their relatively high levels of critical reporting. Therefore, the correlation between positive and negative reports is not necessarily inverse, suggesting different motives behind these reports.

Several other patterns are also notable. *Zero Distance* and *ABC* have large percentages of reports that cover disputes between citizens or between citizens and businesses. *ABC, Number One News*, and *Live Broadcast Nanjing* have high percentages of reports that cover accidents, such as traffic accidents and fire. *Xi'an Zero Distance* has the lowest percentage of reports that criticize citizens and businesses for violating policies, such as citizens violating traffic rules or businesses scamming consumers.

Intensity

To understand the intensity of critical reporting, the frequencies of the following two categories of critical reports are examined: (1) all critical reports and (2) critical reports that feature misbehavior correction. The former includes the latter. Figure 1.2 shows the monthly averages of critical reports by these two categories. On average, *Xi'an Zero Distance* has the highest number of critical reports, whereas *ABC* has the lowest. However, *Xi'an Zero Distance* also has the lowest ratio of corrective reports among all critical reports, meaning that a relatively large number of critical reports did not end with a positive outcome. However, it is likely that follow-up reports broadcast in the next day or so feature resolutions. This pattern is unusual compared to the other programs, suggesting the local leader's intentional push for critical reporting that empowered journalists to criticize local officials.

To put critical reports into the context of television news, figure 1.3 shows the monthly averages of reports in the categories of governance problem (all critical reports), governance achievement, and new policy. The new policy category is coded to include reports that propagate, explain, or discuss new government policies. For example, Xi'an municipal government implemented a vehicle restriction policy in late 2016 to reduce air pollution. This policy limits the number of days when citizens can drive personal vehicles, and the rule is based on license plate numbers. On different days, vehicles with license plates that end with certain numbers would not be allowed on the road. From November to

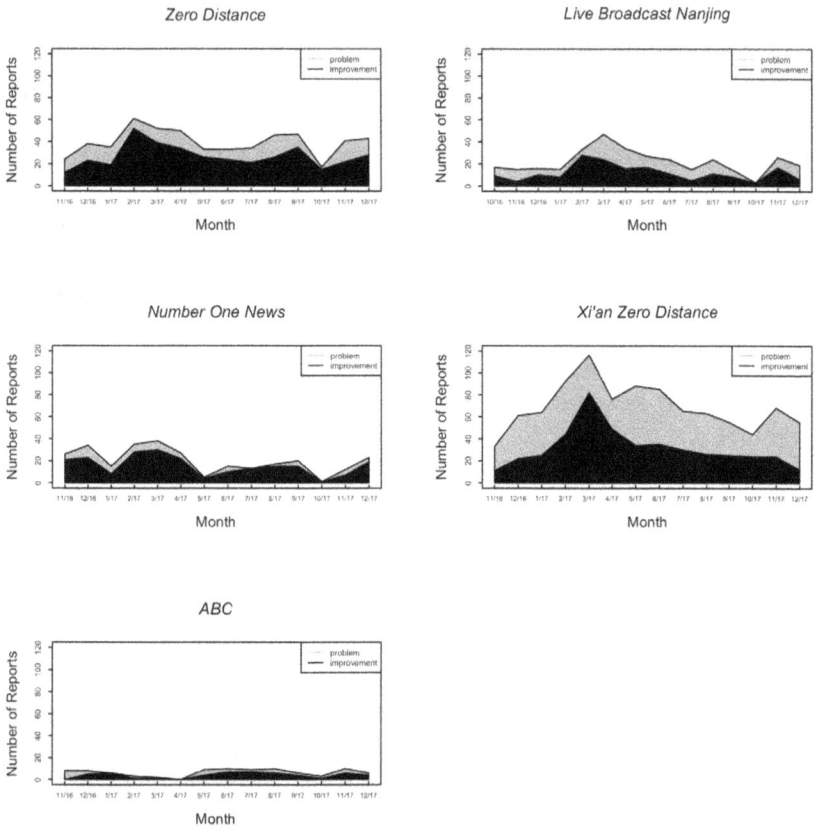

Figure 1.2. Criticism and Improvement. *Source*: Author's dataset.

December in 2016 *Xi'an Zero Distance* aired a series of reports to explain and discuss this policy. In figure 1.3, the new policy category provides a benchmark for comparison. Typically reports that fall in this category are generic reports that provide needed information without being overly critical or adulatory. In comparison, reports that fall into the categories of governance achievement and governance problem have a more obvious tone of criticism or praise.

Several patterns are shown by the data. First, *Xi'an Zero Distance* has the highest average numbers of both critical and positive reports. This indicates an intentional use of the media by the local leader to discipline subordinates as well as to showcase governance achievements.

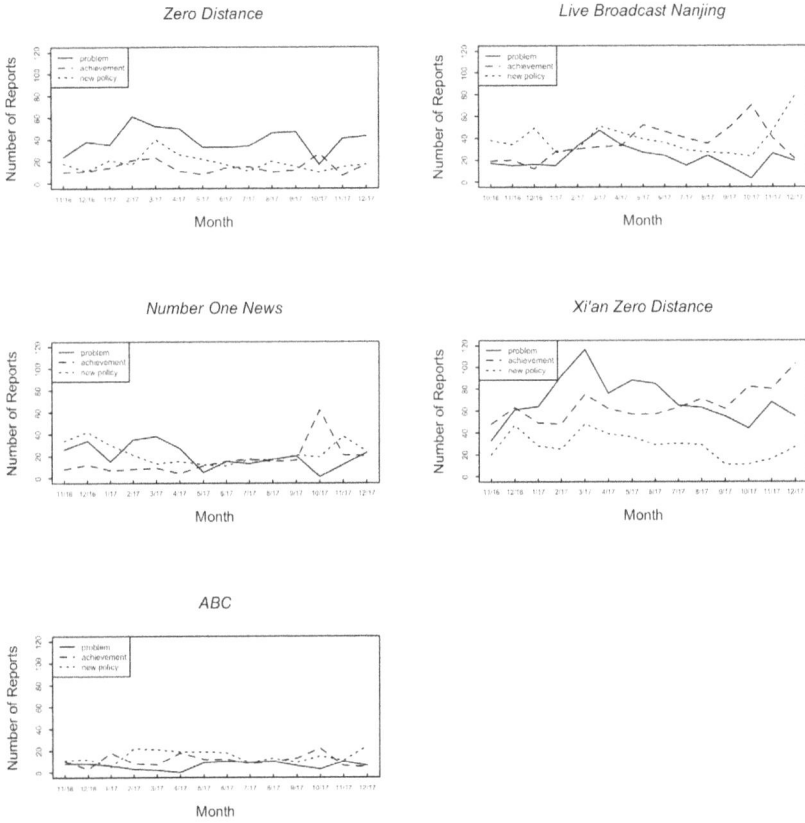

Figure 1.3. Reporting Intensity. *Source*: Author's dataset.

The monthly averages of critical reports were higher than those of positive reports until July 2017, when the two lines crossed, after which there were more positive reports than critical ones. On the contrary, ABC has low levels of both critical and positive reports, and these two lines did not fluctuate much compared to the other programs.

The data also show that all five programs broadcast more positive reports in October 2017, indicating a concerted effort at showcasing governance achievements during the 19th Party Congress, a time when President Xi Jinping acquired his second term and further consolidated his power. Local news programs joined the nationwide effort to create a flattering discursive environment highlighting the achievements of the party-state at both central and local levels. However, *Xi'an Zero Distance* is unique among the five programs; after October 2017 the number of positive reports went up even further, while other programs saw recoils in the number of positive reports. This indicates an intentional use of the media by the local leader in Xi'an—Wang Yongkang—to showcase his achievements after one year into his tenure as the municipal party secretary. More details about this case are provided in the following chapters.

Comparing the numbers of critical and positive reports within each program, *Zero Distance* has more critical reports at all times except October 2017, while *Number One News* and *Xi'an Zero Distance* have more critical reports for most of the time. In contrast, *Live Broadcast Nanjing* and *ABC* have more positive reports for most of the time, indicating vast differences in the amount of critical reporting across news programs. The vivid variations in critical reporting reveal the intricate and interactive forces of bureaucracy, governance, politics, and the media. The following sections outline these forces.

Bureaucratic and Political Conveniences

Given the increasingly complex urban governance, media criticism provides informal power that enhances bureaucratic control for local leaders to tackle governance problems, thus advancing their political careers. In this way, media criticism can be bureaucratically and politically convenient. Before laying out the key mechanisms of these conveniences, it is important to first define whom "local leaders" refers to. In China, the vast bureaucracy that the party-state relies on for effective rule is comprised of various political actors with diverging interests and incentives. The theory of convenient criticism focuses on provincial and municipal party secretaries—the local party bosses that oversee all affairs in their jurisdictions. They have monopolized power to manage the local media, a key reason for them to be the theoretical focus. Being the "first hand" (一把手) differentiates local party secretaries from other high-ranking politicians within the local party-state, who also have tremendous power but not a final say in media matters. Therefore, the theory of convenient criticism does not apply to officials in lower-level positions who do not have the authority to capture the local media. For example, media criticism is not necessarily convenient for the vice provincial or municipal party secretaries, because they cannot override their bosses' decisions regarding the local media. Put differently, they do not have the authority to influence the media to the extent of advancing their careers. Media criticism is also not convenient for street-level bureaucrats or their immediate superiors often targeted by critical reporting.[4]

Being the party bosses, local leaders are typically driven by career ambitions to achieve higher-level leadership positions, and they have the authority to use the local media as a governance instrument. Local leaders' motivations are often twofold: the inadequacy in their formal power rationalizes the bureaucratic convenience, while the opacity in the rules of cadre promotion substantiates the political convenience. The remainder of this section outlines these incentives. To be sure, local leaders have other effective tools to improve governance, and media criticism is just one among many informal maneuvers that some leaders choose to employ. The uneven adoption of media criticism in part explains the variations in local critical reporting. Individual-level differences among the local leaders are also discussed in this section and further in chapter 3.

The Principal-Agent Problem

In the reform era, the CCP attempted to transform itself from a revolutionary party into a governing party (Lieberthal 2004). After a series of bureaucratic reforms, one of the persistent problems is local noncompliance. Also referred to as a principal-agent problem, local officials, or state agents, have interests that incentivize them to behave in a way that may be inconsistent with the expectations of the higher-level leadership, who are the principal of the local agents (Minzner 2018, 69–73; Gallagher 2017, 32–33). Local officials bending policies and regulations are common. The literature on uneven policy implementation uncovers exactly the inadequacy in political leaders' formal power to ensure compliance, sometimes to the benefit of constituents whose rights and liberties would be undermined by relevant policies (Cai 2015; Chung 2000; Edin 2003; Göbel 2011; Lampton 1987; Lieberthal 1992; Mertha 2006; O'Brien and Li 1999; Shi and Kennedy 2016).

The reasons leading to the principal-agent problem are manifold. Institutionally, the cadre management system allows lax and biased evaluations

(Edin 2003) and induces pernicious gaming behavior (J. Gao 2015). Even for policy areas where clear numeric targets are set, implementation may still suffer from noncompliance when measurement is nontransparent, monitoring is insufficient, and cyclical behavior is tolerated (Kostka 2016). Individually, some officials choose noncompliance due to concerns over competing priorities and local conditions (D. Liu 2019; Zhang and Cao 2015; Zheng et al. 2014), policy flaws (Shi and Kennedy 2016), insufficient state capacity (Zhan, Lo, and Tang 2014), local business interests (Luo 2008; Van Aken and Lewis 2015), and corruption (Birney 2014; Ong 2012).

Local noncompliance has become such a serious problem that *People's Daily*, the mouthpiece of the CCP Central Committee, published a series of opinion editorials criticizing this phenomenon. In a discussion section published on May 25, 2015, titled "Local Cadres Discuss Official 'Inaction' Phenomenon: Laziness, Stupidity, and a Lack of Courage Are the Reasons," a selection of essays written by local cadres discusses the reasons why local officials' inaction is so prevalent.[5] Among the discussed reasons are a lack of courage by local leaders, a lack of necessary knowledge by mid-level local officials, and inaction by both entry-level officials and upper-level leaders. This extensive discussion indicates the prevalence and seriousness of noncompliance.

More important, noncompliance obstructs local leaders' pursuit of governance results, which then undermines their career advancement. Media criticism can mitigate the insufficiency in local leaders' formal bureaucratic power. Publicizing street-level bureaucrats' wrongdoing on television creates public humiliation, which is powerful at inducing correction and compliance. Organic criticism allows local media to function as a bottom-up input channel. Journalists help aggrieved citizens articulate their demands and strategize about potent but acceptable bargaining narratives, sometimes leading to correction of official misbehavior. In this process, local leaders are rarely involved, but their tolerance of criticism allows the media to help improve governance. In comparison, orchestrated criticism allows local leaders to direct journalistic focus to key governance issues. By launching what essentially amounts to a media campaign, local leaders can ensure that key governance issues receive ample coverage and that street-level bureaucrats—the implementers on the ground—are pressured to diligently perform their duties. Local leaders' direct involvement enables orchestrated criticism to achieve immediate governance results.

Opaque Political Selection

Local leaders' need to create governance records for career advancement is amplified by the opaque political selection process. Political leaders in China are appointed by their superiors through the *nomenklatura* system, which is used to exercise control over the vast group of party cadres and government officials (Burns 1989, 1994; Y. Huang 1995; Manion 1985). Introduced from the Soviet model, "the *nomenklatura* is a list of leading positions over whose appointments the Party exercises full control" (Edin 2003, 44). In China's *nomenklatura* system, the organization department of the party committee at each administrative level has the authority to make personnel decisions—including promotion, dismissal, and transfer—at one or two levels down the administrative hierarchy (Y. Huang 1995).[6] As a result, leaders at lower levels are held accountable to their superiors. John Burns (1999) points out that the Chinese party-state remains Leninist today partly because of the *nomenklatura* system, which maintains the party's control over the government.

While the authority to make political appointments is clear, the considerations in making those decisions remain opaque. The existing studies have identified two broad categories of factors that shape local leaders' career paths: factional connections (Shih, Adolph, and Liu 2012; Meyer, Shih, and Lee 2016) and governance records (Landry 2008; Li and Zhou 2005). Factional loyalty is conceptually clear, but the diverse goals in performance evaluation mean that local leaders must distinguish themselves from their competitors through notable governance records. After all, factional connections only help an official's career prospects when essential performance targets are met (Jia, Kudamatsu, and Seim 2015; Li and Gore 2018), and the recent documents issued to further reform the cadre management system suggest even higher standards for cadre promotion. For example, a 2015 document issued by the General Office of the CCP Central Committee emphasizes that incapable leaders should be demoted; the top issue areas in cadre evaluation also evolved from the previously paramount economic development to good governance, such as reducing environmental pollution. As the governance context becomes more complex and challenging, further expectations start to arise. For example, local leaders are expected to have an innovative and problem-solving mentality and adroitness in dealing with the media, discussed in detail in chapter 3. Therefore, local leaders are incentivized to go the extra mile in delivering a performance that can help earn fast-track career advancement. In this context, media criticism is an appealing instrument for local leaders to discipline their subordinates and generate immediate governance results. Furthermore, media criticism provides unique value to project an image of a competent leader who appears honest and serious about improving ordinary people's livelihood. As the data analysis in chapter 5 shows, this mechanism is at work for media-savvy leaders who are strategic about media criticism; they leverage critical reporting at the beginning of their tenures and pivot away from this strategy about a year later when they prepare for the next promotion.

As local leaders' media literacy grows, they have come to understand media criticism as an effective instrument that can help achieve governance objectives. This mechanism reinforces the importance of performance legitimacy, performance as both governance outcome (Gilley 2008; Holbig and Gilley 2010; Yang and Zhao 2015; D. Zhao 2009; Yuchao Zhu 2011) and political theater (Hwang and Schneider 2011; Sorace 2016; B. Xu 2012). As discussed earlier, improving governance by way of media criticism is superficial; the political constrains on critical reporting mean that the quest for real governance improvement is pretended. However, media criticism can generate immediate governance results by correcting misbehaving street-level bureaucrats, while performing political reprimand through public humiliation. The uninstitutionalized, informal nature of media criticism allows local leaders to change and adapt, better serving their career interests. Therefore, media criticism provides potent bureaucratic and political conveniences for local leaders to improve governance and advance their careers.

Leadership Style

The above incentives arise out of the institutions of cadre promotion, and they are only part of the explanations for the variations in critical reporting. While local leaders share these institutional incentives, individual-level characteristic of leadership style also shapes their propensity to use the media in an unscripted way. Leadership style, especially the orientation toward the media, is another key factor in explaining not only the existence of media criticism, but also the differences in the level of critical reporting across time and region.

In general, leadership style can be differentiated based on a dimension ranging from risk averse to risk acceptant, suggested by studies in the field of foreign policy decision-making (Bueno de Mesquita 1981, 1985; Keller 2005; Keller and Foster 2012; Kowert and Hermann 1997; Zand 1997, 43). According to Nathan Kogan and Michael Wallach (1964, 214), risk acceptant or risk averse can be seen as "a generalized disposition to treat diverse situations in a consistently risky or conservative manner." Recently, scholars started to apply the concept of individual leadership style to understanding Chinese politics. For example, Sara Newland (2018) finds that local leaders in China can be understood as innovators and implementers when it comes to managing NGOs. While innovators use civil society partnerships to gain attention and approval from higher-level leadership for career advancement, implementers seek stability and security and see little benefit in collaborating with nonstate actors. Jessica Teets, Reza Hasmath, and Orion Lewis (2017) find that individual-level factors such as having an "innovative personality" partly explain local officials' preferences for policy innovation, and that individual preferences interact with institutional incentives to influence policy experimentation outcomes. Applying leadership style to understanding orientation toward the media, this book argues that risk acceptant leaders are more aware of the potential benefits brought forth by embracing controlled media criticism, while risk averse leaders are more resistant because their judgment accents risks associated with media criticism. This individual-level factor is further discussed in the following chapters.

Media Convenience

The second beneficiary group of actors essential in the process of producing critical reporting includes media organizations and their journalists. Media organizations such as local television stations have to fulfill propaganda tasks, but they also operate under the immense pressure to generate profit. Based on my interviews with a number of television producers and reporters, the goals of propaganda and profit have very little overlap. While propaganda tasks are nonnegotiable, an excess of them alienates audience and undermines profitability, which can be tied to journalists' compensation and job security. Critical reporting, at least within the news section of television broadcasts, is an essential way toward profitability. On the other hand, since the emergence of the unique journalistic model of livelihood news two decades ago, television journalists have formed strong professional identities that motivate their work, advocating for ordinary citizens. In this way, the commercial interests of local television stations and the professional aspirations of television journalists align in pursuing limited critical reporting.

Both of these factors—commercial and professional—can only be satisfied, however, when television livelihood news is beneficial to local governance and relevant political interests. The inevitable reliance on politics for viability means that local leaders perceiving the utilities of limited critical reporting is the premise of journalistic agency. Television journalists understand well that their professional aspirations as well as personal livelihood depend on serving relevant political interests. While this prerequisite seems rather compromising from an outsider's point of view, for these journalists who lack access to alternative journalistic models, this prerequisite defines the only way they know how to operate, and their decades-long experience allows them to see it not as limiting but enabling. Serving relevant political interests can boost the legitimacy and longevity of their unique brand of advocacy journalism and create opportunities to satisfy their professional aspirations. This unique position where television journalists reside is a result of not only political domination but also journalistic agency and adaptation. The political expropriation of criticism thus invigorates, rather than diminishes, the impact of critical reporting and the journalistic satisfaction derived from it. Therefore, in the theory of convenient criticism, selective critical reporting also dispenses commercial and journalistic conveniences to local television stations and their journalists, though these conveniences are conditional on the bureaucratic and political conveniences discussed earlier.

Commercial Interests

The reform era ushered in a series of media reforms that transformed the television industry; the resulting immense commercial pressure not only catalyzed the creation of livelihood news in the late 1990s, but also sustains this news production model by tuning into social and economic ills and pursuing the amicable goal of governance improvement. Against the backdrop of rapid urbanization and the associated governance problems, television livelihood news programs pursue critical reporting to absorb citizen grievances and demands. By doing so, they have earned approval and trust from citizens, which translates into program ratings and advances their commercial interests. Based on my interviews, in the news section of local television broadcasts, livelihood news programs often attract major advertisements compared to traditional news programs, serving as a pillar in generating profit. On the other hand, the success of these programs indicates an eager market for media advocacy, as aggrieved citizens continue to resort to television journalists for help, evidently shown by the ample news leads offered in the forms of hotline calls and social media posts. These abundant news sources allow journalists to produce higher-quality news stories, enhancing their productivity.

Taken together, critical reporting in livelihood news delivers commercial convenience to local television stations by increasing productivity in journalists' daily news production, by contributing profits through program ratings, and by harvesting public trust and social impact. Besides media organizations, journalists' own professional identities and pursuits are also fulfilled by the success of livelihood news.

Advocacy Journalism

In the process of developing, adapting, and consolidating the model of livelihood news, some television journalists have developed strong professional identities centered on "helping ordinary folks solve problems" (帮老百姓解决问题), a slogan shared by many livelihood news programs. This journalistic mission departs from the conventional journalistic norms of autonomy and objectivity, which are widely recognized in the Western conceptions of journalism (Iyengar 2015, 72). Instead, it explicitly takes the side of ordinary citizens, rather than maintaining an objective and neutral position, suggesting a populist flavor of advocacy journalism. The notion of "populist" here simply refers to the divide between "the people" and "the elite" (Mudde and Kaltwasser 2017), who may be at odds with one another due to different status in power, wealth, and influence. In Chinese, the word "ordinary folks" (老百姓), prevalently used in television journalistic discourse, has a strong connotation of being on the opposite side of the elites.

Besides departing from the norm of objectivity, Chinese television journalists also lack autonomy. Though the restricting political environment makes this departure rather obvious, the journalistic agency has interacted with the political conditions and shaped the norm that was to replace autonomy. Many journalists see their role as a "bridge" between the government and the people—not autonomous but also not a mere mouthpiece. Within the strict yet expandable political boundaries and conditional on the local leadership and governance context, journalists try to advocate for average citizens using existing policies and agendas, absorbing and diluting local tension arising out of problematic governance. In this way, journalists build a bridge that benefits the government, first and foremost, and also citizens, to a certain degree. Television journalists' mission to help the "ordinary folks" is blended with their view on the government's role in their work. The bridge analogy is premised on the deep-seated view that the government, not civil society groups or other nongovernmental entities, is the rightful authority with the capacity to resolve issues for citizens, which is consistent with the predominance of stateness and the fusion of state and society in China's political history (Gilley 2014). Survey results presented in chapter 4 illustrate this populist-flavored advocacy journalism held among many television journalists.

Judging from my fieldwork at local television stations, this brand of advocacy journalism has been notably successful. A former producer of a popular livelihood news program in Yunnan told me that his program earned such approval and appreciation from the local communities that journalists affiliated with this program were offered free meals at restaurants and free taxi rides. At Xi'an television station, hanging on the wall of the shared journalist office were a dozen or so pennants (commonly used in China by individuals and organizations to express praise or gratitude), all coming from ordinary citizens who received help from *Xi'an Zero Distance*. These pennants are clear indications of genuine gratitude for the program and a strong media reputation in the local communities.

Not only can political power compromise journalistic autonomy, however; so can street-level bureaucrats and businesses. Existing studies have found instances of news extortion, "paid-for news," and other forms of media corruption (Lin 2010; Wang, Cho, and Li 2018; Y. Zhao 1998; Zhou 2000). More relevant to the theory of convenient criticism is the potential for journalists to be captured by street-level bureaucrats, in addition to the local leadership. If street-level bureaucrats tainted by misconduct have built personal relationships with television journalists, wouldn't that reduce the likelihood of critical reporting about those bureaucrats?

The media capture by the local bureaucracy, rather than the local leadership, is certainly possible, thus offering a potential alternative explanation for the variations in critical reporting. However, at least two factors present barriers to a prevailing effect of the local bureaucracy and accentuate the dominance of the local leadership. First, the frequent personnel changes both within the local bureaucracy and within the local television stations reduce the propensity of media capture by the local bureaucracy. Personnel changes demand additional time and concerted efforts, which are not always available, to build new relationships. Second, to terminate a critical report that would otherwise be produced requires not one but several accomplices, due to the professionalized process of news production that involves broad participation of reporters, program producers, and channel directors. Such broad participation raises the stakes of street-level bureaucrats interfering in the news production process. This may generate adverse career impact for street-level bureaucrats, because the capture of the local media is an extension of local leaders' institutional and political power, thus exclusive and not to be shared with their subordinates. If anything, street-level bureaucrats are the targets of local media's critical reporting, when such a news model is seen by local leaders as advancing their governance agendas. Therefore, street-level bureaucrats would overplay their hand if they try to influence the media to cover up their own misconduct. They can, however, build relationships with higher-level officials who then lobby on their behalf to terminate critical reports. The effectiveness of this mechanism depends much on the reach of the political connections and the nature of the misconduct, both are rather fluid factors offering no guarantee. Chapter 2 elaborates on the multilevel nature of the local bureaucracy and its implications for convenient criticism.

Citizen Convenience

Citizens are the protagonists of livelihood news. This news production model, though primarily allowed to advance political interests, also benefits ordinary citizens whose grievances are redressed through the media power of publicity. This is especially significant given that, in a time of growing disparity, livelihood news has become one of the few effective channels of redress left for the lower classes, while the upper classes have multiple channels at use. As Carl Minzner (2018) eloquently puts it:

> Elites have means—both formal and informal—to ensure their voices are heard, their grievances handled. The powerful mingle with their classmates from Beijing University (or Yale). The wealthy can buy access to their local congressman (or

> Party secretary). As elsewhere, it is a different story for the
> poor. Faced with an abusive encounter with police resulting
> in broken bones, or a lengthy land dispute that endangers
> family finances, their choices are limited. Many simply lump
> it. Lack of information or resources means that only a small
> fraction of disputes ever reach the official justice system. (90)

While the wealthy and powerful shun being the focus of local television news, the poor and the disempowered see few reliable and effective allies to redress their grievances other than the local media. Past research shows that connections with local government officials not only shelter families from grievances in the first place, but also mobilize legal resources to resolve grievances (Michelson 2007). In contrast, studies on protests and other collective action in China found that contacting the media to publicize grievances has become an important "trouble-making" tactic for protesters to elicit an effective response from the local authority (X. Chen 2009, 2012). Meanwhile, local media's steering of their journalism toward a populist and advocacy-minded mission has facilitated the tacit alliance between citizens and journalists. As discussed earlier, livelihood news programs rely on news leads from citizens, and their effectiveness in redressing grievances propels citizens to continue to resort to the media for help.

The theory of convenient criticism is built on the bureaucratic and political incentives that allow critical reporting to exist, vary, and persist. While the media convenience is an aiding factor in this theory, the citizen convenience is a collateral effect. Local leaders' need for a competitive governance record takes into account, by way of authoritarian accountability, the need to redress citizen grievances. Citizen interests and demands often are an afterthought, rather than an issue in their own right, that fits into the actionable plan to advance the status quo. Furthermore, addressing citizen grievances publicly on television enhances the symbolic power and literal dominance of the current political system, which deeply shapes the discursive space in the society.

Calibrating Expectation and Reinforcing Hegemony

The sequential steps in livelihood news production and the ensuing governance improvement demonstrate a mechanism of how "consent" is "secured" (Lukes 2005) in China and how political "hegemony" (Gramsci [1926–37] 1971) is reinforced. In this Gramscian notion, the source that gives rise to and maintains hegemony can be cultural and ideological, as well as material. Adam Przeworski (1985) points out that consent, a foundation of hegemony, "corresponds to the real interests of those consenting" (136). Steven Lukes (2005, 8) argues that "Gramsci's ideological hegemony has a material basis and consists in the co-ordination of the real, or material, interests of dominant and subordinate groups."

In China's reform era, the ideological realm undergoes transformation and realignment, with communism giving way to a confluence of traditional and nationalist ideas that are revived and renewed. At the local level, however, subsistence and livelihood remain central in what politics is about, often eclipsing the ideological hold of politics. The dominance of material interests allows the desirable outcome of grievance redress to engender an irresistible appeal to consent to the existing political arrangement that makes this outcome possible. As Luigi Tomba (2014) insightfully argues, "Legitimacy appears less as the result of an elaborated understanding of the good and bad of a certain regime and more as the consequence of one's assessment of the acceptability of everyday governing practices and of the moral discourses that justify such practices under a variety of material conditions" (12). The process of media-induced governance improvement, especially the steps prior to the eventual rectification, albeit appearing undermining due to the acknowledgment of mistakes and incompetence, actually adds additional layers of discursive power that reinforces the political hegemony.

These prior steps strengthen political dominance by calibrating expectation and thereby maximizing the power of correction. Expectation is an underexplored yet captivating dimension of politics. When perceived reality exceeds or disappoints the expectation, which in and of itself is a result of political forces, the implication for political attitudes and behavior can be so powerful that discernable patterns emerge. For instance, a recent study finds that unexpected protests increased trust in government in Russia, because those most likely to be surprised by the permission to hold protests updated their beliefs about the trustworthiness of the government (Frye and Borisova 2019). In a comparative study of 258 authoritarian regimes between 1948 and 2011, Adrián Lucardi (2019) finds that the *expectation* of competitive elections dissuades citizens and elites from engaging in anti-regime behavior during nonelection periods. Researching the role of the economy in generating satisfaction with democracy, a comparative study of 34 countries finds that economic *expectation*, in addition to past and current economic conditions, drives satisfaction with democracy (Nadeau, Arel-Bundock, and Daoust 2019). The authors find that the allure of the "American Dream" for a better tomorrow can be especially potent for the wealthy, as well as those who expect to become wealthy. Studying legal reforms and labor rights in China, Mary Gallagher (2017) finds that the law on the books, which sets the expectation, does not fully represent the law in reality. This unmet expectation subsequently undermines long-term political stability.

In the case of convenient criticism in China, the process of selecting, producing, broadcasting, and redressing citizen grievances calibrates expectation so that when it is exceeded, powerful reactions ensue. First, citizens afflicted with grievances might, in theory, expect outcomes ranging from immediate resolution of the issue at hand to policy reforms and institutional changes addressing its root cause. However, the state's power to control information flow, to erect barriers to advocating for systematic change, and to manufacture political discourse that subdues truthful views and narratives molds citizen expectations for acceptable and satisfactory outcomes, lowering them to a level that can be easily surpassed. As articulated by Steven Lukes (2005, 27), not only are decision-making and non-decision-making during overt or covert conflicts forms of power, but the "power to get another or others to have the desires you want them to have—that is, to secure their compliance by controlling their thoughts and desires" constitutes the third dimension and the supreme exercise of power. In local politics in China, that disempowered and aggrieved citizens choose to ponder, articulate, and struggle for rather narrow and short-term material interests is a result engineered by the political hegemony. These citizens, without enough wealth or political capital to redress their grievances, are forced to confront the system without any backing except the belief that their demands are rightful, which further deflates their expectation for resolution.

The plea for help is directed at the media typically after, not before, the effort at appealing to government officials fails. At this point, the unsuccessful attempt at resolving grievances through permitted means corroborates the overwhelming sense of disempowerment, further lowering the expectation for what can be achieved. Then, media criticism unleashes two powerful turning points. First, the decision for journalists to investigate citizen grievances and the eventual broadcast of the stories demonstrate an unmistakable admission of wrongdoing by the political authority. Television news, despite the media reforms and evolving journalistic norms, still represents the government and its official stance; thus, the mere broadcast of critical reports is a powerful signal to the disempowered that their grievances and struggles are publicly acknowledged. Adding to this promising first sign of change, the second turning point arrives when correction takes place. Correction of misbehaving officials not only redresses citizen grievances, but also unequivocally demonstrates the willingness and effectiveness of the political authority to make positive changes. Together, these two turning points contrast with the prior failure of other mechanisms of redress and fulfill unexpected promises.

This process of twists and turns exhibits a formidable capacity of hegemony. It not only defines citizen interests, but also calibrates their expectations regarding whether and how their demands are to be satisfied. Without conceding power, the political hegemony wins willing consent by lowering the expectation for what can be achieved. In doing so, it grants citizens a false sense of empowerment over misbehaving local officials—the belief that even the ordinary folks can hold government officials accountable, thanks to the support from the rightful party-state.

Meanwhile, the consistent narrative of critical reporting advances the normative justification of the political legitimacy of the CCP. In her insightful article on the importance of political ideology in China, Heike Holbig (2013) points out that the constant adaptation of political ideology, including the correct language and the most current phrases, serves the ongoing process of legitimation of the authoritarian rule. In television livelihood news programs, the narrative of blaming misbehaving local officials for failing policy implementation or inadequate public service provision implicitly but unmistakably reinforces the status of the CCP as the rightful ruling party. Reprimanding the lack of adherence to its policies legitimizes those policies, because any undesirable outcome cannot be blamed as inherent flaws or biases of those policies. Blaming local officials for governance failures exonerates not only CCP policies, but also the policy-making process and the political system in general. The hasty but conclusive verdict on misbehaving local officials inhibits truthful examination of wider and deeper systemic issues. Therefore, the narrative of critical reporting that blames local officials reinforces the perception that higher political authorities and their policies are benevolent and beneficial to ordinary citizens, appealing to the deeply rooted Confucian moral view that rulers shall advance the welfare of citizens (Perry 2008).

Furthermore, the process of calibrating expectation also solidifies the crucial aspect of *positioning* in the grand scheme of consent and hegemony. The third dimension of power, according to Steven Lukes (2005), lies in the very production of interests, desires, and wants. For autocrats, the key to manufacturing a resilient system of interests and desires consistent with their rule is to position the ruled within a confined narrative where their interests are defined. In this way, it would be more difficult for the ruled to redefine their interests and challenge the hegemony, because alternatives are not readily available. A quote from George Orwell's *1984* ([1949] 1961) makes this point clear:

> All that was required of them was a primitive patriotism which could be appealed to whenever it was necessary to make them accept longer working-hours or shorter rations. And even when they became discontented, as they sometimes did, their discontent led nowhere, because, being without general ideas, they could only focus it on petty specific grievances. The larger evils invariably escaped their notice. (74–75)

In the case of disempowered citizens in urban China, the narrative that misbehaving and disobedient local officials are responsible for governance problems, repeated in media reports and shown in the public opinion of "hierarchical trust" (D. Chen 2017b; L. Li 2004, 2016), not only spares the higher political authorities criticism, but also deceivingly elevates the disempowered by placing them in a position of assigning blames. Plagued by mistreatment and oppression, citizens gain a false sense of empowerment when their grievances are affirmed and the purported perpetrator is identified, criticized, and rectified. Their suffering ends with a made-up display of power—the perpetrator's mistakes are corrected, a subtle yet powerful implication of which is that such correction happens only in the current system, not any other.

To be clear, the party-state does not make it easy to consider alternatives. Its ruthless elimination of any potential alternative channels of interest articulation and aggregation leaves little chance for disempowered citizens to seek alternatives. Existing literature on authoritarian rule and democratic transition suggests that a successful and relatively peaceful democratic transition requires a competent opposition force. In Taiwan and South Korea, legitimate opposition forces were in development decades before the institutional transition marked by free and fair elections and a peaceful transfer of power. Similarly, in India "the emerging political opposition took the form of reformists rather than revolutionaries. Pressure was channeled into—not out of—formal legal and political institutions" (Minzner 2018, 155). In China, however, impactful opposition forces do not exist. While opposing voices occasionally bubble up, such as the New Democracy Party (1998), Falun Gong (1999), and New Citizens Movement (2013), they are unfailingly and sometimes preemptively suppressed, thus lacking organization, influence, and legitimacy (Minzner 2018, 173). Alternative social forces and political movements, when they exist, could not mount any plausible challenge against the current system, nor could they supply a credible vision for what a replacement would look like.

When both expectation and outcome are defined by the party-state, hegemony perpetuates itself. However, the arguments here shall not imply the "radical" view of power articulated in the Foucauldian notion of the panopticon, where "there is no escaping domination, that it is 'everywhere' and there is no freedom from it or reasoning independent of it" (Lukes 2005, 12). Instead, both expectation and outcome are fluid. Indeed, neither is constant or guaranteed.

Expectation is malleable contingent upon the context; it can be dominated by the insidious and permeating manifestation of state power, but it can also be defined by underground, alternative discourses. Further, the party-state's own policy and institutional reforms raise expectations that may be subsequently unmet. For example, legal reforms raised expectations regarding protection of labor rights, yet persistent labor disputes show that these expectations are typically not met in reality, "exposing the gaps between law on the books and law in reality" and jeopardizing the state's goal of political stability and long-term survival (Gallagher 2017, 38).

Outcome is also not guaranteed, not least because of the "half-hearted" (Gallagher 2017, 38) intention at resolving governance problems and individual grievances. More important, the multilayered and deeply fragmented bureaucracy in China has long been characterized by uneven policy implementation, let alone the variations in local leadership and governance context. As Sebastian Heilmann and Elizabeth Perry (2011, 24) argue, the "guerrilla policy style," though resilient and adaptive, has fundamental flaws, including the lack of political accountability and undue administrative discretion.

Not all citizen grievances are reflected in the local news and resolved by it and not all local leaders are inclined to use media criticism, but the persistent focus on redressing citizen grievances has sustained the reputation of livelihood news programs and the belief that officials' wrongdoing can be corrected. Consequently, the mechanism of convenient criticism in its current form perpetuates the political hegemony, though conditions fostering change and challenge are manifold. Figure 1.4 summarizes and visualizes the constitutive pieces in the theoretical framework of convenient criticism.

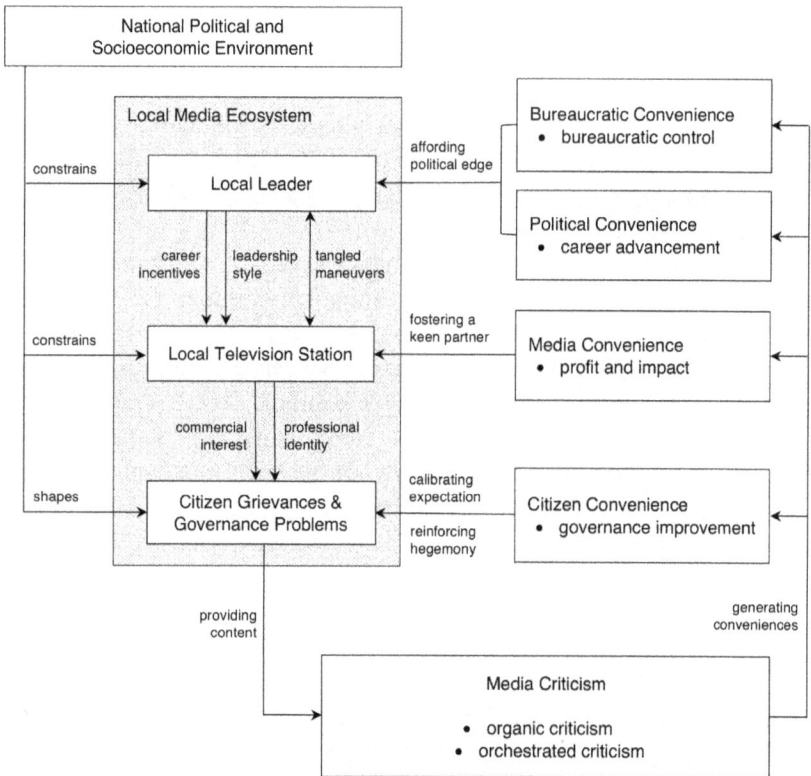

Figure 1.4. Convenient Criticism.

Conclusion

Instead of conceptualizing media criticism as a result of journalistic victory over censorship, this chapter delineates an alternative perspective that situates media criticism in local governance. Critical reporting can provide powerful conveniences to local leaders, the premise of the longevity of the livelihood news model. Local leaders' need to rein in street-level bureaucrats and to create competitive governance records for promotion can be effectively met by selective critical reporting on citizen grievances and governance problems. Meanwhile, these incentives interact with and shape television journalists' professional pursuits that attend to citizen interests and demands in an era of problematic urban governance. These professional aspirations overlap with their media organizations' need for profitability. Uniting the interests of local leaders and local media, critical reporting participates in the local governance process by disciplining street-level bureaucrats, a role that expands beyond the media effects on public opinion. Furthermore, the immediate result of grievance redress calibrates citizens' expectations on governance and satisfies their interests, reinforcing the hegemony of the party-state. Of course, critical reporting is subject to political control and the governance context, and not all local leaders are inclined to use media criticism as a governing tool. Chapter 2 contextualizes and expands on the theoretical mechanism of convenient criticism and outlines its effects, as well as limits, by exploring how things fit together in the day-to-day business of news production.

Chapter 2

Tangled Maneuvers

With local leaders' permission or encouragement, local television stations can play a supervisory role to correct street-level bureaucrats' misbehavior, redress citizen grievances, and improve governance. When seen through a theoretical lens, the conveniences afforded by media criticism to local leaders are clear, but, in reality, varied interests and incentives interact, propelling different actors to react in diverging directions. Though media criticism can offer political advantage, it is a double-edged sword that not only some local leaders are wary about but intermediary actors within the bureaucracy are often resistant to. So, how do the diverging political interests and incentives align in selective critical reporting? How do journalists learn, adapt, and maneuver in this rather complex and dynamic political environment to fulfill their duties and aspirations? In other words, how do things fit together in the reality, not just the theoretical framework, of convenient criticism? By tracing the process of news production and shedding light on the intricate and unspoken interactions, this chapter puts some flesh on the bones of theoretical and abstract interests and incentives. The fluidity in the news production process demonstrates that media criticism, despite its utilities, varies greatly. The qualitative, in-depth examination of the variations in media criticism in this chapter is further illustrated with quantitative data on a more systematic scale in chapter 5. To better understand the tangled maneuvers in the local news production process, this chapter begins with a discussion of the rules and structures that regulate the news industry.

Media Control and Critical Reporting

Despite the rich findings from existing studies, there are two unresolved issues central to understanding media control in China, as discussed in the introduction. First, critical reports are common despite effective media control. The existing explanations are limited by a lack of attention to the interests of local leaders, who are *directly* responsible for the *day-to-day* management of the local media. The second issue concerns the varying levels of critical reporting across time and region. Although recent studies in the area of online censorship have greatly advanced our understanding of the logic behind controlling critical information online (e.g., Gueorguiev and Malesky 2019; King et al. 2013, 2014, 2017), critical reporting done by journalists who are affiliated with official, semiofficial, or commercialized media organizations (Stockmann 2013) follows a different pattern. Some studies suggest that uncertainty and ambiguity regarding the boundaries of permissible reporting lead to journalists' self-censorship (Hassid 2008; Stern and Hassid 2012; Stern and O'Brien 2012), yet still leaving open the question on what explains the varying levels of critical reporting.

The answers to both issues can be drawn from understanding local party secretaries' institutional career interests and individual leadership style differences, which are further discussed in chapter 3. Importantly, these factors lead to different media preferences at the local level. This chapter argues that the synchronization between local leaders' media preferences and local media's news production process is a main explanation for the varying levels of media criticism. The highly institutionalized process of how television producers manage their programs strongly suggests the power that local leaders hold over local news reporting.

For television programs, government control takes the form of ex ante examination and ex post review (Miao 2011). Entertainment programs including television series and variety shows are subject to strict and meticulous ex ante examination, while most television livelihood news programs are broadcast live and reviewed by officials from the local propaganda department during and after the broadcast. Television news programs are monitored and controlled differently than entertainment programs, in part due to the fast pace of daily news production and the political sensibility of reporters, program producers, and high-level executives at local television stations.

Based on my fieldwork, I have found that a television news producer is the person directly in charge of a news program and the first gatekeeper that directs and supervises reporters. Working under channel directors and other higher-up executives, the producer decides which news stories to pursue for each day's programming. Typically, the producer is fluent with the rules regarding news reporting, including both broad guidelines and specific taboos. For breaking and sensitive news stories that are hard to judge, the producer may consult with channel directors before and during the news production process. After broadcast, the local propaganda department regularly reviews program content and provides feedback. Typically, the producer holds weekly (or more frequent) meetings with reporters to review their work from the previous week and to deliver any comments from the local propaganda department. This is the fine-tuning process that synchronizes local reporting with the local leader's media preference.

If the local propaganda department sees any report as crossing the political line, warnings would be duly conveyed to the specific news program and its reporters. Depending on the seriousness of the case, warnings may take the form of phone calls, meetings, written notice, demotion, and even dismissal. The first two types of warnings are the most common, yet, in general, warnings do not happen frequently. Television executives are loyal to the party-state, at least outwardly, and they have excellent political judgments. These gatekeepers are appointed to their positions in part for their political loyalty and competence. Some television executives are also government officials at the local propaganda department, holding concurrent positions at the local television station (interviews 17-XZ and 37-WL). Furthermore, if warnings from the local propaganda department happen frequently, it would indicate ineptitude of the responsible producers and channel directors, who then would likely be demoted or replaced before long. Therefore, the local propaganda department's warnings tend to be very effective, because television executives are sensitive listeners and loyal agents.

The close control that local leaders have over local news reporting strongly suggests that local leaders' media preferences, a derivative of their career interests and leadership styles, in part explain the varying levels of critical reporting. As local leadership changes every few years, local media's ability to learn facilitates the "break-in" period after a new leader assumes his or her post, a process that fine-tunes local news with the local leader's preference. However, the synchronization between local leaders and the local media occurs in a multilevel bureaucracy, which engenders diverging interests but also journalistic opportunities to affect media criticism. The next three sections further explain how critical reporting could occur in the multilevel bureaucracy, how journalists' learning process synchronizes their reporting with local leaders' media preferences, and how journalists might exert limited impact on critical reporting.

Sorting Layered Incentives

In China's elaborate party-state system, there are several layers of bureau-cracy involved in the process of media control during the day-to-day news production. The analogy of *tiao* (条) and *kuai* (块), or lines and pieces, captures the "cross-hatching of horizontal and vertical lines of authority" in China's multilevel bureaucratic system (Lieberthal 2004, 187). Mirroring the horizontal structure within the central party-state that consists of party departments and state ministries in charge of various issues areas, the local party-state has a similar setup of institutions, thus forming the "cross-hatching" structure. From local leaders' perspective, they control and steer the local media through the local propaganda department, which is part of the local party-state. This aspect signifies *kuai* or pieces in the horizontal dimension at the local level. Meanwhile, the local propaganda department is also under the control of the central propaganda department led by the central party-state, and it signifies *tiao* or lines in the vertical dimension that extends from the center to the grassroots. The local party secretaries themselves are also under the control of the higher-level party-state through the cadre management system.

The *tiao/kuai* analogy indicates fragmented authority within the authoritarian political system (Lieberthal 2004; Mertha 2009). In an example of a municipal propaganda department, the vertical line (*tiao*) means that it is under the direction of the provincial and central pro-paganda departments, and the horizontal piece (*kuai*) means that it is under the direction of the municipal party-state. Therefore, the municipal party secretaries ought to weigh the provincial and national preferences of news reporting before they allow or pursue limited critical reporting (Guan, Xia, and Cheng 2017). Meanwhile, they also need to consider local politics and governance conditions in directing news reporting, resulting in occasional incoherence in censorship preferences between these bureaucratic levels (Y.-W. Lei 2016, 26).

Local leaders' media preferences, as regulated by the *tiao/kuai* system, have more influence over affiliated television stations during the *day-to-day* news production process, despite the vertical control from propaganda departments at higher levels.[1] As mentioned earlier, television producers hold frequent meetings with reporters to convey remarks from the local propaganda department. These comments often refer to specific news reports and attend to their details, suggesting that these comments are unlikely to originate from higher-level propaganda departments; the details in the comments most likely reflect the preference of the local leadership. Therefore, despite that local leaders have to consider the broader political environment, their capacity to shape local news reporting remains formidable. Chapter 5 presents quantitative evidence showing that local leaders' media preferences play a significant role in shaping the level of media criticism, after accounting for regional and national variables. This pattern reveals the importance of piece (*kuai*) in media control at the local level.

The *tiao/kuai* system also has implications for journalists when they pursue organic critical reporting. Because television stations are officially designated as a mouthpiece for the party-state at the matching administrative level, television news programs hold power from their administrative ranks when they interact with government officials at lower levels. For example, a provincial television news program has more power to criticize municipal-level government officials than does a municipal television news program, because the latter is at a parallel, rather than higher, administrative rank. Similarly, a municipal television news program has power to criticize county- and township-level officials. Furthermore, the longer the distance between the administrative ranks, the more power journalists can leverage to supervise officials at lower levels. This is because television stations, being the mouthpiece of the party-state at the same level, are perceived, by officials at lower levels, as an extension of that higher-level party-state. Therefore, the lower-level officials don't have the authority to censor reports from a higher-level television station; occasionally, they may have the political capital to lobby higher-ups to censor reports on their behalf. This mechanism is crucial in understanding organic critical reports; it also explains why street-level bureaucrats are the most criticized group of government officials in livelihood news. This dynamic indicates the importance of line (*tiao*) in critical reporting at the local level.

Recent studies on the print media reveal a similar mechanism of *tiao/kuai* at work. In their study of the *Beijing News*, a prominent newspaper known for investigative reporting, Ke Li and Colin Sparks (2018) find that

> Guo Feng, an investigative journalist in the team, told us that an important strategy in gaining interviews with local officials, especially county-level and town-level officials, was to inform them that the *Beijing News* was a central-level newspaper whose reporting would attract central government attention. This status often intimidated the officials and made them think they could not refuse an interview. (419)

Figure 2.1 further illustrates how the multilevel bureaucracy affects media criticism. When local officials are criticized in a news report, their natural reaction to resist and obstruct critical reporting is regulated by the *tiao/kuai* system. For a hypothetical Municipality A, its propaganda department manages the affiliated municipal television station, under the direction of the municipal party secretary and higher-level propaganda departments. In the current bureaucratic system, township is two levels below the municipal level. If an official in Township D is criticized in a news report, this official may not have the political capital to petition leaders in the municipal propaganda department, which is two levels above, to censor the report, especially when facts are solid and the wrongdoing is undisputable. However, if an official from the education bureau in District C has a close relationship with a leader in the municipal propaganda department, which is more likely given that there is only one-level distance between their administrative ranks, then censoring a critical report about this education bureau official would be likely with the right kind of political connection. Therefore, the hierarchy in the bureaucracy that allows critical reporting may be diminished by political connections cross-cutting the *tiao/kuai* system, extending the privilege in media control over to officials at lower levels.

The fluidity in how the multilevel bureaucracy affects critical reporting means that there is space for journalistic maneuver as well. When criticized officials have connections with higher-level leaders, they may try to pressure the producers to drop critical reports. Depending on their

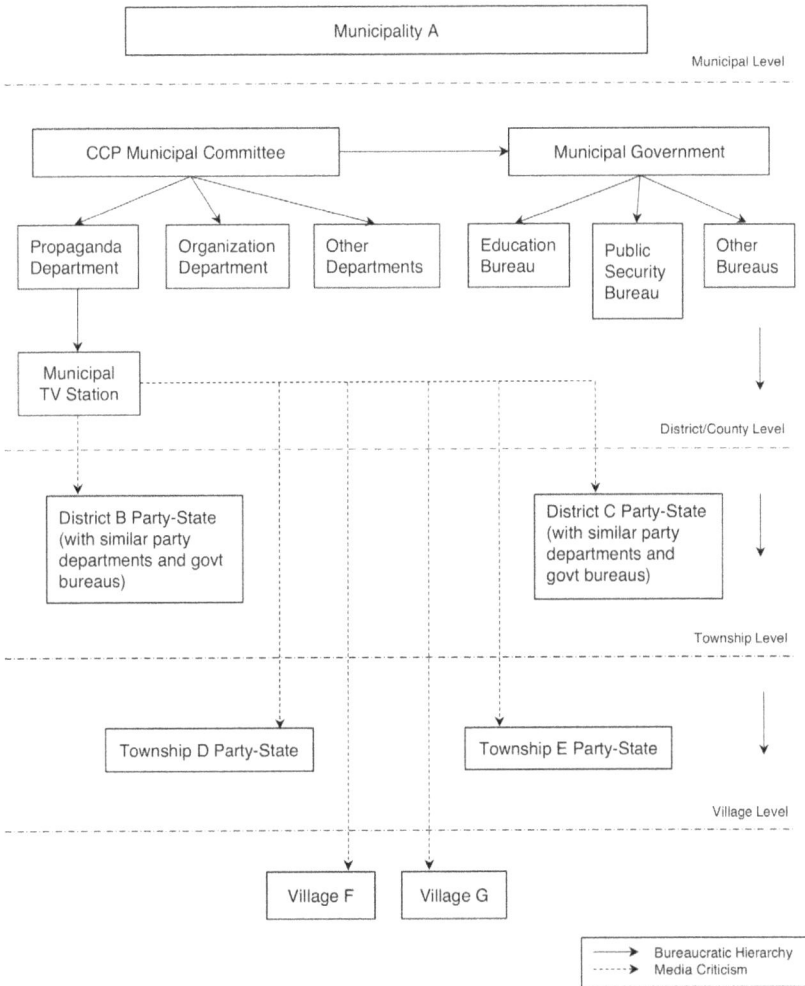

Figure 2.1. Administrative Ranks and Media Criticism.

judgment on the nature and reach of those political connections, some producers may choose to double down on their critical reporting and embrace a potential political fight. For example, based on my interviews, a producer at Xi'an municipal television station routinely turned off his cell phone during the last few hours before live broadcast to avoid calls from government officials requesting cancellation of critical reports. Other producers may be more cautious about critical reporting and give it up more easily when challenged to avoid a potential political backlash, as the second case later in this chapter shows. Therefore, journalists' political judgment may also affect the space for critical reporting, which is further complicated by the frequent leadership changes at the local level. However, journalists' diligent and continual learning allows them to be proficient in understanding local leaders' media preferences.

Shifting Media Preferences and
Journalistic Learning

The centrality of local leadership in understanding local critical reporting requires an understanding of how local leaders' media preferences, evolving both with changing interests at different stages of a tenure cycle and with the frequent leadership turnover, are accurately translated into news reporting. The synchronization between local leaders' media preferences and local news reporting is primarily carried out by producers and reporters, who actively and continually learn the shifting boundaries. In their study of Chinese television entertainment programs, Wenna Zeng and Colin Sparks (2019) reached a similar conclusion about television producers' competence at understanding the political boundaries by finding that "almost as much as in news production, part of the skill of an experienced and successful entertainment producer is to know what cannot be said and done, what needs to be handled carefully and what it is safe to represent. This knowledge, much more than external censorship, is the major mechanism by which political conformity in Chinese television is reproduced on a daily basis" (65).

　　Journalists' learning process can be understood as consisting of two general components. The first component sets clear boundaries, comprised of comments, directives, and orders conveyed from the local propaganda department. These instructions may be a reaction toward a critical report already produced; they may also be unprompted, reflecting changes in media strategy from the local leadership. With these hard rules delineating the space for critical reporting in broad strokes, ex ante examination does not completely restrict the content of news. This leaves room for the second component to exert influence, which is informal and varied, comprised of maneuvers during the news production process, especially for those journalists who allow their sense of agency to push for more space for critical reporting. This type of critical news production is fraught with tentativeness, negotiation, frustration, and compromise, to which performance rich with coded gestures and unspoken rituals is integral. However, it also indicates "a willingness to accept the convention" in the context of "an underlying threat of state violence" (Weller 2017, 171), that is, the disciplinary punishments available for journalists in instances deemed recalcitrant.

Therefore, journalistic learning is not entirely passive or merely reflective of local leaders' media preferences; journalistic agency, though constrained, seeks to expand the space for critical reporting through negotiating with lower-level officials, over whom journalists may have the power to supervise. As discussed earlier, the multilevel bureaucracy provides opportunities for journalists to criticize misbehaving bureaucrats at lower administrative levels. Television journalists' clear understanding of the elasticity in their supervisory power, a source of their journalistic agency, equips them with an acute sense of political judgment and an enhanced ability to learn, knowing when to reach for more and when to call it off. Therefore, through both accepting the hard boundaries set by the local propaganda department and maneuvering, not overreaching, when interacting with lower-level officials, journalists try to exhaust all spoken and unspoken space available for critical reporting. Eventually, this proficient understanding of political boundaries synchronizes news reporting with local leaders' shifting media preferences.

The mechanism of journalistic learning also implicates that self-censorship derives more likely from a clear understanding of the changing political boundaries than from an overwhelming uncertainty about it (Hassid 2008; Stern and Hassid 2012; Stern and O'Brien, 2012).[2] However, this is not to say that existing findings about uncertainty and ambiguity steering self-censorship are to be rejected; in fact, uncertainty and ambiguity are essential properties of media control exercised by the *central* party-state. Facing unforeseen challenges from an increasingly complex socioeconomic and political landscape, the central party-state has to rely on uncertainty and ambiguity to retain effective control over the vast media industry. *Local* leaders' control over the *local* media, however, does not fit the same pattern, because local leaders have a different set of interests than that of their superiors at the national level, one that is more specific and immediate. Furthermore, lower administrative levels and smaller jurisdictions mean less degrees of fragmentation, allowing local leadership to form and exert more straightforward, if less sophisticated, media preferences. In fact, for some media-savvy local leaders, it is desirable for their media preferences to be understood clearly by journalists, so that the news production can be in full synchronization and serve their interests, as the following in-depth cases show. Before delving into the day-to-day news production process to demonstrate the preceding analysis, it is analytically beneficial to first delineate some common journalistic tactics for maneuver, key to the process of journalistic learning.

Journalistic Tactics of Maneuver

My fieldwork reveals that the following tactics are widely used by television journalists. First, journalists choose to focus on criticism at lower bureaucratic levels. As discussed earlier, journalists have more supervisory and negotiating power when criticizing officials at a bureaucratic level much lower than that of their television station. Second, journalists use flattering follow-up reports to end the initial criticism with a positive outcome by highlighting misbehavior correction and governance improvement, which has become a prominent feature of livelihood news. Chapter 5 systematically examines the determinant factors in producing this type of follow-up improvement reports. This tactic tries to balance critical reporting with positive reporting to keep the overall tone in news reporting from being overly critical. Along the same logic, journalists may spread out critical reporting over a longer time period, so as not to create an impression that the program is highly critical. They may also try to balance the bureaus and officials they criticize, rather than concentrating on specific bureaus or officials from the same township or village.

The third tactic concerns the rhetorical frames journalists use to gain leverage. Similar to the logic of "rightful resistance" (O'Brien and Li 2006), journalists make requests that are "legitimate by definition in a rhetoric that even unresponsive authorities must recognize, lest they risk being charged with hypocrisy and disloyalty to the system of power they represent" (O'Brien and Li 2006, 5). Journalists often invoke existing laws, policies, and principles, such as citizens' right to know (公民知情权),

to elicit a positive response from local officials and to hold them accountable (X. Zhang 2007). This tried and tested tactic is acceptable to higher-level political authorities because it reinforces the authority of the party-state. Citizens demanding local officials to abide by the policies from the higher-up bolsters the norm of compliance. Along the same logic, journalists may also "ride the wave" of local governance campaigns or initiatives, choosing to focus their critical reporting on topics of the local government's priority. In this way, local governance agendas legitimize critical reporting.

Finally, television journalists may report on negative news stories that have already been discussed online or reported by other news programs. This cross-media agenda-setting effect allows a different censorship standard to stretch the reporting boundaries at the local level. In an interview, a channel director revealed to me that social media posts are a very effective tool to expand the space for critical reporting. The argument is that if a critical report is already in the public discourse, then it would not make much difference to broadcast an already-public story. Meanwhile, such critical reporting creates opportunities to generate profit through increased ratings. Exploiting different censorship standards in different jurisdictions and media space, journalists can sometimes expand local reporting boundaries.

Demonstrative Cases

To illustrate these intricate, fluid, and unquantifiable aspects of media control and critical reporting, I employ two demonstrative cases of livelihood news programs, one at the provincial level and the other at the municipal level. By tracing the process of news production and revealing the behind-the-scenes journalist-official interactions, these cases show a precarious process of news production, accounting for instances of both successful and failed attempts at critical reporting. Both news programs are also included in the original dataset used in chapter 5, allowing these cases to put flesh on the bones of the quantitative analysis presented later in the book. Both cases are based on interviews and secondary data; the second case is also based on ethnographic observation. To protect my sources, in the second case study I use pseudonyms and withhold information that may reveal identities.

Encouraging Critical Reporting

The first case examines a nationally known provincial livelihood news program called *Zero Distance in Nanjing*, already discussed in previous chapters. This case focuses on the initial year after the program's launch by the Jiangsu television station city channel on January 1, 2002. It delineates the formation of a journalistic identity anchored on supervising government officials, under the auspices of the local leader at the time. Though the boundaries for critical reporting have changed since then, the initial year of encouraged critical reporting shaped and consolidated the journalistic identity. This case then analyzes the declining space for critical reporting as the local leader proceeded further into his tenure as the provincial party secretary, suggesting a strategic and selective use of media criticism.

In the early aughts, Jing Zhigang, a news producer at Jiangsu television station, was promoted to be the director of the local channels. At the cusp of structural transformations in the television industry after the media reforms in the previous decade, this promotion gave Jing the power to create a new form of television news, with an ambitious aim to not only increase ratings and profits but also lead the revolution that was to come in the Chinese television news industry. Seizing the opportunities offered by deregulation and commercialization, Jing recognized that two key elements were missing in Chinese television news at the time: a plain, colloquial language, rather than a hollow propaganda oration, and a focus on ordinary people, rather than political leaders. These became essential features of television livelihood news.

In addition to a vivid style, Jing also realized that, by focusing on ordinary people, the topics of local news would reflect and reinforce the media's supervisory role, so that the news program could truly connect with ordinary people by showing a deep concern over justice and welfare. Engaging in critical reporting, then, became an important ingredient to earn popularity, success, and impact. This was a bold but not implausible idea. By the early aughts, the policy of "supervision by public opinion" (舆论监督) had already made critical reporting possible for about a decade, discussed in detail in chapter 3. Furthermore, the success of supervisory news programs in the 1990s produced by the central-level CCTV, such as *Focus* (焦点访谈)[3] and *News Investigation* (新闻调查), provided guidance for the potential of this recipe for local news production. All considered, Jing decided to create a news program that could distinguish itself with its local focus, colloquial language, and critical reporting. On January 1, 2002, *Zero Distance in Nanjing* was launched on the Jiangsu television station city channel.

While Jing was the designer for *Zero Distance in Nanjing*, without the support from Li Yuanchao, at the time concurrently the party secretary of Jiangsu province and the party secretary of its capital city Nanjing, this program would not be successful at critical reporting. As discussed earlier and elaborated in chapter 3, the formal and informal rules of cadre promotion and the shorter tenures generate strong incentives for local leaders to produce competitive governance records for career advancement, especially at the beginning of their tenure cycles. In this case, Li turned to critical reporting for governance achievements when he was appointed to Nanjing after serving in various positions within the central party-state in Beijing. My fieldwork reveals that, shortly after the initial launch of *Zero Distance in Nanjing*, Li personally visited the newsroom and encouraged the news crew to be "bold" (大胆) in criticizing local officials and holding them accountable. Li even specified that cadres up to the county chief level (县处级) could be criticized.[4]

With the strong encouragement, *Zero Distance in Nanjing* devoted a substantial amount of airtime to critical reporting, most of which centered on bureaucratic ineptitude. According to a content analysis, only 5 of the 170 news reports in 2003 by *Zero Distance in Nanjing* were positive reports about the government and its officials; 93 reports were critical and the remaining reports were nonpolitical or neutral (L. Chen 2004). Subsequently, its ratings skyrocketed, and its dramatic success created a nationwide sensation. As mentioned in chapter 1, its enviable ratings led to substantial revenue gains for Jiangsu television station.

At *Zero Distance in Nanjing*, the primary news source was hotline calls from ordinary citizens reporting unresolved grievances, disputes, or governance problems. Based on my interviews, on average this program received more than 100 hotline calls per day, offering ample leads to facilitate journalistic work. Reporters carefully selected leads from these calls to follow up and produce reports. With Li's encouragement, critical reporting was the focus. For example, in 2003, *Zero Distance in Nanjing* reported that a highway tollbooth worker tried to charge a fee from a firefighter truck that was on its way to put out a fire, constituting preposterous misconduct. Another report exposed the scandal that a national cultural relics protection site, which was applying to be included in the World Heritage List selected by UNESCO (United Nations Educational,

Scientific and Cultural Organization), was rented out by local officials to small businesses, suggesting abuse of power and corruption (L. Chen 2004).

The journalistic vision of *Zero Distance in Nanjing* accorded well with Li's strategic use of media criticism, resulting in a higher level of critical reporting. However, about a year later, Li made comments directly to this news program again. According to my interviews, instead of encouragement, this time Li made it clear that criticism was "enough" and that the news program should scale back its critical reporting. This action suggests a careful, selective use of media criticism, which is to be jettisoned after its intended utility is achieved. As a result, the frequency and intensity of critical reporting declined. However, journalists at *Zero Distance in Nanjing* had already formed a strong identity of helping ordinary folks redress grievances and restore justice. They realized that this was the reputation that they had built among the local audience, which was essential to the program's continued success. Though the space for critical reporting contracted as the local leader's media preference shifted, the focus on advocacy journalism remained intact. The detailed examples of recent critical reports in chapter 5 further show that journalists have developed effective skills to negotiate with local officials and to hold them accountable while operating within an acceptable space for critical reporting. Journalistic agency, in this case, though limited by the local leadership, shaped the trajectory of the program's evolution and preserved its identity on advocacy.

Coinciding with the decrease in critical reporting relative to its heyday, the ratings of *Zero Distance in Nanjing* gradually declined, albeit remaining above the ratings of many other livelihood news programs. Based on available data, in 2007, its average rating was 8.26%, which dropped to 7.13% in 2008 and 6.93% in the first quarter of 2009 (Zhang and Wang 2012, 11). For reference, at its peak, the ratings averaged 9.2% between January and April 2003 (Miao 2011, 103). To revert the trend, this program experimented with several adjustments. In May 2009, to preempt the competition from online and social media, *Zero Distance in Nanjing* was "upgraded" and renamed to *Zero Distance*, incorporating both traditional and new media for close interaction with the audience (Zhang and Wang 2012, 10).

Despite the gradual decline in ratings, *Zero Distance* remains an influential news program in the local media market. The *2015 China Radio and Television Yearbook* reported that *Zero Distance* remained the highest rated livelihood program in the Nanjing media market as of

2014. Its continually dominant status suggests consolidation of the symbiotic relationship between journalists and citizens. The real impact from television reports in redressing grievances has earned *Zero Distance* a strong reputation and deep trust from the citizens; meanwhile, citizens continue to turn to the media for help, which sustains program popularity and impact. This mutually beneficial relationship depends on continued grievance redress, which requires journalists to tread the political boundaries carefully, so that the space for critical reporting remains open and flexible. As the descriptive statistics in chapter 5 show, the level of critical reporting by *Zero Distance* remains one of the highest compared to other livelihood news programs, indicating a consistent reputation for critical reporting. Early in the program's history, the local leader's temporary encouragement for criticism paved the way for *Zero Distance* to explore the model of livelihood news, fostering and consolidating its unique brand of advocacy journalism.

This case shows that the local leader strategically and selectively encouraged media criticism to advance his career interests, after which the space for critical reporting contracted. The clear directives from the local leader, as well as journalists' political competency, ensured that the news production was sensitive to the shifting boundaries. The next case focuses on the informal practices in the day-to-day news production, offering a close examination of journalistic learning and maneuvering.

Limiting Critical Reporting

The second case shows how a risk-averse leader restricted the space for critical reporting, as journalists were learning about his media preference. The livelihood news program *ABC* was launched in 2001 in Municipality X in eastern China. *ABC* is the flagship livelihood news program at the municipal television station, sharing a similar style of television news as *Zero Distance in Nanjing*—a colloquial language and a local focus on critical reporting. Also similar to *Zero Distance in Nanjing*, after its initial launch, *ABC* achieved ratings success. However, in the mid-aughts, the ratings declined gradually and stabilized at a lower but still influential level.

Against this background, Zhao was promoted to the producer position in charge of *ABC* in 2011. As the new producer, Zhao was ambitious in expanding the success and impact that *ABC* had had thus far. Prior to the promotion, Zhao had been a reporter covering government affairs at the television station for ten years, understanding proficiently the shifting boundaries of political reporting. However, he also subscribed to the diagnosis that the media's supervisory role was what could draw more audience attention to enhance the program's popularity and reputation.

During my fieldwork, Zhao shared with me how he evaluated his reporters at ABC. Monetary rewards were used to incentivize reporters to produce quality reports. As the producer, Zhao graded each report at ABC; reporters' grades were then averaged every month to decide the monthly bonuses. Furthermore, the ranking of the monthly grades and bonuses was made public, posted on the wall of the large office shared by 20 or so reporters. While this level of transparency would not be acceptable at many other media outlets in China, the purpose of making this information public, according to Zhao, was to motivate the reporters to work harder.

The criteria Zhao used in grading reports were twofold. First, a report has to meet basic professional standards such as no typos or grammatical mistakes in the scripts; it also needs to abide by the professional code of conduct, such as presenting verified information and protecting the privacy of informants through blurring their faces or changing their voices. Second, a report has to attract the audience's attention, such as capturing a unique angle to a news story to make an idiosyncratic incident look interesting and appear useful to others who may encounter similar situations. For example, a hotline call received in 2013 concerned a senior citizen who was scammed to buy expensive medicine that turned out to be counterfeit. The reporter assigned to this story framed it as a lesson for all senior citizens, who are easy targets of medical frauds.

Another strategy to attract audience attention is to focus on reports that help ordinary citizens solve problems or redress grievances, the common topics of critical reporting. A reporter at ABC named Zhang told me that the news media should serve ordinary folks by building a bridge between them and the local government, so that their grievances can be better addressed. Zhang was civic-minded and compassionate toward the "vulnerable social groups" (社会弱势群体) in Municipality X, such as migrants and laid-off workers (Thornton 2017). He told me that he hoped to help as many people as possible by covering their stories. Perhaps not coincidentally, Zhang was ranked number one in the monthly ranking of grades and bonuses during my fieldwork, and two of his reports from May 2013 received praise from high-level executives at the television station.

In Municipality X, the current party secretary, hereafter referred to as XYZ, was appointed in February 2012, after serving as the deputy party secretary and mayor for three years. Since Zhao had been covering the municipal government for the past ten years, he was familiar with XYZ and described him as a "cautious" and "steady" leader. Knowing that XYZ has a relatively distant attitude toward the media, Zhao was careful when it came to critical reporting. He focused on government officials at township and village levels; when higher-level officials were involved, he framed critical reports in a way that did not implicate specific government bureaus or officials. For example, in June 2013, ABC covered a story that the major roads in the city were flooded because the city's ill-designed drainage system was unable to handle the rain. Instead of blaming specific officials or bureaus in charge of facilities, the anchor commented innocuously that "we hope relevant government bureaus and leaders can quickly solve this problem."

Despite his political sensitivity, initially after XYZ's appointment, Zhao had a steep learning curve when he tried to grasp XYZ's media preference, which can be illustrated by two key learning moments. First, in 2012 ABC covered a story that some government officials were using public cars for private trips. This was already a common phenomenon in China at the time. In this report, Zhao was discreet to specify no officials' names nor relevant bureaus. It was a generic report on this common phenomenon of abuse of power, as it was happening in Municipality X. The day after the broadcast, Zhao and other senior executives at the television station were called over to the municipal propaganda department to be "criticized and educated" (批评教育). This was a warning that such reports were off-limits.

The topic of using public cars for private trips, however, was already a national issue that even the central leadership had sent strong signals to resolve. *People's Daily*, for example, published an opinion piece in 2011 arguing for institutional reforms to eradicate this "persistent disease" of power abuse (Jie Jiang 2011). Another opinion piece went further, arguing that installing GPS on public cars is necessary to monitor and eradicate this problem (Shichuan Wang 2011). In places like Guangzhou, regulations were already rolled out in 2011 to monitor and prevent private use of public cars (Qiu 2011). Therefore, Zhao's intention, as he told me, was to cover an issue that already received national attention, so that it would be less risky politically but more appealing to the audience. The strong reaction from the municipal propaganda department was a learning moment relaying a clear message that this municipal leadership was strict in managing the media, even on topics already reported elsewhere.

The second key learning moment came during the news production process. This news story involved officers from the city management bureau (城市管理局) at the district level. The city management bureau was established at the municipal level and below; it is in charge of enforcing administrative regulations and laws, with an overarching aim of ensuring effective urban governance (Zang and Pratt 2019). Its extensive responsibilities include managing public sanitation, zoning, urban planning, and maintaining public order. For example, removing street vendors deemed as illegally occupying public space is part of its responsibility. Due to the confrontational nature of their work, such as removing and confiscating properties from street vendors, city management officers often become the target of controversy in public discourse (Huang, Xue, and Li 2014; Ramzy 2014; Swider 2015).

At ABC, a news story came from a hotline call in June 2013. The caller complained that his neighbor, a municipal people's congress delegate, illegally built a sunroom that blocked sunlight for his own apartment. This caller said city management officers had already ruled that this delegate violated relevant regulations on illegal construction, and that the sunroom was to be revised or demolished. However, this delegate ignored the ruling, and nothing had changed.

I shadowed Zhang, the top reporter at ABC, to the city management bureau office the next morning. It was a large office with eight cubicles. The city management officers, who were all in uniform, were unfriendly to Zhang once they saw the camera in his hand, refusing to answer any questions. One officer waved his hand in the air while yelling, "Go away!" Zhang was not willing to give up easily and tried to talk to this officer, but this officer refused to even look at Zhang. In the meantime, five or six other officers started to approach us, trying to kick us out. The atmosphere was very tense. After a short standoff, Zhang gave up, as he did not see any possibility of even having a conversation with the officers, let alone on-the-record interviews.

While we were walking out of the building, an officer that we did not meet before chased us. This officer greeted Zhang and was very friendly. In that moment I realized that the previous unfriendly officers were most likely street-level bureaucrats who were fed up with being the target of controversies; in contrast, the officer who stopped us was probably a mid- or high-level leader who had to be careful about the image of the bureau, especially when dealing with the media affiliated with the municipal party-state. He invited us to an air-conditioned conference room and made us tea. He first asked us why we were there. Zhang told him about the hotline call and clarified that, as a reporter, he did not mean to make trouble; he simply wanted to report the truth about this dispute. After hearing this, the officer said he understood Zhang's request and would invite officers who were directly involved in this case to provide more information.

About ten minutes later, the friendly officer brought in three other officers—one was responsible for dealing with the media, and the other two dealt with this case. These officers were fairly cooperative. They even offered a cigarette to Zhang, a friendly gesture common in professional settings in China, which tend to be male-dominated and structured around informal conversations.[5] Social smoking, in this context, was a subtle but important way to build rapport, so much so that those who don't smoke or quit smoking often feel obligated to accept cigarettes to show appreciation and affinity. As the officers told Zhang details about the case, the conference room was quickly filled with smoke; the details corroborated with the caller's story.

After the conversation, Zhang asked the officers to go on the record and explain the ruling that the sunroom should be revised or demolished. After the interview was over, we were leaving. Right before we walked out of the building, the officer who was responsible for dealing with the media stopped us and asked Zhang, "Do you *have* to broadcast this?" As a seasoned reporter, Zhang responded, "We don't *have* to." Zhang knew that the officer was just being polite, and the real intention was to kill the story. Zhang said he would consult with his producer. After we left the city management bureau, it was time for lunch. During lunch, Zhang received a phone call from Zhao, after which he said the story was killed. The efforts at the bureau where Zhang spent a whole morning were all for naught.

Later, I asked Zhao about this story, and he said it was too sensitive to be pursued. However, this was not the attitude when he assigned Zhang to investigate the story. If Zhao thought this story was too sensitive, why would he send Zhang to the city management bureau in the first place? Zhao then told me that a leader from the city management bureau called and requested that the report not be broadcast. Zhao decided to drop this report without a fight. Given the solid evidence of illegal construction

and the lack of enforcement of the city management bureau's own ruling, Zhao could have chosen to bring the case to higher-level leaders
in the municipal party-state, if the city management bureau continued
to protest it. However, the conservative attitude toward news reporting
that this municipal leadership had shown thus far made Zhao decide
to steer away from a potentially unworthy political fight, which may
jeopardize his own reputation as a reliable media executive in the eyes
of the municipal leadership.

This case also shows that, even when supervising officials at lower
levels, journalists' attempt at critical reporting is not guaranteed to succeed.
The precarious news production process can be shaped by variable factors
from all parties involved, and local conditions may allow some factors
to exert oversized influence. In this case, besides the journalists' learning
of the municipal leadership's media preference, the city management
officers present another key variable, which is political connection. If
the city management officers had solid connections with higher-ups in
the municipal party-state who might help lobbying to censor the report,
then dropping the story would spare Zhao the futile efforts. But it was
unclear whether solid political connections existed. If Zhao cared to
acquire information on this variable, it may have helped him make a
more informed decision on this report. However, the local leadership's
conservative attitude toward the media had an oversized influence on
Zhao, compelling the circumspect decision to drop the story. The political sensitivity that Zhao displayed may be a result of his decade-long
experience covering local political news.

Conclusion

This chapter demonstrates that in carrying out media control at the
local level during the process of news production, bargaining takes place
between involved actors with diverse political and professional interests
in the crosshatching bureaucratic system of *tiao* and *kuai*. Not only are
the political boundaries shifting with local leaders' changing political
interests and frequent leadership turnover, but the interests of lower-level
officials may also exert influence on critical reporting through political
connections with higher-ups in the multilevel bureaucracy. These uncer-
tainties and dynamics are aptly absorbed by journalists' competent and
continual learning, where their coded performance functions as a nimble

detector for the shifting boundaries of critical reporting. This mechanism synchronizes local news reporting with local leaders' media preferences, which in part explains the varying level of critical reporting. Chapter 3 zeroes in on the central role played by local leaders, contextualizing the political institutions that regulate local leaders' career interests and elaborating on the individual characteristics that introduce further variations into their approach to media criticism.

Chapter 3

Political Edge

L ocal leaders use media criticism adroitly to gain a political edge in career advancement. This unique maneuver of media politics did not arise out of a vacuum. This chapter starts with an overview of the historical legacies and evolving policies that comprise the institutional backdrop, against which local leaders leverage the opportunities to shape and use media criticism in unscripted ways. Delving into both formal and informal rules in the cadre management system, this chapter analyzes similar and different career interests of local leaders at provincial and municipal levels. Political leaders' use of media criticism to discipline subordinates has a decades-long history, though its specificities and intentions have evolved along with the dramatic changes in how politics is operated both within the party-state and before the population.

Historical Use of Media Criticism

Criticism has played an important role in the creation and consolidation of the CCP. Mao Zedong, a founding leader, was a proponent of using criticism and self-criticism to correct thoughts and reinforce party ideology (Mao [1929] 1951). Criticism was also an important way to accomplish the "mass line" policy by heeding opinions from the masses, so as to achieve consistency between theory and practice (Mao 1944). In fact, criticism and self-criticism constitute one of the CCP's "three great superior traditions," the other two being "seeking truth from facts" and "the mass line" (Y. Zhao 2011, 221). However, extreme and distorted criticism culminated during the Cultural Revolution (1966–76), taking the form of fabricated and exaggerated accusations against party cadres and ordinary citizens, and leading to abuse, death, and chaos. In the post-Mao era, Deng Xiaoping, the second-generation leader, further theorized the importance of criticism and self-criticism in constructing intraparty unity and democracy (Deng 1983). Most recently, Xi Jinping, the current Chinese leader, has pointed out that criticism and self-criticism are potent weapons that can rid the party of impure and degenerate thoughts, individuals, and other elements (Xi 2016).

While the idea of using criticism to maintain party unity and legitimacy can be traced back to its founding in the 1920s, using the media to publicize criticism has been practiced since the initial years after the founding of the People's Republic. During the Maoist period, criticism and self-criticism were exercised mainly in leader speeches and newspaper articles. For example, Mao himself often criticized and corrected other party cadres' thoughts and actions in his speeches, according to *China Discipline Inspection News*, the mouthpiece of the Central Discipline Inspection Commission of the CCP (X. Liu 2017). In April 1950, the central leadership issued *The Decision to Launch Criticism and Self-criticism in Newspaper Publications* (关于在报纸刊物上展开批评和自我批评的决定), formalizing media criticism. The *Decision* specified that all criticism was to be published independently by reporters and editors, and that as long as the criticism was factual, it could be published without the knowledge or consent of the criticized officials (X. Liu 2017). Immediately following the *Decision*, a critical report was published in *People's Daily* regarding a case of graft and bribery committed by the former Hebei provincial leaders Liu Qingshan and Zhang Zishan, who were executed a month later. Although it is apparent that this particular critical report on the first major corruption case in the People's Republic history was orchestrated by the central leadership rather than resulting from journalistic investigation (Wang and Zhang 2009), this example nonetheless signifies an early use of media criticism to target and discipline lower-level officials.

In the Xi Jinping era of tightening controls over the party and the society, media supervision, by partially reflecting citizen voices, continues to feature prominently in politics and governance (Andreas and Dong 2017, 146). During the ongoing anticorruption campaign launched in 2013 by Xi, tens of thousands of officials have been disciplined, dismissed, or convicted, and televised confessions have been used to prosecute high-level officials for corruption, such as Zhou Yongkang, and to persecute dissenting individuals, such as the bookseller Gui Minhai and the Swedish human rights activist Peter Dahlin.[1] The targeted audience of these staged, televised confessions is far-reaching, including both citizens and government officials. Although these confessions do not fall in the same category as self-criticism, they suggest the importance of the media in the party's tactics to achieve its political objectives. The visuals of televised confessions present a foreboding image that displays the party's power and will in eliminating all dissenting or otherwise inconvenient individuals and voices. The mass communication capacity of the media makes an indispensable force in creating a sense of awe in the party's strategic use of criticism. Without the media, confessions and other forms of criticism and self-criticism would not achieve the same level of subjugating effect. As the old Chinese saying goes, kill the chickens to scare the monkeys. Publicity, which can only be achieved through the mass media, is an essential component in disciplining party cadres and other individuals.

Supervision by Public Opinion

Given its importance, media criticism was formalized as a governing principle by the party when the policy of supervision by public opinion (舆论监督) entered the CCP lexicon in the late 1980s. This policy makes media criticism of party cadres and government officials, in principle, acceptable, further elevating the role of the media in the CCP's rule. While the primary media role remains propaganda and thought work, the target of which is the population, the media now can also be used to supervise local officials.

The first official use of the term "supervision by public opinion" was in the 1987 *Report to the 13th Party Congress*. Party General Secretary Zhao Ziyang stated:

We should use all kinds of modernized news and propaganda tools to increase reporting on government and party affairs, to allow supervision by public opinion to play a role, to support the masses' criticizing the weaknesses and wrongdoings in our work, and to struggle against bureaucratism and other kinds of unhealthy tendencies. (Z. Zhao 1987)

Since then, supervision by public opinion has been mentioned in every Party Congress report. Legally, supervision by public opinion became a part of the *Regulations on Intraparty Supervision of the Chinese Communist Party* (中国共产党党内监督条例) implemented in 2004. Article 33 states:

> Under the leadership of the CCP and according to relevant rules and procedures, news media should play the role of supervision by public opinion through either internal or public reports. Departments and cadres at all levels should emphasize and support supervision by public opinion, listen to criticisms and suggestions, and improve their work.

As argued by other scholars (Chan 2002; Repnikova 2017a), supervision by public opinion is fundamentally about strengthening the CCP rule rather than decentralizing power. Further, in addition to the disciplinary effects, media criticism is also an effective way for the party-state to proactively shape the narrative on its governance performance, in light of increasingly complex and challenging governance issues arising out of rapid urbanization. Although investigative journalism, an important form of media supervision, has been declining due to increasing pressures from the CCP and defecting advertisers (Tong 2011, ch. 4; Tong and Sparks 2009; Wang and Sparks 2019), television livelihood news, which continues to feature critical reporting on a local and limited scale, remains prevalent and continues to shape the public discourse on local governance issues.

The current leader, Xi Jinping, has reemphasized the importance of supervision by public opinion, though what exactly he means by media supervision needs to be parsed. Xi pointed out in his speech at the party's news work conference in April 2016 that "supervision by public opinion and positive propaganda are consistent with each other. News media should confront and disclose problems in government work, while at the same time making sure that critical reports are accurate and objective" (Cui 2016). In juxtaposing critical and positive reporting, this quote unites the two elements in the media's political role so that both aim at strengthening the party's rule. The key to this unity, as implied, is to make sure that "critical reports are accurate and objective." Accuracy and objectivity, however, can be understood as euphemisms for reporting that unambiguously defends the CCP rule, thus allowing arbitrary judgments on the scope and intensity of media criticism. Adding these qualifying properties to the long-standing policy that started the era of media supervision, Xi's interpretation of supervision by public opinion seems to caution against excessive criticism and reorient the media's role toward that of a mouthpiece, so that there is little possibility for a media betrayal against the party. To further understand Xi's interpretation, it is helpful to examine how some local governments and media organizations understand this policy in the Xi era.

In May 2016, immediately following Xi's speech, previously mentioned, the Sichuan provincial party committee issued an administrative order—*On Strengthening Public Opinion Supervision and Persisting in the Implementation of the Central Government's Eight Provisions* (关于加强舆论监督持之以恒落实中央八项规定精神的实施意见). A joint interview with a director from the Sichuan provincial propaganda department and a director from the Sichuan provincial discipline inspection commission reveals that this administrative order is intended to encourage the media to supervise and discipline government officials. It specifies that local governments in Sichuan ought to cooperate with the media and not to withhold information from or lie to the media (S. Chen 2016). Therefore, the Sichuan provincial government sees media supervision as a way to discipline government officials at lower levels, which would advance the central government's campaign on strengthening party discipline. This interpretation is ostensibly more liberal in attaching less strings to media supervision than what Xi's speech seems to imply.

Party Literature (党的文献), the official journal of the CCP Party Literature Research Office (中共中央文献研究室), an institution focusing on theory development for the CCP, offers a slightly different interpretation of supervision by public opinion. It argues that under Xi's leadership media supervision should be integrated with intraparty supervision so that supervision from both within and outside the party can advance the goal of strengthening party unity and discipline (Yin 2017). This analysis uses the legitimacy of intraparty supervision to justify media supervision coming from outside the party. It argues that the synergy of double supervision will best advance "the strict rule of the party" (从严治党). The emphasis, therefore, is more on party loyalty and cohesion, and less on specific government work or governance outcome. In general, this interpretation is also fairly receptive toward media supervision, focusing on the benefits that media supervision can bring.

Chinese Journalists, an official journal published by the state-owned Xinhua News Agency, emphasizes the importance of objectivity and accuracy in media supervision and the media's loyalty to the party, according to an article published to discuss Xi's treatise on news and public opinion work (L. Zhang 2016). This article cites Xi's earlier speech made in 2004 at the Zhejiang provincial news propaganda work conference, stating that the notion of the Fourth Estate is to be rejected because this concept would negate the party's control and guidance over news work. The distinction made between supervision by public opinion and the Fourth Estate clarifies what supervision by public opinion is not, emphasizing that ideological loyalty remains the most important attribute of the news media. This article also cites Xi's speech made in February 2016, stating that critical reports should be objective and accurate, the meaning of which is interpreted as setting the limits of critical reporting. This article then cites Xi's speech made in 1989 in Fujian, stating that certain topics should be off-limits to media supervision, especially problems that are hard to resolve aptly due to limitations in government work. By limiting specific kinds of critical reports, media criticism can be ultimately "constructive" and "positive" for the party. Compared to the previous two interpretations, this is arguably the closest to the original meaning in Xi's speech, emphasizing the limits of critical reporting.

These interpretations demonstrate the nuances in the multidimensional, malleable notion of supervision by public opinion: the Sichuan provincial government emphasizes using media supervision to improve governance; the Party Literature Research Office emphasizes using media supervision to enhance party loyalty and cohesion; the state news agency emphasizes the limits of critical reporting, defining media supervision by what it is not. These differences also demonstrate how the inherent flexibility of this policy allows different interpretations and practices. Although the Xi era has seen tightening rules, a decentralized approach to media criticism remains, as shown by the Sichuan provincial government's interpretation. Therefore, supervision by public opinion continues to provide an institutional opportunity structure that legitimizes media criticism for the ultimate goal of strengthening the party rule. Meanwhile, several other media-related policies consolidate this opportunity structure by providing a more conducive environment for media criticism.

Other Media-Related Policies

In the mid-1990s, the central leadership started to emphasize the issue of increasing government transparency. The report to the 15th National Party Congress (1997) states that "the government should publicize its administrative affairs and budgets. . . . Departments that deal with the mass's interests should publicize their procedures" (Jiang 1997). Since then, the importance of increasing government transparency and public participation was mentioned in the report to every National Party Congress. In 2000, the CCP Central Committee General Office and the State Council issued *The Notice on the Full Implementation of the System of Open Government Affairs in the Township Governments and Enterprises* (关于在全国乡镇政企机关全面推行政务公开制度的通知). This initiative was then promoted from township governments to higher-level governments, according to *The Outline to Comprehensively Promote the Implementation of the Administrative Programs* (全面推进依法行政实施纲要) issued by the State Council in 2004. Under these initiatives, local governments rolled out their local regulations on making government information more transparent. Guangzhou and Shanghai implemented *Regulations on Open Government Information* (政府信息公开规定) in 2003 and 2004, respectively, before the national regulation on open government information was implemented in 2008.[2] Building on the momentum, in 2011 the CCP Central Committee General Office and the State Council issued *Opinions on Deepening Open Government Affairs and Enhancing Administrative Services* (关于深化政务公开加强政务服务的意见) to consolidate and innovate the ways to publicize government affairs. The use of the Internet for government affairs was promoted. Government websites, online complaint systems, and the "mayor's mailbox" are exemplary initiatives intended to increase government transparency and encourage public participation (Distelhorst 2017; Chen, Pan, and Xu 2016; Meng, Pan, and Yang 2017; Pan 2019).

Parallel to these changes made to the government, within the CCP, the initiative to open up party affairs (党务公开) also became part of the transparent government initiative. Open party affairs was formalized in the *Regulations on Intraparty Supervision of the Chinese Communist Party* (中国共产党党内监督条例), issued in 2004, and later emphasized in *The Outline on the Implementation of a Comprehensive System to Punish and Prevent Corruption through Education, Institution, and Supervision* (建立健全教育、制度、监督并重的惩治和预防腐败体系实施纲要), issued in 2005. Under these initiatives, a news spokesperson system and a system of open power and transparent operation at the county level were established (C. Liu 2013).

This series of institutional and policy changes provide a conducive environment by making it easier for journalists to conduct investigation and accentuating the role of media supervision in local governance. The Nanjing municipal government provides an example. According to Hao Jiming, the dean of the party school of the CCP Nanjing committee, the Nanjing municipal government and the CCP Nanjing committee experimented with and eventually succeeded in establishing a "sunshine government" that emphasizes transparency, serving the public, preventing corruption, increasing efficiency, and advancing development (Hao 2013). Media supervision played an indispensable role in establishing this sunshine government. In 2001, the Nanjing municipal government launched the annual event of Ten Thousand Citizens Evaluate Government Bureaus, the results of which were broadcast live by the Nanjing television station, highlighting the media's role in supervising the local government. In 2009, the Nanjing municipal government launched an online complaint platform, which is shared with local media outlets including the Nanjing television station, Nanjing radio station, and *Nanjing Daily*. Citizens can lodge complaints using this platform, and the media outlets will choose news sources from these complaints. According to Hao (2013), in 2010 this platform received 3069 emails, among which 1978 were suggestions and 1091 were complaints. The response rate was 85% and the satisfaction rate was 92%.

Overall, the institutional opportunity structure for media supervision consists of a series of policies at central and local levels. Against this institutional backdrop, to understand whether and how local leaders choose to engage in media criticism requires a close examination of their interests and incentives. The following sections analyze how media criticism can function as political reprimand to advance the distinct career interests of leaders at provincial and municipal levels, and how individual leadership style differences recalibrate the political appeal of media criticism.

Local Leaders' Career Interests

Formal Institutions of Cadre Promotion

As discussed earlier, political leaders in China are appointed by their superiors through the *nomenklatura* system. Provincial leaders such as provincial party secretaries and governors are appointed by the Central Organization Department. Leaders at lower levels, including municipal,[3] district, county, and township levels are appointed by their superiors at the next level up, referred to as the "one-level-down management" model (Landry 2008, ch. 2; O'Brien and Li 1999). For example, a county party secretary's appointment is typically decided by the organization department of the municipality to which that county belongs and approved by the provincial organization department. This one-level-down management model has been revised in recent years, a result of the party's continuous efforts at reforming the cadre management system. For example, in 2009 the Central Organization Department implemented a revision to the one-level-down model so that county party secretaries are directly appointed by provincial organization departments, rather than municipal organization departments. The main motivation for this reform was the lackluster performance by county party secretaries in general, including corruption scandals and unresolved local conflicts that escalated into protests (Jiamin Wang 2009). The purpose of the reform was to increase control over county party secretaries so that competent and loyal cadres are placed in positions that oversee important governance responsibilities. Analysts argue that this reform also allows competent county party secretaries to be promoted to higher-level positions through a faster track. Therefore, local leaders are incentivized to please and impress their superiors for career advancement.

Another component of the cadre management system is cadre rotation. The rule of cadre rotation is intended to curb localism. In June 1999, the Central Organization Department issued *Regulations on Cadre Exchange*, which specifies that (1) county and municipal top leaders should not be selected from the same region, (2) those who head a county or a city for over ten years should be transferred elsewhere, and (3) provincial leaders should be transferred more frequently to another province or the central government (C. Li 2001, 65–66). Furthermore, the rule of avoidance (回避制度) was revived after 1978 to place effective constraints on localism (Eaton and Kostka 2014, 362).[4] The rule of cadre rotation means that promotion can take a political leader to a different locality; the higher the position one has been promoted to, the broader the geographic area one's career trajectory tends to cover. An important implication is that, when a leader is parachuted to a different locality where he or she may have little political connection, mobilizing all resources available, including the media, to establish personal authority and promote effective governance becomes a strong career incentive.

Promotion decisions, however, are based on evaluation criteria that are not entirely transparent. The literature on Chinese elite politics focuses on two broad categories of evaluation criteria—performance (Landry 2008; Li and Zhou 2005) and factional loyalty (Shih, Adolph, and Liu 2012; Meyer, Shih, and Lee 2016). Integrating these criteria, a recent study further finds that the lower the administrative level, the more important economic performance is, and the higher the administrative level, the more important factional loyalty is; these strategic criteria allow ruling elites to achieve economic performance while ensuring loyalty (Landry, Lü, and Duan 2018). More recently, differentiating the types of competence, Don Lee and Paul Schuler (2020) find in their comparative study that technical competence is rewarded in autocracies in East Asia as long as political competence is not seen as a threat to the existing rule. This mechanism dovetails the dual importance of loyalty and performance.

While factional loyalty is conceptually clear, especially during the Xi era of tightening control and centralized power, performance is a more ambiguous goal that can be measured with a diverse set of metrics. Furthermore, factional loyalty only helps when performance is satisfactory (Jia, Kudamatsu, and Seim 2015; Li and Gore 2018). The relative importance of various governance goals in performance evaluation evolves as the socioeconomic and political conditions change. In general, the emphasis on hard economic output is gradually giving way to good governance and quality growth, which emphasizes issues such as reducing environmental pollution and providing public services. Several important documents issued by the central leadership reflect this evolution in cadre performance evaluation. At the beginning of the reform era, in November 1979, the Central Organization Department issued *The Decision to Establish Cadre Evaluation System* (中共中央组织部关于试行干部考核制度的意见), introducing explicit targets and performance contracts that bear on promotional decisions (Edin 1998, 2003; Whiting 1996, 2004). In the late 1980s, the cadre evaluation system set up quantitative goals, or "hard targets," that must be met (O'Brien and Li 1995, 764). The new measures also included introducing competition among bureaucrats, using economic incentives to encourage goal fulfillment, and using third parties to measure government performance (Edin 2003, 37). Performance evaluations based on hard targets were used to assign jobs and determine remuneration (O'Brien and Li 1999, 172; Heberer and Trappel 2013). The goals of cadre management were twofold: to increase governing efficiency and to more ably control local officials (Edin 2003).

In the Xi Jinping era, the Central Organization Department issued new documents on performance evaluation that continue to shape cadre promotion. In December 2013, *The Notice to Improve Local Party Leadership and Cadre Performance Evaluation Work* (关于改进地方党政领导班子和领导干部政绩考核工作的通知)[5] was issued to deemphasize the role of economic performance while emphasizing other areas of governance including sustainable development and livelihood improvement. In January 2014, the Central Organization Department issued and updated *Regulations on Party Leadership and Cadre Promotion Work* (党政领导干部选拔任用工作条例),[6] replacing an earlier version issued in 2002 and emphasizing promoting "good cadres" who are loyal to the party. In July 2015, the General Office of the CCP Central Committee issued *Several Regulations to Further Leading Cadres' Ability to Fulfill Requirements* (推进领导干部能上能下若干规定),[7] emphasizing party control over personnel and explicitly recommending incompetent leaders be demoted. This series of documents outlines the evolving notion of good performance as a result of changing politics and governance priorities. In the 1990s and the first decade of the new century, when the economy was taking off, economic performance was primary among the evaluation criteria, despite diverging external factors beyond local leaders' control, such as global market conditions and the size of nonstate and state sectors in the local economy (Landry 2008, ch. 2; Whiting 2011; Heberer and Schubert 2012). In the Xi era when the economy is slowing down, efficient and quality governance is emphasized, especially in light of rapid environmental degradation and growing public discontent.

Informal Politics of Getting Ahead

The complex and evolving criteria of cadre evaluation and promotion are not all that dictates local leaders' career interests. On paper, local leaders are evaluated based on the formal targets and goals outlined above. They have to "govern well" (Landry 2008, 82) to advance their political careers. In reality, however, local leaders also face incentives to game the system through impressing the right superiors for a quick climb up the bureaucratic ladder. This makes informal politics, such as distinctive political accomplishments (政绩) (Cai 2004) and image building (Pan 2019), particularly important.

Recent studies find that superiors' recognition and appreciation are crucial in promotional decisions (Li and Gore 2018), indicating that merely completing the targets and goals may not be enough to earn superiors' attention and praise. Christian Göbel and Thomas Heberer (2017) observe that, the recent "mass line activities" launched by Xi Jinping essentially project a new type of "clean" cadres who would "both prioritize the needs of the people and develop a 'learning,' 'innovation,' and 'problem-solving' mentality in order to enhance overall state capacity" (293). Furthermore, "while target fulfillment requires cadres to administer and manage, policy innovation requires more—it requires entrepreneurship" (303). This over-the-top expectation outside the formal rules of cadre evaluation drives local leaders to go the extra mile to advance their political careers.

Mastering the art of getting ahead through informal politics is not easy, however. Though local leaders try to meet and exceed expectations from higher-up for political survival and advancement, the result is often featured by overreach and disarray. A recent development in Beijing provides an example. According to a report by Chris Buckley and Keith Bradsher (2018) of the *New York Times*, Xi ordered Beijing to reduce its population, and his protégé Cai Qi, the newly appointed Beijing party secretary, used a deadly apartment fire to push for mass demolition, resulting in tens of thousands of migrants losing their homes and a subsequent public outcry. The authors refer to this and other similar incidents as "a confounding mix of overreaction to orders and reluctance to act on one's own initiative." Local leaders often wield discretionary power to impress, but they must also bear the possibility of miscalculation and backfire.

Adding to the complexity is the increasing importance of "dealing with the media" (应对媒体) in an era that gives prominence to political communication. Since the first training sessions for spokespersons were held in September 2003, the CCP has mobilized media scholars to contribute insights on political communication strategies. In 2006, one of the first government-sponsored books on this topic, *The Study of Government and News: How the Government Should Deal with the Media* (政府新闻学——政府应对媒体的学问), was published by the party-affiliated Jiangsu People's Publisher. In the foreword, Ye Hao, then director of the municipal propaganda department of the CCP Nanjing committee, emphasized the importance of training party cadres and government officials to correctly understand and deal with the media (F. Chen 2006). In an article that Ye later published in *Jianghai Journal*, the communist theory journal affiliated with the Jiangsu social science academy, he discussed the way the American government deals with the media and what party cadres and government officials can learn from it (Ye 2008). He argues that a positive and proactive attitude is key to "guiding" the media to the advantage of the party-state.

Considering both the formal institution of cadre evaluation and promotion and the informal politics of getting ahead, it becomes clear that the expectation for a successful political career is quite high. One has to generate the right kind of governance outcomes while presenting a competent media performance. These incentives motivate some local leaders to use media criticism to increase bureaucratic control and to advance their governance agendas. Although media criticism is not the only instrument for local leaders to employ and it is not the most fitting for all politicians, the political appeal of media criticism is further elevated by the reality of frequent leadership turnover, which impels local leaders to generate governance outcomes on a short deadline. The urgency underscores the appeal of the media power of publicity.

Frequent Leadership Turnover

In recent decades, shorter leadership tenures have added a layer of urgency to the informal politics of getting ahead. At the municipal level, the majority of municipal party secretaries and mayors move on to the next position within two to four years, shorter than the prescribed term of five years. According to Sarah Eaton and Genia Kostka (2014, 362), an analysis of 898 municipal party secretaries between 1993 and 2011 shows that the average tenure was 3.8 years, and that 23% of municipal party secretaries spent two years or less in their positions, while 25% stayed for 5 years or more. Pierre Landry (2008, 90) finds that between 1990 and 2001, mayors' average tenure declined from 3.2 years to 2.5 years. At the provincial level, Gong et al. (2015) find frequent leadership turnover in both provincial party secretary and governor positions from 1980 to 2011; the average tenure was 3.6 years for provincial party secretaries and 3 years for governors. The frequent leadership turnover has important consequences for governance; it breeds short-term decision making and undermines accountability.

In their study of environmental policy implementation, Sarah Eaton and Genia Kostka (2014) detail the negative consequences of frequent leadership turnover. Because of the short time horizons, local leaders are likely to choose quick, low-quality tactics to implement environmental policies, barring thoughtful and long-term approaches to environmental protection: "The immense pressure of a short term in office, during which time leaders must produce results to be considered for promotion, incentivizes local leaders to select highly visible projects that deliver outcomes during their own tenure periods, while long-term complex initiatives are often sidelined" (360). Indeed, local leaders complain about frequent turnover. According to Pierre Landry (2008, 90–91), a member of the standing committee of the Liaoning provincial people's political consultative conference complained that one locality had had six party secretaries in seven years. In their recent study, Baoqing Pang, Shu Keng, and Lingna Zhong (2018) find that "sprinting with small steps," referring to the phenomenon where officials who have held a series of key positions briefly are more likely to be promoted to higher levels, constitutes a common track of cadre promotion, in addition to the track where officials earn their promotion through regular and longer tenures.

Indeed, the frequent leadership turnover and shorter tenures create urgency to produce governance results in time for promotion. Studying China's mayors, Pierre Landry (2008, 102) finds that as their tenures near the end of a full five-year term, their exit is more likely than promotion, suggesting the importance of showcasing performance early in the tenure cycle to advance one's political career. Jennifer Pan (2019) finds that county-level leaders in their early tenure cycle tend to project images of benevolence and attentiveness to citizens' concerns through government websites to promote their careers, and that late-tenure county-level leaders tend to show competence by highlighting their achievements. These findings suggest that local leaders' tenure cycle affects how they use the media. Considering the utility of media criticism in generating immediate governance results, the incentive for local leaders to use critical reporting should be stronger at the beginning of their tenures.

The former Jiangsu provincial party secretary, Li Yuanchao, provides an illustrative example of how a local leader uses media criticism to advance career at the beginning of the tenure cycle, as discussed in the previous chapter. Immediately after being promoted to the Jiangsu provincial party secretary position in 2002, Li turned to media criticism to help increase bureaucratic control and improve governance, by personally visiting the newsroom of *Zero Distance in Nanjing* and encouraging the journalists to supervise government work. However, about a year later, Li changed course and instructed the program to scale back critical reporting, suggesting a strategic and selective use of media criticism. This example shows the appeal of the governance effects of media criticism to a newly appointed leader.

Differing Incentives at Provincial and Municipal Levels

Despite the shared incentive to use media criticism as part of the informal politics of getting ahead, leaders at provincial and municipal levels face some different career incentives due to their ranks, which shape their career paths going forward. Earlier studies find that "provincial leadership is both a training ground for national leadership and a battleground for various political forces" and that "the post of provincial chief has been the most pivotal stepping stone to top national leadership offices in post-Deng China" (C. Li 2010, 2–3). The percentage of Politburo members with provincial chief experience has gone up from 50% in 1992, during the 14th Party Congress, to 76% in 2012, during the 18th Party Congress (C. Li 2013). This increasingly common career path for provincial leaders, however, hinges on an established but informal rule of age limit. The retirement age for Politburo members is 68 or older, and this rule has been followed since the 16th Party Congress in 2002 (Miller 2016). If one is 68 years old, then a promotion to the Politburo is unlikely and retirement is expected. If one is 67 years old, then a promotion to the Politburo is possible and retirement is expected after completing a term when one is older than 68. According to Cheng Li (2010), the majority of provincial chiefs (80.7%) are aged between 56 and 65. Therefore, many provincial leaders have 11 years and less to prepare for further promotion to the top national leadership, and the urgency rises as one's age approaches late 60s.

At the provincial level, age limits were formally established in 1982 when a mandatory retirement system was introduced; provincial leaders were required to retire at the age of 65, although this rule was not enforced across all provinces until the first decade of the new century (D. T. Liu 2018). In the 2010s, age has become one of the most important indicators of a politician's career prospects (C. Li 2012). If a provincial party secretary is not promoted to a post in the central leadership, typically in the Politburo, before the age of 65, he or she then must retire. The implications are twofold. First, leaders approaching 65 but still young enough to retain the prospect of promotion have stronger incentives to utilize all formal and informal means, including media criticism, to increase the chance of promotion. Second, leaders very close to or already 65 may become "lame ducks" who lose motivation for better governance performance due to the slim prospects for promotion (D. T. Liu 2018). Therefore, leaders in this elder age range should have weaker incentives to utilize media criticism.

Municipal leaders of similar ages, however, do not face such urgency, because their career paths would most likely take a different trajectory. Positions below the provincial level also have age limits, and they follow the general retirement age rule of 60. If a municipal leader is already 59, then the dim chance for further promotion would reduce the incentive to engage in informal politics of getting ahead. Therefore, with an age in high 50s, municipal leaders' incentive to use media criticism should be weaker than provincial leaders, who in the same age range should strive for promotion until they reach an age close to 65. With an age in the low 50s, both provincial and municipal leaders should have a strong incentive to engage in informal politics, including media criticism, to get ahead. The quantitative analysis in chapter 5 provides empirical support for these hypothesized age patterns. Leaders who are savvy about the media may even take a step further and orchestrate critical reporting to achieve governance goals.

At the age of 53, Wang Yongkang was appointed to be the party secretary of Xi'an, the capital of Shaanxi province, on December 9, 2016, after spending most of his career in the eastern coastal Zhejiang province.[8] Within a month after his appointment, Wang initiated the creation of a new television news program called *Daily Focus* (每日聚焦) that first aired on December 23, 2016. This program is devoted to supervising and criticizing various bureaus within the municipal government. The topics covered are the municipal government's governance priorities, such as curbing environmental pollution and cracking down on illegal construction. As I found in my fieldwork, the discipline commission of the municipal party committee deployed special personnel to temporarily station in the Xi'an television building to provide detailed instructions for the day-to-day critical reporting. According to an article published by the Zhejiang television official website,[9] Wang, who was a top provincial leader in Zhejiang, intended to emulate the "Zhejiang model" where the media play an important supervisory role in local governance. This article states that by being personally involved in the creation of *Daily Focus*, Wang intended to use this program to discipline government officials and improve governance in all districts, counties, and towns in Xi'an.

As a daily news program, *Daily Focus* is only about five minutes long, but it examines a single issue in-depth.[10] To justify its critical reporting, this program often cites Wang's speeches and the priorities of the Xi'an municipal government. On the basis of direct support from Wang, this program is a mouthpiece of the municipal leadership that publicizes vexing governance issues so that street-level bureaucrats feel the pressure to resolve those issues competently. In this way, *Daily Focus* has become an effective, informal instrument outside of the formal institutions of bureaucratic control to achieve governance outcomes.

For example, in its report aired on January 5, 2017, *Daily Focus* criticized government officials who worked at the service windows of a district police bureau for their poor attitude. These officials are examples of street-level bureaucrats because they work at the grassroots of the administrative hierarchy and they directly deal with citizens. This report specifically criticized the officials responsible for processing household registration documents. Journalists disguised themselves as ordinary citizens in need of household registration, and their requests were declined by these officials for unclear reasons. The video footage obtained by a hidden camera shows that some officials were impatient while talking to the disguised journalists, and they were distracted by chatting with each other when they were supposed to focus on handling citizens' cases. The issue of household registration was selected because it was a priority issue for the Xi'an government to attract talent by making it easier to obtain an urban household registration and settle down in Xi'an. At the end of this report, the anchor cited Wang's speech about correcting government officials' service attitudes toward citizens, justifying the critical report and presenting to the viewers that the municipal government is attentive to citizens' concerns.

Two days later, *Xi'an Zero Distance*, a livelihood news program also produced by Xi'an television station, as discussed earlier, aired a follow-up report stating that those misbehaving officials had been criticized and educated. Furthermore, their district police bureau submitted a self-criticism report to the municipal party committee, detailing their mistakes and plans for rectification. Specifically, the district police bureau decided that the annual target performance evaluation would incorporate media criticism as a measure. Under its jurisdiction, if a township police bureau were criticized by the media once, that bureau would be demoted in the annual target performance evaluation; if a township police bureau were criticized by the media twice, it would be demoted again in the evaluation; if a township police bureau were criticized by the media three times, responsible officials would be dismissed. Furthermore, all police bureaus at district and township levels in Xi'an convened organization-wide meetings to educate their bureaucrats about discipline and serving the people.

My interviews with journalists at the Xi'an television station clearly show that, since Wang became the municipal party secretary, the television station has become an important actor in the local governance process. The news production model has evolved under Wang's leadership; now a complete problem-solution chain—from discovering problems, reporting on them, to solving them within a matter of days—has become the hallmark narrative and almost guaranteed result of critical reporting, thanks to Wang's direct support. This news production model is markedly different from the previous examples where journalists had to be careful about whether to pursue certain critical reports, let alone their resolution. This change has empowered journalists to devote more airtime to critical reports on key governance issues and the follow-up reports covering subsequent resolutions.

The municipal leader's heavy involvement, therefore, has closely steered the direction of critical reporting in Xi'an. Unlike organic criticism where local leaders allow journalists to supervise street-level bureaucrats through a regular news production process, in this example, Wang directly participated in the news production process by assigning journalists with specific governance topics, essentially becoming a behind-the-scene news producer. The purpose is to orchestrate critical reporting that targets specific issue areas and government bureaus to help generate desired, visible, and immediate governance results. Furthermore, this example shows that a different news program can pick up the topic covered by the more critical *Daily Focus*. This between-program agenda-setting effect allows temporarily higher tolerance for media criticism to spill over and enable other news programs to reap the commercial and professional benefits.

Wang's savvy use of media criticism comes from his previous governing experience in Zhejiang where he held the position of municipal party secretary of a prefecture-level city, Lishui. In China the eastern coastal provinces are generally perceived, though not always accurately, as being at the forefront of reform and development, thus expected to share successful experiences with inland provinces. Wang's invoking the notion of the "Zhejiang model" suggests a shrewd leadership style; as an externally appointed leader parachuted to Xi'an, Wang embraced his prior experience and used it as an advantage to establish personal authority under the name of "learning advanced experiences" (学习先进经验). Casting media criticism as a core component of the "Zhejiang model," his proactive and adroit use of critical reporting suggests a careful calculation to help him get ahead in a fiercely competitive career.

Around July 2017, about half a year into Wang's tenure, instead of continually reporting on new governance problems, *Daily Focus* started to shift gears and devote more airtime to review the improvements and accomplishments that this municipal government had achieved thus far. Other news programs produced by Xi'an television station followed suit and the number of positive reports increased. Relevant descriptive statistics are already presented in chapter 1. Although the level of critical reporting remained higher than before Wang's tenure, the level of positive reporting increased as Wang's tenure proceeded. This important change indicates the strategic and temporary nature of orchestrated criticism. Once governance goals are perceived to be accomplished, local leaders scale back criticism and calculate other ways to use the media or other elements of informal politics to advance their careers. Therefore, the level of critical reporting fluctuates, as it is an uninstitutionalized instrument of governance.

From a different perspective, governance results achieved through media criticism are mostly short-term; they may redress some citizen grievances and dilute local tension, but the root cause of governance problems is unlikely to be fully addressed. Long-term solutions require careful considerations and rigorous policy-making, which are not provided by media criticism in its current form. However, these concerns are likely beyond the scope of local leaders' considerations, especially in an age of shorter tenures. The unique power of media publicity allows critical reporting to provide exactly what local leaders look for when they recruit the media as extra help—immediate and visible improvements on key governance issues.

Individual Differences in Leadership Style

So far, this chapter has demonstrated that the institutional interests and incentives derived from the cadre management system regulate local leaders' behavior toward the media. However, these interests and incentives are faced by all local leaders, thus they do not fully explain the varying levels of critical reporting, which requires a further examination of individual-level factors.

Media control is an issue area that amplifies the impact of individual-level characteristics such as leadership style toward the media. Unlike issue areas where concrete, numeric targets can be set and met, such as economic growth and environmental protection, the work of managing the media is more fluid, defying objective or uniform standards. Because media policies from higher-level leadership often contain broad and vague goals, such as to "organize, coordinate, and direct provincial propaganda work in cultural, broadcast, radio, news, publishing, and other relevant agencies,"[11] in the case of the Jilin provincial government, or to "tell a good Sichuan chapter of the China story, so as to create a beautiful, prosperous, and harmonious Sichuan image,"[12] in the case of Sichuan provincial government, these media policies necessitate local discretion in interpretation and implementation, which allows local party secretaries' leadership style toward the media to drive the focus and tone of media reporting.

As discussed in chapter 1, this book employs a framework based on the level of risk acceptance to categorize and understand local leaders' approach to the media. This framework has resonance in the literature. In their study of political personalities in China, Reza Hasmath, Jessica Teets, and Orion Lewis (2019) find that there are three baseline personality types—authoritarian, consultative, and entrepreneurial—based on a series of original surveys with local policymakers. This categorization is also primarily based upon risk tolerance. Furthermore, the authors find that these personality types interact with institutional incentives to shape the propensity for policy innovation. Local officials innovate when they perceive that it may advance their career prospects or solve local governance problems. Along a similar logic, this chapter has laid out the institutional incentives for local leaders to govern well, which then induce different media strategies that are shaped by individual leadership styles.

Because of the inherent risk of media criticism in an unfree political system, risk averse leaders tend to be cautious about media criticism, exerting strict control over local media outlets; risk acceptant leaders tend to be savvy about using media criticism strategically and selectively, treating it as an instrument of governance to rein in subordinates and to generate governance achievements. Therefore, the shared institutional incentive to perform well and to impress superiors can lead to two diverging strategies regarding media control. Incorporating the institutional incentives discussed earlier, we should expect risk acceptant leaders to have stronger incentives to use media criticism at the beginning of their tenures, a time when they need to establish authority for immediate governance outcomes. We can also expect that toward the end of their tenures, the incentive to use media criticism becomes weaker, because that is the time to showcase governance records for promotion. Conversely, we should expect risk averse leaders to tolerate less critical reporting throughout their tenures.

Therefore, local leaders' intentional use of media criticism suggests fluctuation in the level of critical reporting, and that high levels of critical reporting are transient. Furthermore, too much criticism will have negative implications for stability maintenance, a top goal for which a lack of satisfaction could lead to adverse career impact for local leaders (Minzner 2018, 92, 97–100; Wang and Minzner 2015; Lee and Zhang 2013). Media criticism is not intended to truly supervise the local government but is strategically and selectively used by savvy politicians. Chapter 5 provides further quantitative evidence supporting the correlation between a risk-acceptant, media-embracive leadership style and a higher level of critical reporting at the beginning of tenure cycles.

Conclusion

The media have been an important actor not only controlled but also manipulated by the party-state to advance political interests. The career incentives that local leaders face propel them to resort to informal politics, including media criticism, to get ahead in a fiercely competitive career. Using media criticism as an effective instrument to achieve immediate governance results satisfies local leaders' need to generate notable governance records on a short deadline, due to the opaque selection rules of promotion and frequent leadership turnover. Media-savvy leaders may even orchestrate critical reporting as concentrated efforts to discipline subordinates for governance improvement.

While sharing the common incentive to use media criticism for career advancement, local leaders at provincial and municipal levels also face different promotion rules separating their career trajectories. Provincial leaders have a relatively higher likelihood to be promoted to central leadership positions, but the age limit may propel them to use media criticism more as they approach their late 60s. Municipal leaders face lower age limits for positions below the national level, indicating that they have a weaker incentive to use media criticism as they approach their late 60s. Therefore, given the same age range between mid-50s and mid-60s, provincial leaders tend to have a stronger incentive to use media criticism for career advancement. Chapter 5 demonstrates the statistical significance of these factors in explaining varying levels of critical reporting.

Allowing or orchestrating criticism to discipline street-level bureau-crats, local leaders use the media to undergird their authority, generate governance outcomes, and impress their superiors. However, the political logic is only part of the theory of convenient criticism. The market logic and journalistic agency are crucial factors in absorbing and reflecting citizen grievances and governance problems that arise during rapid urbanization. It is to these topics that the next chapter turns.

Chapter 4

Keen Partner

The concept of media market came into prominence among news professionals after the media reforms started in the 1980s. Prior to that, almost all media organizations in China received complete state funding and thus were under microscopic state control (Miao 2011, 92). After the media reforms, state funding receded substantially, and media organizations had to rely on advertising and other sources of revenue to maintain operations (Chan and Qiu 2002; De Burgh 2003; Esarey 2005; Shirk 2011; Volland 2012). Meanwhile, deregulation, commercialization, and partial privatization (Stockmann 2013), all part of the media reforms, granted more autonomy in the management structure within media organizations and more decision-making power in the news production process. The subsequent sharp increase in the number of news outlets led to intense competition for audiences and changing style and content of news.

In the television industry, the overnight success of livelihood news programs demonstrated a model of profitable news production. Critical reporting that supervises and corrects local officials helps establish a strong media reputation among audiences, who have come to treat livelihood news programs as an effective channel to seek help and redress grievances. This mutually beneficial relationship sustains the model of livelihood news that makes up a large portion of organic criticism existing in the Chinese media discourse. The model of livelihood news, which started in the late 1990s and the early aughts, also paved the way for orchestrated criticism that started in the late aughts, when local leaders learned to capitalize on the media power of publicity and take control of critical reporting to achieve governance goals.

This chapter examines the convenient criticism argument from the media perspective, unraveling how livelihood news programs have evolved into a keen partner in the local governance process. Although local leaders may perceive career benefits from corrective critical report-ing and thus allow or encourage it, journalistic agency emanating from commercial pressures and professional aspirations is the animating force of news production. This chapter first outlines the media reforms that led to the fierce competition in today's media landscape, setting up the backdrop that spurred transformational changes in the television news industry. Then, it examines the unique journalistic values that emerged in the context of rapid urbanization. By taking the side of the disempowered, journalists channel citizen grievances through limited critical reporting. This pursuit is simultaneously shaped by the political forces that direct journalistic energy to street-level bureaucrats, which facilitates effective and immediate rectification within the bureaucracy. To enrich the context of television critical reporting, the final section of this chapter discusses the common issues of citizen grievances and governance problems covered by livelihood news programs.

Media Reforms and Competition

After the epoch-making policy of reform and opening was adopted in the late 1970s, the wave of reforms started to move beyond the economic sector. In 1992, the 14th Party Congress officially adopted the concept of "socialist market economy," after which the State Planning Commission officially categorized the news industry as part of the service industry. As the state funding for media organizations receded, the news media started to rely on advertising and other sources of revenue to survive and thrive. For television stations, advertising revenue, which is closely associated with program ratings, became a chief revenue source (Hong, Lü, and Zou 2009, 44). The commercial pressure coupled with deregulation allows more control over news production by journalists, leading to increasing diversity in news content. As a result, the media evolved from a pure political instrument of propaganda to a commercialized entity that also needs to serve the market. Meanwhile, a series of reforms restructured the television industry, leading to fierce market competition.

Using data from the China Statistical Yearbooks published by the National Bureau of Statistics and the China Radio and Television Yearbooks published by the State Administration of Radio and Television, figure 4.1 shows the numbers of television stations in China from 1978 to 2014. In 1983, the central leadership issued the policy of "four-level television stations" in the number 37 document that approved the *Reporting Outline for Radio and Television Work* (关于广播电视工作的汇报提纲). According to this document, governments at the central, provincial, municipal, and county levels shall have affiliated television stations (Huang and Zhou 2003, 31). This led to a rapidly growing number of television stations, which peaked in 1997 with 923 stations. The vast television landscape generated problems such as limited local audiences, especially for county-level stations, low-quality television programming, and an increasingly diverse media market that became more difficult for the party-state to oversee (Huang and Zhou 2003). In 1998, the State Council issued the *Notice to Strengthen Radio and Television Transmission Network Construction* (关于加强广播电视传输网络建设管理的通知), halting further expansion of television stations. In 1999, the State Council further issued *Opinions on Strengthening Radio and Television Cable Network Construction Management* (关于加强广播电视有线网络建设管理的意见) to streamline the structure of the television industry. Consequently, many county-level radio and television stations were disbanded, although some continue to operate and broadcast programs till today (Miao 2011, 92). Following this restructuring was a sharp decrease in the number of television stations. At the end of 2014, there were a total of 159 television stations in mainland China.

Despite the decreasing number of televisions stations, the competition in the television industry has only been growing. Each television station has multiple channels, to allow localization and diversity of program content. Therefore, even with the decreasing number of television stations, the number of television channels has been growing steadily, from 219 in 1985 to 3,360 in 2016, a 14-fold increase in 31 years, as shown in figure 4.1. Many county-level television stations that were disbanded in the late 1990s were eventually absorbed by municipal-level television stations as additional channels.

On the other hand, the penetration rate of television in China has grown from 78% in 1989 to 98.99% in 2016, shown in figure 4.2. Importantly, there was very little difference in television penetration rate in recent years between rural and urban areas, indicating broad and even coverage of television programming. This broad influence is not yet shared by other forms of media, including print and online media outlets. Since

Number of Television Stations

Year (1978–2014)

Number of Television Channels

Year (1985–2016)

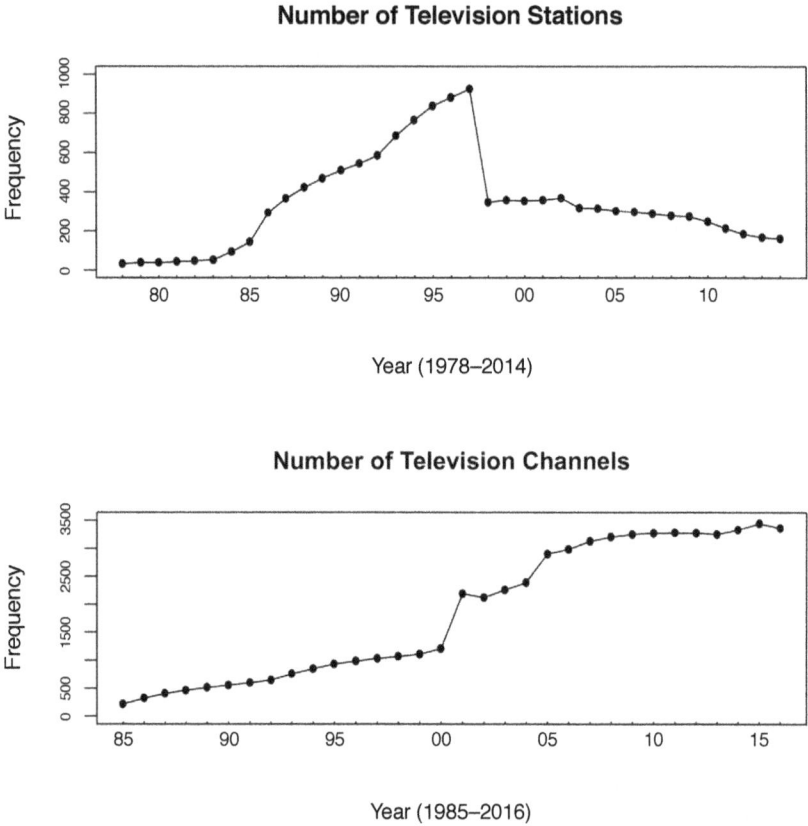

Figure 4.1. Television Stations and Channels in China. *Source*: China Statistical Yearbooks and China Radio and Television Yearbooks.

2004, the television penetration rate in China has remained above 95%. Given the shrinking room for the penetration rate to grow further, the rising number of television channels and the growing number of staff clearly suggest mounting competition.[1]

Booming in the television industry are not only news programs but also entertainment, educational, and other programs. To isolate news programs, figure 4.3 shows the number of television program hours produced in the past two decades. The overall television programming has been increasing, and the speed is higher in the first decade of the new

Television Penetration Rate

Year (1989–2016)

Size of Television and Radio Staff (10,000 people)

Year (1984–2016)

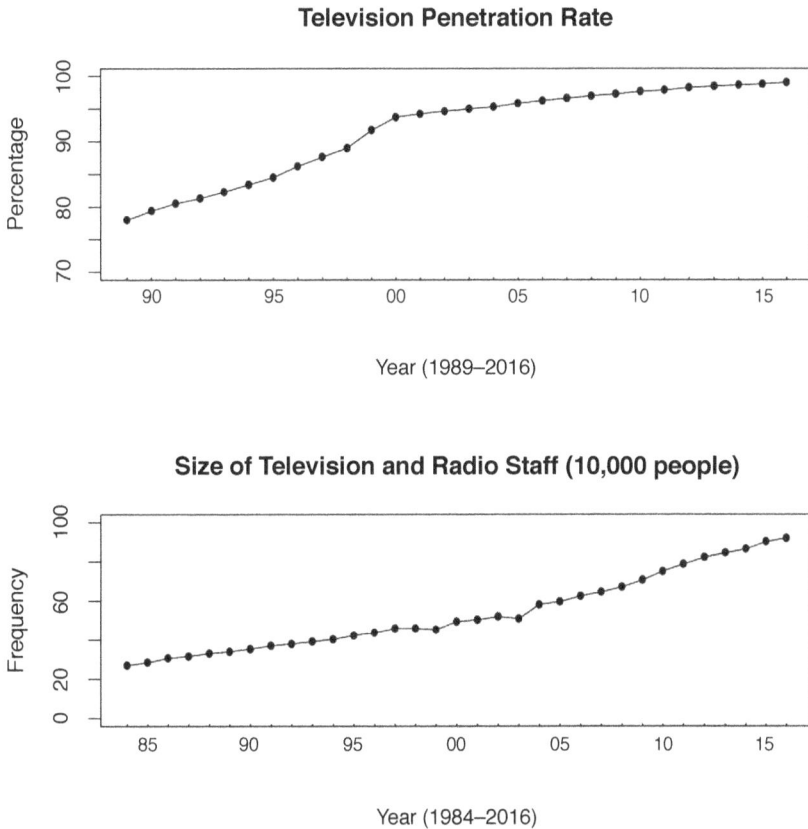

Figure 4.2. Television Industry in China. *Source*: China Statistical Yearbooks.

century. Due to the inconsistent television program categories documented in the China Statistical Yearbooks and the China Radio and Television Yearbooks, I only show three categories that were consistently documented throughout the years—news, variety shows, and special programs—in figure 4.3. While all three categories have been growing in the past two decades, variety shows peaked in the late 1990s, and special programs peaked in the following decade. Starting from the late aughts, news programs have been growing with the highest number of production hours among the three categories, indicating persistent importance of news

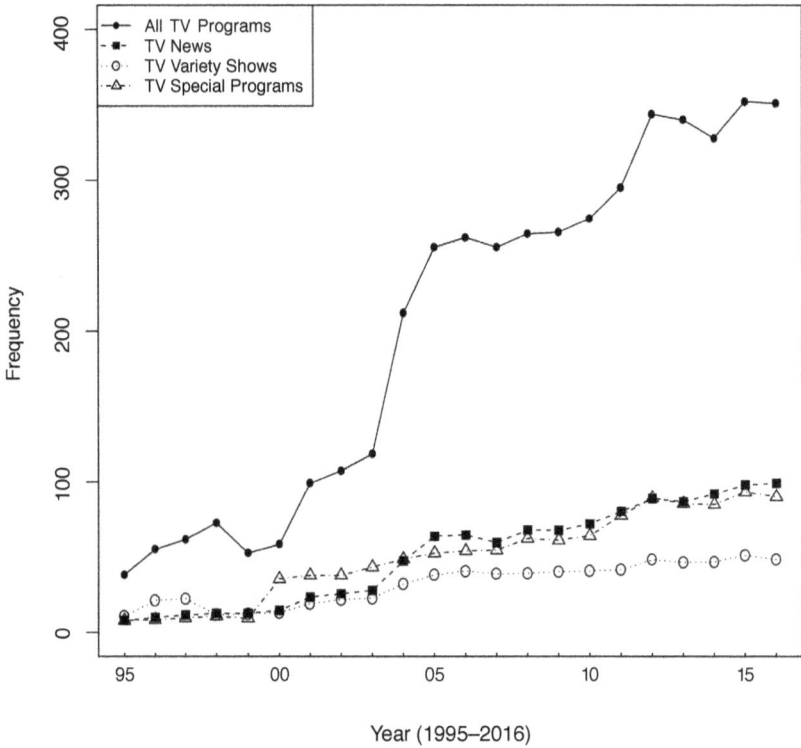

Figure 4.3. Television Program Production (10,000 Hours). *Source*: China Statistical Yearbooks and China Radio and Television Yearbooks.

in the television industry and political communication in general. This growth in news production also indicates increasing market competition, given the limited airtime and finite media market.

Reforms in the management system within television stations constitute another important change in the television industry. Limited autonomy was granted as a result of deregulation, enabling television professionals to nimbly adjust content production for media competition. Prior to the management reforms, there was very little room for journalists to make decisions regarding programming content; news programs mainly carried state propaganda. In the mid-1990s, the management reforms started in the central-level CCTV when the "producer system" was introduced (Hong, Lü, and Zou 2009, 43). Under the producer system, mid-level television executives could make decisions regarding program design, content, budget, and staffing (Sun 2003). By the late 1990s, the producer system was introduced to all television stations in China (Hong, Lü, and Zou 2009, 44). With this newly granted autonomy, television news innovation took off, resulting in pioneering livelihood news programs such as *Zero Distance in Nanjing*.

In light of these transformational changes in commercialization and deregulation, the party-state needed to find an effective way to manage the media industry that was only to grow larger and more complex. After a series of documents issued by the central leadership in the late 1990s and the early aughts, the state media were restructured to adopt the group operating model (集团化运营模式), combining and consolidating media outlets across different industries and regions. Private sources of financing were also incorporated into the reformed radio and television industry. *Opinions on Strengthening Radio and Television Cable Network Construction Management* (关于加强广播电视有线网络建设管理的意见) issued by the State Council in 1999, as mentioned earlier, not only provided guidelines to streamline the television industry, but also required each province to create a provincial radio and television group, formalizing the model of group operation. In the following two years, the State Administration of Radio and Television issued directives to specify the requirements of group operation, including combining radio, television, and film; combining cable, wireless, and education television stations; and streamlining provincial, municipal, and county level radio and television stations (Zhang and Zhang 2012, 40).

In the first decade of the new century, as the media reforms continued to take shape, the need became apparent that the profitable components of radio and television content production, such as entertainment programs, films, and television series, should be separated from the core business of news and propaganda. *Opinions on Deepening Cultural System Reform* (关于深化文化体制改革的若干意见), issued in 2006 by the CCP Central Committee and the State Council, articulated this goal. Being a main carrier of propaganda, news programs are not the most profitable section of the radio and television industry; however, they are the core business, because they serve the party-state as a propaganda disseminator. To satisfy the need of the media industry to be profitable and to encourage the development of the cultural industry, *Opinions* adopted the policy of separating production from broadcasting (制播分离). Under this policy, the production of films, television series, and other entertainment programs can be done by third-party companies, which would increase competition and generate more popular and profitable content. According to *Opinions*, the entertainment section can be operated under market principles, and it is to be separated from the core business of news production, which remains to be produced by television stations under the direct management and control of the local party-states. In this way, television continues to be a key propaganda instrument for the party-state and "remains the most tightly controlled type of media in China" (Miao 2011, 96). Its ability to simultaneously transmit text, sound, and visual components of a news story and its near-universal penetration in China make it a top priority in the party-state's political communication strategies and a key player in local politics and governance.

These complex and consequential reforms, unfolding since the 1980s, shaped the formation of professional journalism, which in many ways departs from party journalism exercised both before and after the reforms. The commercial pressure to be profitable and the professional aspiration to be reputable and impactful propelled television journalists to pursue limited critical reporting outside of propaganda tasks,[2] which are often seen as irrelevant and a ratings-killer. Given these competing priorities, how has journalism evolved as a concept and practice?

Redefining Television Journalism

In the reform era, Chinese Journalists, or "news workers" as they are referred to by the CCP, have been exposed to the professional ideals existing in liberal democracies, including the norms of objectivity and autonomy. The small group of elite print journalists aspires to produce the kind of journalism that would put them on a par with their democratic counterparts, had they been given the political space (Hassid 2015; Repnikova 2017a). But most Chinese journalists are pragmatic journalists, trained to closely abide by party principles, most importantly. The concept of journalism, defined by the CCP and executed in journalism education by Chinese universities and news outlets, contrasts with the norms of objectivity and autonomy.

Before 1978, all forms of media were seen by the CCP as tools of propaganda and instruments of political power. According to Alan Liu (1971, 6), the most important function of the mass media in Leninist states is to "transmit the Party's or state's programs and instructions to the masses." As a result, the media "are adjunct to the Party apparatus and must be controlled completely by it" (6). Put differently, the media were supposed to serve only the party-state. After 1978, under the overarching policy of reform and opening and after the series of media reforms, "media were intended to serve both the state and the market" (Stockmann 2013, 50). Zhu Hong (朱虹), the former spokesperson and director of the Office of the State Administration of Radio and Television (国家广电总局办公厅主任和新闻发言人), summarizes the media evolution as transforming from a traditional mouth-and-throat function to a news propaganda and industry function (H. Zhu 2008).

Despite the media reforms and the state encouragement to develop a profitable cultural industry, the political attribute of the news media to serve the party-state remains primary. The Marxist theory of news (马克思主义新闻观) has been closely followed by the CCP till today. Mao Zedong emphasized the importance of "politicians creating newspaper" (政治家办报), as opposed to journalists, indicating the predominance of political ideology and control over the media (Mao [1959] 1968). More recently, Xi Jinping emphasized that the state media should remember that their surname is the party, and that they exist primarily to serve as a propaganda tool for the party (Wong 2016). These views are remarkably consistent despite the drastic changes in the media industry thus far, and they directly contradict the norms of objectivity and autonomy.

In the era of media reforms, journalism education in Chinese universities has incorporated certain elements from democratic journalism to train future journalists who can advance a dynamic and profitable media industry, offering courses on topics such as professional journalism, investigative reporting, and media law.[3] However, party ideology remains dominant. Courses on the Marxist theory on news remain compulsory, not to mention the close ties between the party units embedded in Chinese universities and journalism schools that implicate restrictions on faculty research, teaching materials, and student learning activities (Repnikova 2017b).

Journalism in Livelihood News

The lack of a strong influence from the democratic conceptions of journalism allowed the dominant party logic to blend with the market logic in the formation of pragmatic journalists' professional identity. The rise of television livelihood news mirrors the emerging journalistic identity, reflecting a redefined television journalism.

Chinese scholars and media practitioners generally agree that two conditions facilitated the rise of television livelihood news. First, local television stations were in a difficult financial situation because they could not compete with CCTV in terms of resource and authority, which steered them to nurture a bond with local audiences in ways that CCTV could not (Zhang and Zhang 2012, 145). Therefore, television livelihood news programs focus on local topics and adopt a colloquial language to successfully forge a path toward profit and reputation. Second, the supply side of the equation suggests that the socioeconomic context of rapid urbanization could provide ample materials for television livelihood news. These topics dramatically diverge from traditional television news, which is flooded with propaganda often seen as irrelevant and unable to absorb the diverse interests and needs that arose during profound socioeconomic transformations (Zhang and Zhang 2012, 146). The copious supply of citizen grievances and governance problems spurred a reconceived model of television news.

In this context, pragmatic journalists' emerging professional identity can be illustrated through the news sources they choose and the rhetorical frames they adopt in producing livelihood news. The dominant news source comes from ordinary citizens, who report their grievances or governance problems through hotline calls and social media posts. Based on my fieldwork conducted at eleven provincial and municipal television stations, over half—sometimes two thirds—of the news stories came from ordinary citizens. When propaganda tasks, such as covering leader speeches and activities, are not overwhelming, the percentage of citizen sources could go as high as over 70%. This is a major departure from traditional television news, where the coverage is mostly on political leaders; livelihood news is mostly about local citizens and their problems.

On the other hand, citizens offer leads to livelihood news programs primarily to seek help. They report grievances caused by local officials or businesses. Journalists typically take the side of aggrieved citizens and use critical reporting to seek resolution. Other citizens turn to the media for help due to personal difficulties, such as when expensive medical bills put families in financial ruin. In these cases, livelihood news programs serve philanthropically to help raise money using their media platform. Some programs regularly launch public interest events (公益活动) to help raise money for different causes, a typical example being to help students in poverty pay for tuitions and fees.

Depending on the problems reflected by citizen grievances, journalists strategically frame news stories so that they compel redress but are still politically acceptable. The primary tactic to negotiate and qualify critical reporting is to use the government's own policies, regulations, leader speeches, and governance campaigns for justification. By trying to hold street-level bureaucrats accountable, the frames of livelihood news indicate advocacy-oriented journalism. Based on my interviews, I found that television journalists pride themselves on helping those in need. Their intentional and heavy involvement in redressing citizen grievances suggests that their advocacy journalism differs from the democratic conception that emphasizes objectivity. Commonly invoking the phrase of "we ordinary folks" (咱们老百姓) that dispenses a strong populist flavor, livelihood news is defined by a firm stance with the ordinary and the less privileged, as opposed to the wealthy and the powerful. Indeed, many livelihood news reports are not exactly news but citizen complaints. In helping aggrieved citizens, journalists proudly take the side of the disempowered. Their desire to use their media power to right the wrong deviates from the notion of journalistic objectivity.

This populist-flavored advocacy journalism also deviates from the CCP's conception of journalism as a party mouthpiece, though the two are not mutually exclusive. The model of livelihood news manifests the role of brokering between the government and the people, without abandoning the political task of polishing the government image. In fact, as previous chapters make clear, this form of controlled critical reporting engenders political conveniences to local leaders and reinforces the hegemony of the party-state. In this way, pragmatic journalists' aspirational desire for positive social impact is satisfied by local leaders' strategic use of corrective critical reporting. This mutually beneficial dynamic enables the party-state to expropriate media criticism and mold television journalism, trapping journalists in the confined reporting cycle of exposure, rectification, and praise. Yet, the inflated sense of journalistic empowerment is potent. From the journalists' perspective, livelihood news programs rightly focus on helping citizens solve their problems, through which to facilitate positive changes and earn public reputation. It is through this unique path of advocacy journalism that television journalists transformed the function of livelihood news. The mission to serve the people using their media power is widely shared among television journalists.

Advocacy and Populism

To demonstrate populist-flavored advocacy journalism, I show descriptive results from a survey I conducted in June 2013 with journalists working at a municipal television station in Jilin province. These journalists worked for three different livelihood news programs, and they did not include people in management positions, such as producers and directors. The respondents were grassroots-level news professionals responsible for the day-to-day news production, including conducting interviews, shooting video footage, writing scripts, and postproduction editing. They account for two thirds of all staff working at the news center of the municipal television station.

Although the survey results are not representative of all television journalists in China, they reveal some shared journalistic values. Using surveys to study Chinese journalists is not yet a common approach, due to political and practical constraints. Among the studies that did use surveys, Zhongdang Pan and Joseph Chan (2003) surveyed journalists in Shanghai working for different types of media outlets, and Fen Lin (2010) surveyed print journalists in Guangzhou. Both studies rely on a framework that only differentiates between party journalism and professional journalism that is defined by democratic conceptions, yet television journalists do not fit neatly in either category. As discussed earlier, television journalists serve the party, but they are not merely mouthpieces; they have professional values that are also not entirely consistent with the journalistic norms of objectivity and autonomy. They are advocacy-minded, heavily involved in resolving disputes and grievances for the disempowered, thus departing from both the journalistic norm of objectivity and the notion of mouthpiece. Meanwhile, they value political stability and meaningful counsel to the local government, thus departing from the journalistic norm of autonomy. My survey with the television journalists, though not representative, probes multiple dimensions of journalistic identity that go beyond the framework of party journalism vis-à-vis professional journalism.

Advocacy—to Bridge the Government and the People

Journalists surveyed in this study were divided on the most valued journalistic norms and the mission of livelihood news, but they coalesced around providing news and information, building bridges between the government and the people, and helping ordinary citizens solve problems, shown in table 4.1. Specifically, answers to Q1 show that only 3.1% of the journalists chose the party's conception of journalism; this result is consistent with Jonathan Hassid's (2011) typology of Chinese journalists, where communist professionals are a minority. The number of journalists who chose news and information as the top value of journalism was higher than the other answers. More significantly, a substantial number of journalists chose answers that can be understood as advocacy journalism; those who chose the third and fourth answers accounted for 25% of the respondents. Additionally, 28.1% of the respondents described their mission as building a bridge between the government and the people, indicating a preference for using governmental channels to advocate for citizens and resolve their grievances.

Table 4.1. Conceptions of Journalism

Description	Percentage
Q1: Which following description is closest to your ideal journalistic role?	
1. Journalists should help the government better publicize policies, laws, and regulations to create a better public opinion environment.	3.1
2. Journalists are bridges between the government and the public. They should facilitate effective communication between the two for the purposes of social stability and prosperity.	28.1
3. Journalists should represent ordinary people, especially the vulnerable social groups.	5.2
4. Journalists should use their media power to help ordinary people solve problems.	19.8
5. Journalists should provide reports with news value to help people understand issues and acquire information.	32.3
6. None of the above can represent my understanding.	3.1
7. Don't know/Refuse to answer	8.4
Observations	96

Source: Author's 2013 survey.

Populism—to Channel Citizen Grievances

If television journalism is advocacy oriented, then we should see a predominant focus on citizens in livelihood news production, lending a populist flavor to these programs. In table 4.2, the survey results show that audience demand is the primary factor in shaping the content of livelihood news. In Q2 and Q3 the majority of respondents chose the audience as the top consideration. The predominant status of citizen demands is further supported by the common topics of livelihood news. The results in Q4 show that the most common topics covered by livelihood news programs concern citizen disputes and grievances. The focus on public service is consistent with the mission to help ordinary people. Additionally, in Q2 the contrast between the second and third answers shows that when it comes to news production at the local level, the local government has a more prominent role than the central government in managing the day-to-day journalistic activities, corroborating the prominence of local leadership discussed in previous chapters.

Political Constraints

Organic critical reports, the news leads of which primarily come from ordinary citizens, are subject to political control; orchestrated critical reports would have local leaders' direct support, yet they rarely occurred at this locality at the time of this research, as indicated by my fieldwork. Survey results in table 4.3 indicate the level of political constraints faced by the journalists.

Unsurprisingly, the question about political constraints (Q5) has the highest number of null responses, which indicates the political sensitivity of this question but also demonstrates the validity of these answers. The majority of the respondents reported frequent government intervention in critical reporting; 28.1% of the respondents chose "several times," and 31.3% chose "often times." These results corroborate the expected political constraints in organic criticism. Answers to Q6 provide further information on the outcome of political constraints; 46.9% of the respondents thought that positive and negative reports had equal share in their own livelihood news programs, and 42.7% thought that most reports were critical, even though these reports typically ended with a positive outcome. Comparing these results with the data I collected from content analysis in chapter 5, this level of critical reporting—half or more of the reports were critical—is unusually high. This may be due

Table 4.2. Factors in Livelihood News Production

Description	Percentage
Q2: Generally speaking, which factor below has the largest influence on the content of television livelihood news programs?	
1. Audience demand	62.5
2. Formal or informal rules from the central government	7.3
3. Formal or informal rules from the local government	16.7
4. Journalists' own judgment	11.5
5. Widely discussed topics online	2.1
6. Other	0
7. Don't know/Refuse to answer	0
Q3: Which of the following sources is the dominant news source for *your* program?	
1. Government bureaus (propaganda tasks)	8.3
2. Audience hotline calls	64.6
3. Widely discussed topics online	9.4
4. Other television stations' reports	6.3
5. Journalists' own materials or topics	8.3
6. Other	1
7. Don't know/Refuse to answer	2.1
Q4: This year which topic was covered the most by *your* program?	
1. Consumer rights defense (消费者维权)	28.1
2. Traffic violations	6.3
3. Citizen disputes (纠纷)	20.8
4. Macro-level social problems and government policies	3.1
5. Crimes and fraud	7.3
6. Government bureaus' work in providing public services	25
7. Other	6.3
8. Don't know/Refuse to answer	3.1
Observations	96

Source: Author's 2013 survey.

Table 4.3. Political Constraints

Description	Percentage
Q5: During the time that you have worked at the television station, are there incidences where news stories could not be aired because they involve government bureaus?	
1. Never	3.1
2. Once or twice	19.8
3. Several times	28.1
4. Often times	31.3
5. Other	1
6. Don't know/Refuse to answer	16.7
Q6: Which statement below most closely describes *your* program?	
1. Most reports focus on the positive news in the society.	7.3
2. Most reports are supervisory reports (輿論監督报道), focusing on problems and raising possible solutions.	42.7
3. About half of the reports are positive, and half are negative.	46.9
4. Other	2.1
5. Don't know/Refuse to answer	1
Observations	96

Source: Author's 2013 survey.

to different understandings of what constitutes a critical report; reports critical of local businesses or misbehaving individuals, rather than just government officials, may also have been counted by journalists when answering this question.

Taken together, the survey results suggest a populist propensity and a strong orientation toward advocacy for the disempowered among the television journalists. This journalistic identity further reveals the unique position of the local media that challenges the binary state-society framework, discussed in the introduction. The ability of the local media to straddle the government and the public places them in between the state and the society. The notion of building a "bridge" between the government and the public captures the common ground in the previously assumed contradicting dynamics of politics and the market in news production.

Indeed, a bridge would not hold without securing both ends. Rather than merely pandering to the demand of the public or that of the government, livelihood news has morphed into a concrete, effective, and bounded notion of advocacy emerging in a time of maturing media industry and growing governance problems. After two decades of media reforms, the initial urgency to increase profitability has receded somewhat, as the livelihood news model matures and the broader direction of media reforms settles. Subsequently, journalistic identity and media reputation started to exert more influence on news production. Reputation has become an essential component emphasized by news producers in my interviews, which goes beyond profit. Indeed, the survey results indicate that the journalistic identity is more than a party mouthpiece or a market machine. Meanwhile, securing both ends of the bridge means transcending the contrasting political and market logics articulated in the literature from the first decade of media reforms (Lee 2000; Y. Zhao 1998, 2008; Stockmann 2013). The bridge is a metaphor for a new narrative that unifies the political and market logics, which was made possible by the context of accruing governance problems. Local leaders and disempowered citizens both have strong and urgent interests to resolve governance problems; livelihood news capitalized on the shared interests and consolidated its role as the bridge between the two through a specific and bounded focus on chastising street-level bureaucrats. To further illustrate how livelihood news unifies the various interests in local governance, the next section discusses some common governance problems covered in livelihood news.

The Governance Context of Media Criticism

China's urbanization process is characterized by its fast speed and heavy state involvement. From 1996 to 2013, the urbanization rate in China increased from 30.5% to 53.7%, with an average year-over-year increase of 1.36%, much faster than the world average (Yiming Wang 2017). However, the institutional infrastructure, including regulations and enforcement capacity, is not keeping pace with the speed and scale of urbanization. In this period of rapid and problematic urbanization, various governance issues emerge, supplying materials for livelihood news. Due to political constraints, most critical reporting aims at disciplining street-level bureaucrats rather than precipitating meaningful policy or institutional reforms. Therefore, citizen grievances and governance problems covered in livelihood news are mostly framed as implementation issues. Selected from the common topics covered in livelihood news, this section discusses three governance problems widely shared by cities nationwide.[4]

Illegal Construction in Residential Complexes

Mushrooming high-rise buildings in residential complexes are an ostensible sign of urbanization. In China, two-thirds of all housing stock was built after 1990, and almost 40% of housing in cities was built between 2000 and 2010 (Khor and Oi 2017, 213). As more people migrate to the cities, the need for urban housing has boosted housing prices, squeezing the middle and lower classes that struggle to afford quality housing. The need for more space, coupled with lax regulation enforcement, incentivizes many residents to build additional rooms or structures on top of or adjacent to residential buildings that they reside in, essentially encroaching on public space. These rooms and structures are considered "illegal construction" (违章建筑) because they are not approved by the local government, causing concerns over safety and zoning.

The reasons for the prevalent phenomenon of illegal construction are complex. In addition to the private motive for financial gains in a time of prohibitively high housing prices, several institutional factors are pertinent. First, the already complex structure of property rights is further complicated by the economic transformation from a state-planned economy to a market economy. Currently, in Chinese cities there are as many as four types of housing for purchase (not counting for renting): commodity housing, formerly public-owned housing, secondhand housing, and economically affordable housing (经济适用房) (Khor and Oi 2017, 213). The first and second types constitute the largest percentage of urban housing for purchase. While commodity housing is newly built and traded on the market between real estate developers and homebuyers, secondhand housing may be traded between homebuyers and real estate agents or homeowners. Economically affordable housing is a state effort to provide low-cost housing under the affordable housing policy.

Formerly public-owned housing is a legacy of the communist era where state-owned enterprises provided housing to their employees. After the reforms, much of this type of housing was transferred to private ownership through payments below the market value. However, formerly public-owned housing tends to suffer from illegal construction the most, due to a lack of clear demarcation of property rights. Especially on the top and bottom floors, many residents built illegal structures to expand their private space; some residents even rent out their illegally built rooms for financial gains (Xu and Ni 2018).

In residential complexes where the demarcation of property rights is relatively clear, illegal construction may still occur if it is not immediately contained and regulated by the government. This brings us to the second institutional factor. The lax enforcement of government regulations incentivizes some residents to engage in illegal construction, regardless of the demarcation of property rights. In addition to bureaucratic ineptitude, the lax enforcement can be attributed to ill-considered regulations, unclear division of enforcement responsibilities among government bureaus, and the sheer volume of illegal construction cases. Although several laws and regulations at different administrative levels deal with the issue of illegal construction, on-the-ground situations vary so greatly that these regulations may not provide clear instructions, especially for buildings with a more complicated history of property rights. As a result, local officials often need to investigate and make decisions on a case-by-case basis. The difficulty in demarcating property rights is compounded by the institutional arrangement where several government bureaus share responsibilities regarding illegal construction. For example, within a typical municipality, the housing and construction bureau (住房建设局), the urban management bureau (城市管理局), and the urban planning bureau (城市规划局) all have responsibilities regarding illegal construction, which breeds inaction when these bureaus evade accountability by claiming other bureaus' oversight. The incentive for inaction is especially strong in complicated and confrontational cases. In most instances, it is the urban management bureau that demolishes illegal construction, after the urban planning bureau verifies whether a structure is illegal. During this process, the housing and construction bureau, which manages property titles, is also involved when titles are required as proof to demarcate properties. This working process requires coordination among these bureaus, which does not always occur, before the eventual demolition of illegal constructions.

Finally, the bureaucratic inefficiency is exacerbated by the sheer number of illegal construction cases and the limited capacity of the enforcement bureaus. Many urban management bureaus, for example, simply do not have enough people to handle all illegal construction cases in a timely fashion, the process of which includes investigation, collecting evidence, issuing decisions, and the eventual demolition. Sometimes residents choose to appeal against a demolition decision or simply obstruct the process because they see illegal constructions as their rightful private properties, prolonging the process.

Given these socioeconomic and institutional obstacles in dealing with illegal construction, some local governments use short-term campaigns and special task forces to generate quick results, especially in locations where illegal constructions concentrate. For example, the Shijngshan district government under Beijing municipality created a special task force to deal with illegal construction in 2017 (G. Zhao 2017). The top leaders in the district government each oversaw a different aspect of this campaign to ensure its effective enforcement. This campaign even created temporary party units in each street committee to ensure enforcement outcomes.

Illegal construction is not only targeted by the local government but also criticized by residents who do not engage in illegal construction. They are concerned with building safety and the encroachment of public space, and they perceive unfair treatment by the local government if certain residents are allowed to benefit from their illegally built structures. These grievances have created disputes and conflicts among residents, who often report illegal constructions to livelihood news programs in seeking resolution.

Television livelihood news programs, through the media power of publicity, can generate immediate results by criticizing street-level bureaucrats responsible for the final stages of enforcement. Media supervision is especially effective when illegal construction is a prioritized governance issue. These immediate results are by no means long-term solutions; the root cause of this problem goes far beyond the media's supervisory capacity. However, media correction that leads to demolition of illegally built structures provides short-term relief to citizen grievances and satisfies local leaders, which are key to the sustainability of media criticism. Such a resolution, though superficial, unites the interests of local leaders, local media, and aggrieved citizens.

Pollution

Pollution of various kinds—soil, water, air, noise, and light—also marks urbanization in China. The party-state is well aware of the political risk associated with pollution, yet the difficulty in alleviating this problem can also, in part, be attributed to the lax enforcement at the local level, besides the perceived conflict between economic development and environmental regulation. Similar to the case of illegal construction, enforcing environmental regulations suffers from a lack of clearly demarcated responsibilities among government bureaus and the lagging regulations that fail to keep pace with rapid urbanization.

Polluted rivers, or "black stinky rivers" (黑臭河), as they are referred to in the public discourse, is a common problem plaguing many cities. This problem was so widespread that a nationwide campaign was launched to clean rivers in urban areas. In 2015, the State Council issued *Action Plan to Prevent and Cure Water Pollution* (水污染防治行动计划),[5] formally elevating this issue to national importance. Following this initiative, the Ministry of Housing and Urban-Rural Development (住房和城乡建设部) issued *Work Guidance to Clean Urban Black Stinky Waters* (城市黑臭水体整治工作指南), requiring each municipality to issue its own plan to clean polluted waters by the end of 2015 and complete the plan by the end of 2017. This task required the housing and development bureaus of each municipality to collaborate with the environmental protection bureaus. This bureaucratic arrangement made this task prone to evasion of responsibilities, due to the lack of a clear division of labor and accountability system. Some local leaders relied on the media to supervise the progress of cleaning polluted waters, as it was in their interest to complete this task on time. For example, *Zero Distance in Nanjing* aired a series of reports in the first half of 2017 to supervise the government work on cleaning the rivers.

Air pollution has instigated broad concerns and public discontent. The frequent occurrence of smog, an extreme form of air pollution, in many Chinese cities has made the word "smog" a key word in public discourse.[6] In 2013, the State Council issued *Action Plan to Prevent and Remedy Air Pollution* (大气污染防治行动计划),[7] officially rolling out a national campaign to clean the air. It was also in 2013 when the government started to publicize its monitoring results of air pollution, including indicators of PM 10 and PM 2.5. In 2015, the Environmental

Protection Law was revised to include more specific regulations about smog.[8] Around the same time, each municipality created its own plan or campaign to reduce air pollution. This issue has wide-ranging implications for factories that emit pollutants, construction sites that produce polluting dust, the use of private cars, and the household use of coal for heat and cooking. To tackle these sources of air pollution also requires concerted efforts among different government bureaus. Media criticism again can be a useful tool to supervise and pressure street-level bureaucrats for immediate enforcement outcomes.

Food Safety

Food safety is a unique issue in China's poorly regulated market economy. China has had several national scandals, including the 2008 milk scandal that affected 300,000 babies and killed at least six infants (Branigan 2008). In 2009, the National People's Congress passed the Food Safety Law, which was further revised in 2015.[9] The revision expanded the state's supervisory scope and increased punishment for violation. However, one of the vexing issues remains problematic enforcement due to overlapping institutional responsibilities. Within a typical municipality, the food and drug inspection and management bureau (食品药品管理监督局), the market supervision and management bureau (市场监督管理局), the commerce bureau (工商局), and the quality inspection bureau (质量检查局) all have enforcement power over issues regarding food safety. It is worth noting that some cities have streamlined these administrative bureaus. In Shenzhen, the market supervision and management bureau was created in 2009, which combined responsibilities under the former commerce bureau, the former quality inspection bureau, and the former food and drug inspection and management bureau.[10] However, in many other cities, the issue of food safety remains under the overlapping responsibility of several bureaus. According to the reports by livelihood news programs examined in this book, these bureaus' work on food safety relies on periodic campaigns that crack down on illegal and unsanitary food production and sales, especially during national holidays and cultural celebrations, when concentrated consumption of food increases the risk of food safety incidents. In these periodic campaigns, relevant bureaus jointly inspect restaurants, food factories, and street stands, and punish those that violate food safety regulations. In these occasions, media criticism can be a useful tool to push through these campaigns for immediate results, recruiting journalists and citizens to play a supervisory role to prevent food safety incidents from happening.

Aligned Interests

These governance issues signal areas where the interests of citizens, journalists, and local leaders align. In addressing these governance issues, even in superficial ways, media criticism channels citizen grievances by not only acknowledging their rightful claims but also aiming at resolution through governmental collaboration, thus functioning as a bridge between the public and the local party-states. To achieve successful resolution, journalists help aggrieved citizens strategize about rhetorical frames of critical reporting that would invite, rather than antagonize, street-level bureaucrats to rectify misbehavior. Positive outcomes from critical reports then enhance the popularity and reputation of livelihood news programs. Finally, savvy local leaders understand that media supervision can facilitate achievement of governance outcomes. Despite the possibility of excessive criticism generating political instability, a basic criterion on which local leaders are evaluated (Wang and Minzner 2015; Lee and Zhang 2013), limited critical reporting, if managed well, has the potential to dilute local tension. Given a compatible leadership style and a fitting governance context, controlled and selective media criticism can help create and showcase a notable governance record, advancing local leaders' political careers.

Conclusion

Most news professionals are under considerable pressure to generate revenues from the news they produce, propelling them to seek ways to attract an audience. In an environment where sharp criticism is rare yet governance problems are mounting, the public needs to release frustration while seeking willing and able partners to pursue resolution without directly challenging the party-state. Media criticism, even only targeting street-level bureaucrats, occupies a unique position to advance this goal. After more than two decades of media reforms, television journalism has evolved to embrace a mission of populist advocacy as urbanization continues to transform Chinese society. The sustained popularity of television livelihood news suggests that critical reporting, though limited and varied, has a large and loyal following. The governance problems covered by livelihood news programs reflect urgent public concerns and align the interests of citizens, journalists, and local leaders to pursue speedy resolutions.

Chapter 5

Criticism and Correction

L ivelihood news has become a defining feature of local television news in China. In this unique model of news production, the media's bounded supervisory role unites the political interests of local leaders, the commercial interests and professional aspirations of television journalists, and the citizen demands to redress grievances. However, the degree to which media supervision features in local governance depends on a web of interactive factors, as this book has demonstrated thus far. This chapter synthesizes the factors previously discussed, providing a big picture that shows how these factors fit together to exert influence and offering explanations for the variations in critical reporting. It does so by analyzing an original dataset consisting of five livelihood news programs produced and aired in Jiangsu and Shaanxi.

Expectations and Hypotheses

Previous chapters discuss factors in four areas that shape media criticism. First, the institutional incentives from cadre evaluation and promotion shape local leaders' career interests. The demanding evaluation criteria exercised over complex local governance conditions and the over-the-top expectations for an innovative and problem-solving mentality, discussed in chapter 3, incentivize local leaders to use media criticism as an effective instrument to create distinguishable governance records for promotion. Furthermore, the trend of shorter tenures drives local leaders to use media criticism at the beginning of their tenure cycles, so that governance records can be generated in time for promotion. To capture this expectation, the leader tenure variable is created to measure the number of months that a leader has held the current position.

Differentiating leaders at different administrative levels, provincial leaders should have more incentives to use media criticism than municipal leaders as they age toward the mid-60s, because of the different age limits and career trajectories. The administrative level variable measures local leaders' rank with three levels—provincial, deputy provincial municipal, and municipal.

On the other hand, chapter 2 suggests that the administrative rank of a television station calibrates its power to supervise lower-level officials. Provincial television news programs should have more power to supervise, for example, township-level officials, than do municipal television news programs. Because local television news programs share the administrative rank of the local leaders, the administrative level variable may lead to different expectations regarding how it affects critical reporting.

The following consideration, however, should clarify how the administrative level variable fits into the actual and statistical models of news production. Local television news programs can supervise lower-level officials only with local leaders' explicit or implicit approval. Otherwise, critical reporting itself is at risk, in which case the administrative ranks of the television stations and of the criticized officials would not matter. This consideration prioritizes the administrative level of local leaders in the actual process of news production. Local media's administrative rank matters only when local leaders tolerate critical reporting. Therefore, the administrative level variable primarily indicates local leaders' interests regarding media criticism. Furthermore, because provincial leaders in their mid-60s, compared to their counterparts at the municipal level, are under greater career stress due to the higher age limit, there should be an interactive effect between administrative level and leader age regarding local leaders' interests for critical reporting. These expectations lead to the following hypotheses.

Career hypothesis: Local leaders tend to encourage higher levels of critical reporting at the beginning of their tenure cycles.

Interaction hypothesis (1): Within the age range from 55 to 65, leaders at the provincial level tend to allow higher levels of critical reporting than leaders at lower levels. Within the age range below 55, leaders do not show difference in their tolerance for critical reporting based on their administrative levels.

Despite the shared institutional incentives to advance career, local leaders' individual orientation toward using media criticism differs. The second factor concerns the individual-level leadership style. When it comes to media criticism, risk-averse leaders tend to be resistant, while risk-acceptant leaders tend to be embracive. The leadership style variable captures this distinction, and its measurement is specified below and further in appendix B. Moreover, this individual characteristic should interact with institutional career incentives. Media-savvy leaders should use media criticism more than media-resistant leaders, particularly at the beginning of their tenure cycles. Toward the end of their tenures, this difference should diminish.

Leadership style hypothesis: Local leaders who are more embracive of the media tend to allow higher levels of critical reporting than local leaders who are resistant to the media.

Interaction hypothesis (2): Local leaders who are more embracive of the media tend to allow higher levels of critical reporting than media-resistant leaders at the beginning of their tenure cycles.

The political logic of convenient criticism also implicates conditions at local, regional, and national levels, which constitute the third factor—governance context. During important national political events, the level of critical reporting should be lower because of political sensitivity, such as during the annual meetings of the National Party Congress and the National People's Congress and during the annual meetings of their provincial and municipal counterparts. Meanwhile, local governments periodically launch campaigns and initiatives to address specific governance problems in a concentrated way, such as cleaning polluted rivers. Under the auspices of these local initiatives, journalists may pursue more critical reporting in the name of governance improvement. To account for these factors, variables of political events and local initiatives are created and details of the measurements are provided in the next section.

Political events hypothesis: The level of critical reporting tends to be lower during important political events.

Local initiatives hypothesis: The level of critical reporting tends to be higher during local initiatives to address governance problems.

Along with the political logic, the market logic also shapes news reporting. The fourth factor concerns the media market. Intense competition in the local media market should drive television journalists toward more critical reporting in pursuit of ratings and profits. This is captured by the media competition variable and its measurement is discussed in the next section. Furthermore, well-known livelihood news programs with a relatively long history, such as *Zero Distance in Nanjing*, created in 2002, should have an advanced sense of journalistic identity and a stronger reputation for critical reporting, compared to the more recently created programs. Therefore, the program age variable captures the historical longevity of livelihood news programs.

Media competition hypothesis: Livelihood news programs that face more media competition tend to have higher levels of critical reporting.

Program history hypothesis: Older livelihood news programs tend to engage in higher levels of critical reporting than newer ones.

Data and Measurements

The data used to test the hypotheses comes from several sources. The primary source is content analysis of five livelihood news programs in Jiangsu and Shaanxi, which measures the level of critical and other reporting. The descriptive statistics have been presented in chapter 1. The following dependent variables are created using the data from content analysis: critical reports, positive reports, unresolved reports, and improvement reports. Independent variables are created using information from local newspapers, government documents, and other media sources, discussed in detail below.

It is worth noting that the critical reports and improvement reports variables do not differentiate between organic and orchestrated criticism. Differentiating the two types of criticism in quantitative measures is beyond the scope of this research, due to the practical obstacle that it would require checking the source of each of the 2,231 critical reports with journalists at different television stations. Given political sensitivity, personnel turnover, and different practices of archiving old reports, it is very difficult to obtain reliable and consistent information on the original news sources. However, the differences between the two types of media criticism are illustrated through qualitative evidence in previous chapters as well as in the last section of this chapter.

Leadership Style toward the Media

Leadership style is an important but amorphous concept to study. As discussed in chapter 3, leadership style can be conceptualized as risk-acceptant and risk-averse. This book is interested in learning about a subset of leadership style that focuses on orientation toward the media. Political leaders who are risk-acceptant tend to be more embracive of the media and are therefore more inclined to use the media in achieving governance goals; political leaders who are risk-averse tend to be more resistant toward the media and wary of the risks associated with excessive media criticism or praise. As the old Chinese saying goes, the shot hits the bird that pokes its head out. Therefore, risk-averse leaders tend to limit the media's role in governance.

The concept of leadership style toward the media is difficult to measure, due to obvious political obstacles; it is virtually impossible to survey or interview local party secretaries in China.[1] To get around these obstacles but still probe the concept, this chapter utilizes an indirect way to capture the variation in local leaders' approach to the media. This measurement ascertains comparative differences among local leaders on a scale, rather than offering an absolute measure of local leaders' media preferences in defined categories. Since this chapter focuses on the relative differences among local leaders, rather than their absolute media preferences, this comparative approach is sufficient for present purposes.

Specifically, how frequent a local leader's name is mentioned in the local party newspaper is used to measure how embracive this local leader is of the media. The higher the frequency, the more media-embracive the leadership style is. In China, each provincial and municipal party committee has an affiliated party newspaper (机关报) serving as the mouthpiece of the local leadership. The local party secretary, holding the highest office in the locality, has the ultimate control over the local party newspaper. Counting the number of articles that mention the local party secretary's name, therefore, captures an important dimension in his or her inclination toward the media. In existing research, Victor Shih (2008) uses content analysis of provincial party newspapers that counts the mentions of national slogans to examine provincial leaders' signaling of loyalty to national leaders. By the same logic, if a local leader's name appears more frequently than other local leaders, then we can reasonably infer that this leader is more embracive of the media. In their recent study, Don Lee and Paul Schuler (2020) measure their concept of political competence through scores of public profiles based on Google/Baidu search data. Essentially, name mentions, or search terms, are used to gauge a politician's political competence in building a popular public profile. Along a similar logic of gauging the public visibility of a politician's name, this chapter uses name mentions in local party newspapers, which local leaders have full control of, as a measurement of orientation toward the media.

Some may argue that a local leader has to be familiar with the media before he or she can embrace them. This is a reasonable postulation, but the lack of access to local leaders means that a compromised, indirect approach to this measurement has to be adopted. Furthermore, because the local party newspapers are affiliated with the local party leadership and are under the control of the local leaders, this approach arguably already takes into account the familiarity with the media. Therefore, this is a reasonably sufficient measure of local leader's orientation toward the media.

To ensure that content analysis of local party newspapers captures different leadership styles toward the media and enables meaningful comparison, I made three choices for the analysis. First, I chose party newspapers from where these leaders were previously appointed, rather than their current positions, to avoid the problem of tautology. If the immediately previous position was not party secretary or governor/mayor, I used a more distant previous position to ensure that the leader had control over the local party newspaper.

Second, I chose to compare local party newspapers from January to March in the last year of the local leaders' previous tenure cycles. Choosing the time range from January to March was a result of two considerations. While a longer time range may present a more comprehensive picture, local leaders' tenure lengths vary greatly, with some being less than a year. Therefore, a longer time range would bias the measurement against leaders with shorter tenures. Given this, the choice of January to March was considered the most appropriate, as this was when the annual meetings of the National People's Congress and the Chinese People's Political Consultative Conference and the meetings of their local counterparts are held. These important political events leveled the playing field by presenting the same national political environment and therefore the same set of institutional incentives to increase positive reporting that highlights national and local governance achievements. In the same context, the different frequencies of leader name mention, then, can be attributed to the differences in local leaders' orientation toward the media. Other factors that would also alter the frequencies of name mention, such as local governance initiatives and other political events, tend to circumvent these important political meetings.

Finally, I chose to count the number of articles that mention local leaders' names, rather than the number of times their names appeared. Due to the differences in writing style, some articles mention a leader's name multiple times, while other articles mention the name only once.

Given this, counting the number of articles is more apt for capturing the differences in local leaders' orientation toward the media.

When articles in local party newspapers mention local leaders' names, they are positive or neutral in tone, and they typically cover the following topics: local leaders' activities, such as visiting special constituents; local leaders' initiatives or policies; theoretical discussion on local leaders' governance philosophy; and local leaders' speeches, policies, or governing philosophies cited by other influential people such as political and business leaders and media professionals.

China National Knowledge Infrastructure (CNKI), a comprehensive database that archives articles from major newspapers, was used to conduct content analysis of local party newspapers. After obtaining frequency counts of articles that mention the names of the local leaders in this database from January to March in different years, I conducted further content analysis to count the articles that mention local leaders in other localities in the same time frame to provide reference points. Since in my dataset all provincial leaders' previous position was governor instead of party secretary, name mentions for provincial governors in all 32 provincial units (excluding Hong Kong and Macau) were counted to provide a national average. Compared with the national average, provincial leaders in this dataset were assigned with a score that indicates which 10th percentile their article counts fall into.

For municipal leaders, I randomly selected 50 municipalities all over mainland China and counted the articles with name mentions for the municipal party secretaries and mayors, respectively, during the same time period. Averages from these 50 municipalities were taken as the national averages to provide reference points. The municipal leaders in this dataset were also assigned with a score that indicates which 10th percentile their article counts fall into. Similarly, municipal party secretaries in this dataset were compared to other municipal party secretaries, and mayors were compared to other mayors. A higher leadership style score indicates a more embracive style toward the media. Additional details are provided in appendix B.

Media Competition

The market logic indicates the importance of media competition in news production. For television news programs, their direct competitors are news programs broadcast in the same television market and in the same time slots. Other media outlets, especially social media, are also considered competitors because they can provide similar news and information regarding local affairs. However, television journalists and their news programs are primarily evaluated by program ratings, thus by focusing on the television market we can sufficiently capture the degree of media competition.

The number of television news programs in the local television market is used to measure the media competition variable. Considering the lack of access to reliable ratings and other media market data, I made two choices regarding this measurement. First, I only counted the number of television news programs broadcast in the same time slot. Most of the news programs were broadcast in the early evening hours between 17 and 19 o'clock, except the pseudonymized program ABC that was broadcast during the prime-time hour between 21 and 22 o'clock. Given the unique nature of airtime, unlike newspaper, the competition for audience primarily occurs during the same time slot and in the same program category.

Second, I used the number of news programs broadcast by both municipal and provincial television stations in the same time slot as a measure of local media competition. Due to the unique structure of Chinese television stations, which mirrors the administrative setup of the party-state, the audience in a municipality typically has access to channels from their municipal television station, their provincial television station, and the national-level television station. The audience rarely has access to programming from other parallel municipal television stations. Under this structure, local news is provided predominantly by the municipal and provincial television stations.

Governance Context

As discussed earlier, local governments periodically launch initiatives to tackle governance problems in a concentrated way. It is thus possible for livelihood news programs to "ride the wave" and pursue more critical reporting under the auspices of fitting governance initiatives. To account for the effect of local initiatives on critical reporting, the local initiatives variable is created to capture official orders on governance initiatives. It is coded as 1 during the two weeks after an initiative is launched to address a specific governance problem; otherwise, it is coded as 0.

Official government documents (省/市政府文件) are analyzed to generate a list of local initiatives. Thanks to the reforms to open government affairs in the first decade of the new century, discussed in chapter 3, all provincial and municipal governments publish their official documents, including orders, notifications, decisions, reports, and correspondence, on their websites.[2] In this study, the rule to capture local initiatives is to count the documents that lay out an actionable plan on a specific problem. For example, some documents are about personnel decisions, which are not counted as local initiatives. Other documents are about building a high-tech industry, which is a plan to fulfill an aspiration rather than solving an existing, tangible problem. These documents are also not counted as local initiatives. Examples of local initiatives include the plan to prevent and cure soil pollution, the plan to improve the water environment, and the order to inspect security measures at construction sites.

In addition to local initiatives, political events at national and regional levels generate politically sensitive times when critical reporting tends to tone down in favor of praise. The political events variable captures the annual meetings of the National Party Congress, the National People's Congress, and the Chinese People's Political Consultative Conference, as well as the annual meetings of their provincial and municipal counterparts. This variable is coded into three levels so that it differentiates these important meetings at national, provincial, and municipal levels.

Finally, the level of economic development also constitutes the governance environment, which may affect critical reporting. The GDP per capita variable (measured in 10,000 yuan) was created using the data from the 2015 China Statistical Yearbook and the 2015 Provincial Statistical Yearbooks.

Explaining Variations

Bivariate Analysis

The descriptive data presented in chapter 1 shows the variations in the level of critical reporting both between programs and across time. As a first step to explain variations in news reporting, this section examines variations between programs in the same time period and variations within the same program under different leadership.

Results from t-tests comparing the daily numbers of critical and positive reports across the five programs show that the level of critical reporting varies at a statistically significant level between programs. Figure 5.1 shows the sample means of the daily reports and their 95%

confidence intervals in the following four categories of reports: critical, positive, unresolved, and improvement. The unresolved and improvement categories are subsets of the critical category, referring to critical reports without a successful resolution and critical reports that end with a positive outcome, respectively. Critical reports that end with a positive outcome are either follow-up reports or original critical reports. Based on figure 5.1, the ranking of general critical reporting from high to low is *Xi'an Zero Distance, Zero Distance, Live Broadcast Nanjing / Number One News*, and *ABC*; the ranking of positive reporting from high to low is *Xi'an Zero Distance, Live Broadcast Nanjing, Zero Distance / Number One News*, and *ABC*. Within critical reports, the ranking of unresolved critical reports from high to low is *Xi'an Zero Distance, Zero Distance / Live Broadcast*

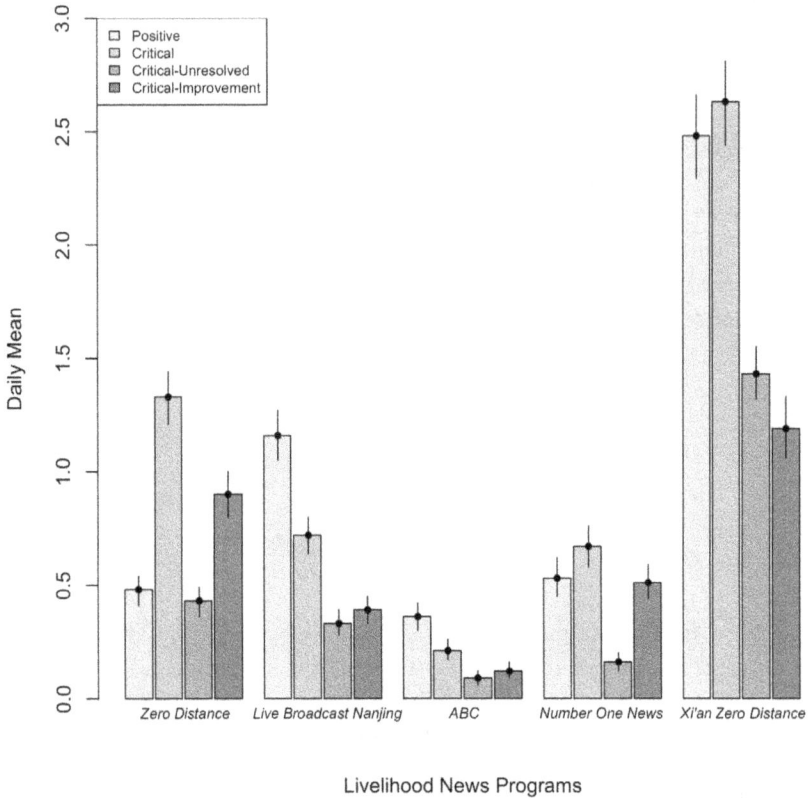

Figure 5.1. Sample Means of Daily Reports. *Note:* The 95% confidence intervals of the sample means are computed using the Student's *t*-distribution.

Nanjing, Number One News, and *ABC*; the ranking of improvement reports from high to low is *Xi'an Zero Distance, Zero Distance, Number One News / Live Broadcast Nanjing*, and *ABC*. Overall, *Xi'an Zero Distance* appears to be the most active program in generating larger numbers of both critical and positive reports, whereas *ABC* appears to be the least active. The other programs vary when it comes to different categories of reports.

When comparing critical and positive reports within the same program but under different leadership, results from t-tests show that, at a statistically significant level, only *Live Broadcast Nanjing* and *Number One News* have different reporting styles under different local leadership. In Nanjing under Wu Zhenglong's leadership, *Live Broadcast Nanjing* had less critical reporting and more positive reporting, compared to Wu's successor Zhang Jinghua. Differently, in Shaanxi under Lou Qinjian's leadership, *Number One News* had more critical reporting and less positive reporting, compared to Lou's successor Hu Heping. In Xi'an there was no significant difference in critical reporting by *Xi'an Zero Distance* under the two leaders, but under Wang Yongkang's leadership there was more positive reporting. More details about the results are provided in appendix B.

It is important to note, however, that due to the limited range of data (November 2016 to December 2017), the amount of information may be inadequate to fully capture the influence of leadership style on news reporting in a bivariate analysis. For example, Wang Yongkang's predecessor only has 2 months of data in this dataset, whereas Wang has more than 12 months of data. While these results suggest that leadership style plays a role in news reporting, how much it matters and how it compares to other factors are further examined in the following regression analysis.

Regression Analysis

In regression analysis, the main dependent variable is the number of critical reports in each day's programming; it is an overdispersed count variable. Other dependent variables—the daily numbers of positive reports, critical reports without a resolution, and critical reports highlighting misbehavior correction and governance improvement—are also overdispersed count variables. Therefore, negative binomial regression is used to model the data, and the results are summarized in table 5.1. To account for the

Table 5.1. Negative Binomial Regression Results

	(1) Critical	(2) Critical	(3) Positive	(4) Positive	(5) Unresolved	(6) Unresolved	(7) Improvement	(8) Improvement
Leader Factors								
Leadership style	0.16*** (0.04)	0.27*** (0.05)	-0.35*** (0.04)	-0.32*** (0.07)	0.19* (0.08)	0.33*** (0.09)	0.16** (0.05)	0.25*** (0.07)
Leader tenure	0.0007 (0.004)	0.08*** (0.01)	-0.0009 (0.004)	-0.05*** (0.01)	-0.0008 (0.006)	0.06*** (0.02)	0.0003 (0.006)	0.10*** (0.02)
Style × tenure		-0.01*** (0.002)		0.007** (0.002)		-0.01*** (0.003)		-0.01*** (0.003)
Leader age	0.02 (0.03)	-0.28* (0.12)	-0.09*** (0.02)	0.34** (0.12)	0.07 (0.04)	-0.06 (0.17)	0.002 (0.03)	-0.50** (0.16)
Admin. level	0.28 (0.21)	-5.18* (2.04)	0.62** (0.20)	8.79*** (2.12)	-0.25 (0.36)	-3.14 (3.34)	0.52 (0.27)	-8.17** (2.70)
Leader age × admin. level		0.11** (0.04)		-0.16*** (0.04)		0.05 (0.07)		0.18** (0.06)
Media Factors								
Media competition	0.71*** (0.07)	1.05*** (0.17)	0.93*** (0.07)	0.45** (0.17)	0.90*** (0.07)	1.02*** (0.25)	0.55*** (0.10)	1.17*** (0.23)
Program age	0.07 (0.04)	0.05 (0.04)	0.36*** (0.04)	0.31*** (0.05)	0.09 (0.07)	0.04 (0.07)	0.04 (0.05)	0.04 (0.05)

Contextual Factors

Political events	0.002	-0.01	0.11***	0.12***	-0.05	-0.06	0.04	0.02
	(0.03)	(0.03)	(0.02)	(0.02)	(0.04)	(0.04)	(0.03)	(0.03)
Local initiatives	-0.07	-0.07	-0.02	-0.008	-0.09	-0.09	-0.05	-0.06
	(0.06)	(0.06)	(0.07)	(0.07)	(0.09)	(0.09)	(0.08)	(0.08)
GDP per capita	-0.20**	-0.22*	-0.84***	-0.65***	-0.23*	-0.15	-0.14	-0.26*
	(0.07)	(0.09)	(0.06)	(0.11)	(0.11)	(0.13)	(0.08)	(0.12)
Constant	-5.35***	7.73	3.88***	-16.43**	-8.72***	-3.40	-4.72***	17.59*
	(1.11)	(5.37)	(0.95)	(5.66)	(2.04)	(7.95)	(1.32)	(7.32)
McFadden Pseudo R-Squared	0.14	0.15	0.14	0.15	0.17	0.18	0.10	0.10
Observations	2086	2086	2086	2086	2086	2086	2086	2086

Notes: Standard errors in parentheses. The number of observations in each model indicates the number of days for all five programs included in the dataset. *$p<0.05$, **$p<0.01$, ***$p<0.001$

Source: Author's dataset.

variation in the number of all critical reports, model (1) shows results consistent with some of the above hypotheses. A more media-embracive leadership style is positively correlated with critical reporting, lending support to the leadership style hypothesis. The media competition variable is also positively associated with critical reporting, lending support to the media competition hypothesis. Higher GDP per capita is associated with lower levels of critical reporting, indicating that media criticism participates in local governance more in less developed areas. However, the leader tenure, administrative level, program age, local initiatives, and political events variables do not seem to affect critical reporting.

Adding a term interacting leadership style with leader tenure and another interacting leader age with administrative level, model (2) shows results lending strong support to the interaction hypotheses. Figure 5.2 plots the interactive relationships using predicted values. The two levels of leadership style plotted represent the minimum and maximum values in the dataset. Media-embracive leaders tend to use media criticism more than media-resistant leaders, but only at the beginning of their tenures, and the gap decreases as their tenures proceed. About 14 months into the tenure cycles, the difference between media-embracive and media-resistant leaders is not statistically significant any more. On the other hand, provincial leaders tend to allow more critical reporting than municipal leaders as they age past 52; the gap becomes larger as the leaders age further. Additionally, the statistical significance of other variables remains the same in this interaction model. The media competition variable remains positively correlated with critical reporting. Therefore, the career hypothesis, the program history hypothesis, the local initiatives hypothesis, and the political events hypothesis are not supported by the regression results. The interactive relationship shows that the career hypothesis only applies to local leaders with a media-embracive leadership style.

To break down different types of critical reporting, models (5) and (6) show the results for critical reports that did not result in a positive outcome. Without interaction terms, model (5) shows that a media-embracive leadership style plays an expected role that positively correlates with unresolved critical reporting, but not any of the other characteristics of local leaders. This result seems to accentuate individual-level characteristics above institutional incentives for career advancement. The statistical significance of other variables is similar to model (1) that accounts for all critical reports.

Predicted Critical Reports with 95% CIs

Predicted Critical Reports with 95% CIs

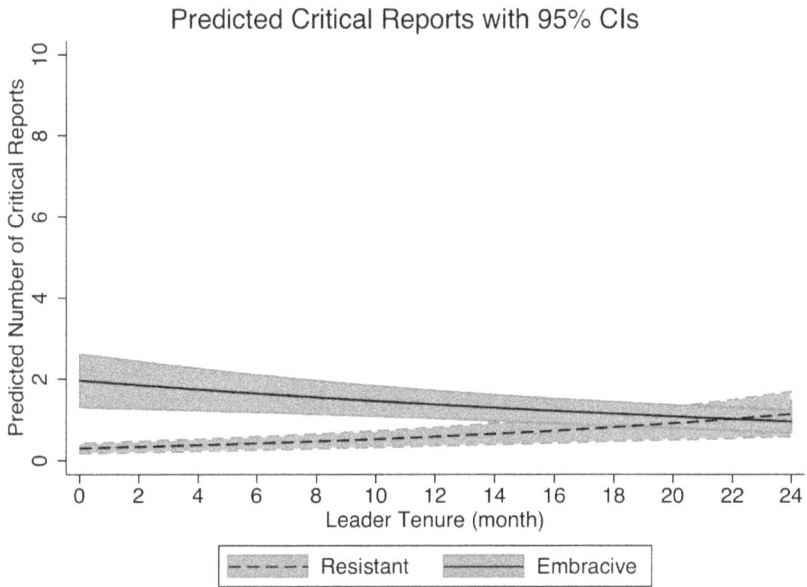

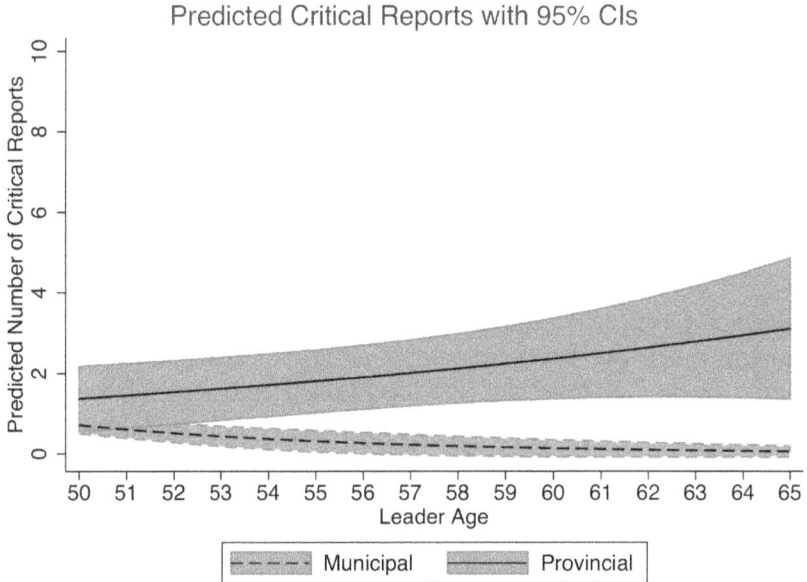

Figure 5.2. Interaction Effects in Modeling Critical Reporting.

Adding the interaction terms, model (6) shows that leadership style is conditioned by leader tenure, so that a media-embracive leadership style positively correlates with unresolved critical reports only at the beginning of leadership tenure cycles. This is similar to all critical reports. However, the difference between provincial and municipal leaders is absent. The contrast between these two sets of interaction variables suggests that allowing critical reports is more a result of a media-embracive leadership style, which is an individual-level characteristic, shaped by career interests of promotion, which are institutional-level characteristics. An important implication is that using media as a governance instrument is not a tactic that all local leaders are inclined to adopt, despite their shared institutional interests for career advancement. Indeed, leveraging the media to one's political advantage is a learned skill; if not used adeptly, it can easily backfire. Furthermore, the absent difference between provincial and municipal leaders suggests that leaders under the age pressure tend not to pursue critical reporting without a positive outcome to advance career; instead, they tend to pursue critical reporting that ends with a positive outcome, as the results from models (7) and (8) suggest. The preference for corrective critical reporting indicates that media criticism is closely associated with local leaders' career interests. Finally, the consistently significant variable of media competition suggests the power of market pressure in news production.

The other type of critical reports results in positive outcomes and thus highlights government responsiveness, referred to as improvement reports. Models (7) and (8) show that, unlike the results for unresolved reports, improvement reports share a very similar statistical pattern with general critical reports, suggesting the influence of individual leadership style, institutional career incentives, age pressure at provincial and municipal levels, media competition, and local governance context. These patterns reveal the strategic nature of using critical reporting to induce correction and improvement. For local leaders embracive of the media, their engagement with critical reporting is carefully and strategically managed, present only when it is convenient to advance their political careers. Media competition plays a similarly important role in driving journalists toward the direction of critical reporting, and less developed areas seem to have more room for this kind of media governance.

Finally, models (3) and (4) account for the variation in positive reports, those that praise local or national governance outcomes and other political achievements. Model (3) shows that leadership style has the opposite effect on positive reporting; a more media-embracive leadership style is negatively associated with positive reporting. Younger leaders tend to be associated with higher levels of positive reporting than older leaders, and provincial leaders tend to be associated with higher levels of positive reporting than municipal leaders. Leader tenure does not seem to affect positive reporting. In media factors, both media competition and program age are positively correlated with positive reporting. These results are discussed further below. The political events variable is positively correlated with positive reporting, suggesting sensitivity around important national and regional political events. GDP per capita is again negatively associated with positive reporting, and local initiatives do not seem to exert influence.

Adding the interaction terms, model (4) shows interactive effects on positive reporting between leadership style and leader tenure and between leader age and administrative level. As shown in figure 5.3, media-resistant leaders tend to be associated with higher levels of positive reporting than media-embracive leaders at the beginning of their tenure cycles, and the gap disappears as their tenures proceed into 18 months. Provincial leaders tend to be associated with higher levels of positive reporting than municipal leaders until they reach the age of 51, when the difference is not statistically significant any more. Due to the large overlapping confidence intervals, a different scale of leader age is plotted in this figure. The statistical significance of the other variables remains unchanged. These results suggest that a media-resistant leadership style correlates with more positive, adulatory reporting, which may be a symptom of a conservative, cautious approach to politics. Among political leaders, more caution and being risk-averse seem to associate with more wariness and skepticism toward media criticism and more confidence in the safe, though less effective, propagandist positive reports. When both provincial and municipal leaders are still years away from the age limits for retirement, provincial leaders engage in more positive reports than municipal leaders, suggesting a more cautious approach toward news reporting at a higher administrative level. Conversely, municipal leaders, compared to their provincial counterparts, seem to exhibit a more open approach to news reporting that is less fixated on adulation. This implication is largely consistent with recent findings in the study of Chinese governance that most innovation and experimentation happen at the grassroots level (He 2013; Heilmann, Shih, and Hofem 2013; Kostka and Nahm 2017; Teets and Hurst 2014) and that the municipal level has more room for governance innovation than the provincial level.

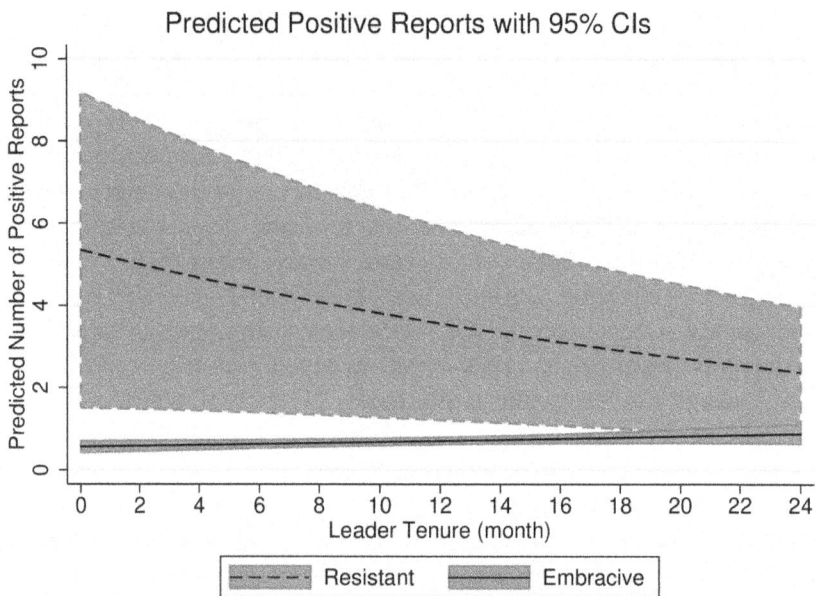

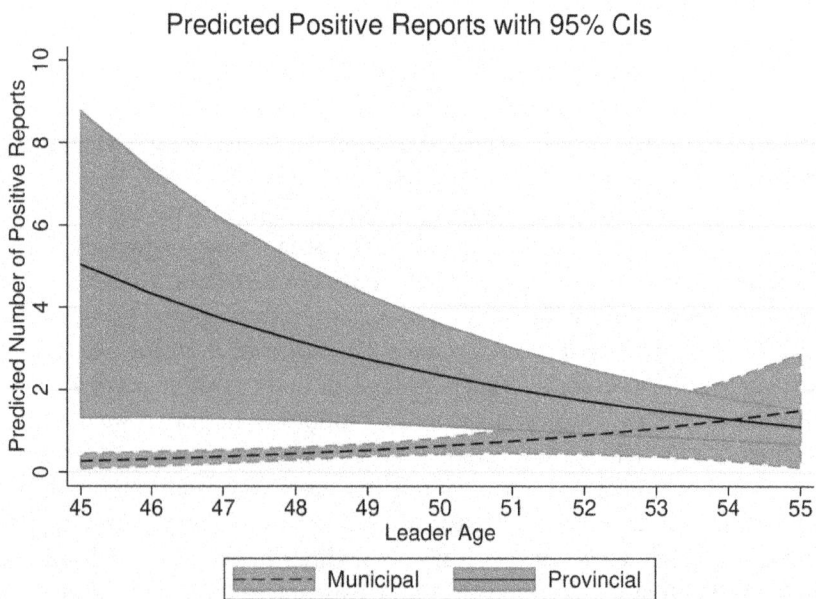

Figure 5.3. Interaction Effects in Modeling Positive Reporting.

Taken together, these regression results show that local leaders' career interests and orientation toward the media shape both critical and positive reporting. The contrasting interactive effects reveal that media-embracive leaders tend to use news reporting more as a governance tool and less as a propaganda instrument, particularly at the beginning of their tenure cycles. Compared to their municipal counterparts, provincial leaders tend to encourage higher levels of positive reporting when they are younger. As provincial leaders approach the age of 52 and older, they tend to encourage critical reporting more than municipal leaders, possibly due to the closing window for further promotion and thus growing pressure to create competitive governance records. Therefore, media criticism is used by some local leaders as a governance instrument outside of formal powers to increase the chance of promotion.

Regarding media factors, media competition drives critical reporting, as expected, but it also positively correlates with positive reporting. The latter correlation may be a deliberate choice for journalists to hedge against the risk of critical reporting, so as to balance criticism and keep the general tone of news reporting acceptable to the local leadership. My interviews with journalists suggest that they are very careful with not only the frame and frequency of critical reports, but also how they are distributed. Journalists avoid concentrated critical reporting, spreading critical reports and filling the gaps in between with positive reports. This pattern helps ease their relationship with local propaganda officials and provides important evidence to defend their political loyalty. Interestingly, though the age of news programs is not associated with critical reporting, it is positively correlated with positive reporting, suggesting a journalistic survival tactic developed over time.

The governance context also affects news reporting. Important political events tend to create phases of higher levels of positive reporting, though they do not seem to decrease critical reporting. Local initiatives, inconsistent with the hypothesis, do not seem to affect news reporting. This result suggests that journalists' tactic to "ride the wave" of governance initiatives to engage in critical reporting may not be adopted systematically across time and region, even though my fieldwork reveals that it is a tried tactic. The level of economic development is negatively associated with both critical and positive reporting, suggesting that the local media are a more active participant in local politics and governance in less developed areas. To shed further light on the mechanisms through which critical reporting occurs, the following section focuses on two news programs included in this dataset and provides in-depth cases of orchestrated and organic critical reports to illustrate their production processes and outcomes.

Demonstrative Cases

The following cases come from the original dataset, helping put flesh on the bones of statistical analysis. They highlight the reactions from street-level bureaucrats, the back-and-forth negotiation between journalists and criticized officials, and the nonlinear process of governance improvement.

Xi'an Zero Distance

Shortly after his appointment in December 2016, Wang Yongkang, the party secretary of Xi'an at the time, was directly involved in the creation of a critical news program called *Daily Focus* (每日聚焦), as discussed in chapter 3. A few months later, Wang formalized the media's supervisory role in local governance (媒体问政) by proposing a "five-party interaction" (五方联动) mechanism, an innovative initiative of his administration. According to *Xi'an Zero Distance*, "five-party interaction" refers to the following five components of media supervision: (1) the municipal leadership creates a list of governance issues; (2) the media supervise lower-level government officials on these issues; (3) average citizens provide leads on these issues; (4) government bureaus ensure rectification (整改); and (5) the local party disciplinary inspection commission investigates misbehaving local officials and publicizes its results through the media.

This initiative, intending to improve governance, involves the public and the media, though the ultimate verdict on official misconduct or incompetence is made by the local party-state. Despite the state involvement in critical reporting, this initiative nonetheless allows the media to play a more prominent role in local governance through both orchestrated and organic criticism, benefiting their commercial interests and professional aspirations. As the following examples show, this ambitious and media-savvy leadership style has wide-ranging impact on the local media landscape. Not only was *Daily Focus* effective in criticizing and correcting misbehaving local officials, but other news programs, including *Xi'an Zero Distance*, were also empowered and included in the initiative of media supervision. Furthermore, journalists working for *Xi'an Zero Distance* learned to "ride the wave" by producing their own critical reports on relevant governance issues. Effectively, orchestrated criticism spilled over to embolden organic critical reporting.

Orchestrated Criticism

As governance issues become more complex, innovations occur at the local level to resolve emerging challenges. Successful innovations are often picked up by the central government for nationwide implementation. For example, Dongcheng District in Beijing pioneered the system of "grid management" (网格化管理) to ensure effective governance in urban areas in 2004; by 2017 this practice had been implemented in about 60% of the cities in China ("China Wants" 2018). The idea is to divide up jurisdictions into grids, which are then assigned to specific individuals to take charge; the goal is to resolve issues quickly within any single grid, aided with clear designation of responsibility.[3] It has been applied to various governance issues, such as cleaning up polluted rivers and cracking down on unpermitted street vendors. Its success was promoted nationwide by the central government in 2013, during the third plenum of the 18th Party Congress.

In March 2017, Xi'an started to implement grid management to improve air quality by cleaning up streets and covering up dirt in construction sites (扬尘覆盖) (Q. Lei 2017). The municipal government referred to this initiative as "iron wrist curing smog through grid management" (铁腕治霾网格化管理). At first, this initiative was carried out with bureaucratic ineptitude; many streets remained dirty and the dirt at some construction sites remained uncovered. In June 2017, the municipal party discipline commission assigned the local media to supervise "grid managers" (网格长). On June 16, 2017, *Xi'an Zero Distance* reported that two grid managers were negligent, because the streets in their grids were covered by construction trash. These managers were interviewed in the report, admitting wrongdoing and promising to clean up the trash. In the following day's broadcast, a follow-up report highlighted the improved conditions in those grids.

In this example, the Xi'an municipal government relied on the media power of publicity to supervise street-level bureaucrats and to generate quick results on key governance issues. Orchestrated critical reporting like this ensures that the resulting rectification is publicized, the real message of which is to highlight the local government's achievements.

Organic Criticism

By April 2017, various governance issues such as river pollution, illegal taxis, littering cigarette butts, and dirty public toilets had been covered in the local news and improvements had ensued. The decision to focus on these specific issues was a result of the Xi'an municipal government's agenda, national governance campaigns, and public concern. For example, to ban littering cigarette butts was a result of Wang's adroit performance during a public appearance.[4] To clean up polluted rivers was welcomed by the public, and to clean up public toilets was part of a national campaign. Without an electoral process, the imbalance between the local government's priorities and average citizens' top concerns provides a powerful incentive for the municipal government to tackle issues originally discovered by organic critical reports.

On April 9, 2017, *Xi'an Zero Distance* aired a report on citizen grievances regarding a real estate dispute. According to a hotline call, a local real estate developer cheated a group of consumers who purchased homes through advance payments in 2008. The promised homes that these consumers already paid for were built only half way, and the construction stopped due to insufficient funds. As a result, the half-built skeletons of residential buildings had been sitting on the construction site for nine years. This phenomenon is so common across the country that it is referred to in the public discourse as "rotten tail buildings" (烂尾楼). A senior lady, interviewed in this report, complained that government officials from the local street committee promised her that this matter would be resolved soon. She bought a home for her son when he was 18 years old, hoping that he would start a family in this home; now her son was 27 years old and still not married. She blamed the lack of home ownership for her son's misfortune. A six-year-old girl from another family was also interviewed in this report, saying that her parents bought a home before she was born; now she was six years old and the home was still unfinished. Finally, a young lady said in the interview that she borrowed large sums of money from her relatives and friends in order to buy a home, but now it seemed impossible to ask for a refund from the real estate developer. She ended up not owning a home and deep in debt. Several other consumers were also interviewed to account for their misfortune.

The tone of this report and the visuals of skeletons of high-rise building structures were clearly sympathetic to the consumers. In a time of real estate boom, insufficient and incompetent government oversight has resulted in many instances of illegal financing that ended up hurting consumers' basic rights. However, this report did not name the responsible government bureaus with the authority to hold the real estate developer accountable. Toward the end of the report, the voice-over said briefly that these citizens hoped that "relevant government bureaus" (相关政府 部门) could stand up and help them resolve this issue.

For this report, *Xi'an Zero Distance* did not follow up due to a lack of resolution. However, the development in the media supervision initiative in the following months, discussed at the beginning of this section, enabled the municipal government to tackle the broader issue of real estate fraud. Fast forwarding to July 2017, the Xi'an municipal government doubled down on the efforts to use the media in local governance, launching new radio programs dedicated to media supervision. Xi'an became among the first in the country to systematically use radio to criticize local government officials. Fast forwarding again to September 2017, a new policy from the municipal government further expanded the system of media supervision by adding an online component. Citizens now can easily lodge an online complaint, which will then be reviewed and reported by television and radio programs. These efforts to use media supervision received praise from the central leadership, according to a report from *Xi'an Zero Distance* on September 22, 2017. In the same episode, *Xi'an Zero Distance* highlighted several cases reported to this multimedia supervision platform (radio, television, online), one of which concerns real estate fraud. In this case, another residential complex also ended up becoming "rotten tail buildings," where the real estate developer cheated consumers by selling them unfinished homes. Although this residential complex is not the same one reported in April 2017, the issue is the same. This time, journalists reviewed this complaint and passed it on to Xi'an Housing Security and Management Bureau. The Bureau replied that the real estate developer had been fined as an administrative punishment, and the district housing security and management bureau, its lower-level counterpart, would take over to further handle this case.

This example demonstrates that the local leader's savvy use of media supervision led to positive developments in uncovering and resolving governance problems. On the issue of "rotten tail buildings," the municipal government responded timely, suggesting the effectiveness of government-sponsored media supervision.

Zero Distance

Zero Distance, formerly *Nanjing Zero Distance*, is a pioneering livelihood news program created in 2002. Its longevity evidently shows its sustained popularity in the local media market. If *Xi'an Zero Distance* under Wang Yongkang's leadership primarily exemplifies orchestrated criticism, *Zero Distance* illustrates the possible scope and impact of organic criticism. My interviews with the journalists at *Zero Distance* in 2012 and 2013 reveal that the majority of the news leads still came from citizen hotline calls and social media posts. Equally important, as a result of its success and reputation in the early aughts, *Zero Distance* has formed a strong journalistic identity that prides itself on critical reporting and helping ordinary citizens, a classic embodiment of the populist-flavored advocacy journalism discussed in chapter 4. Critical reports by *Zero Distance* are different from those by *Xi'an Zero Distance* in several ways.

First, while orchestrated critical reports almost invariably refer to governance initiatives and leader speeches as justification, organic critical reports do so less often. In producing orchestrated critical reports, the reference to local governance initiatives has two intended audiences— the public and the higher leadership. For the public, referencing local initiatives helps create the positive image of a caring government that actually serves the people (为老百姓办实事). For the higher leadership, orchestrated criticism showcases the governance agenda and achievements, benefiting local leaders' political careers. Put differently, orchestrated critical reporting primarily advances local leaders' political interests, while organic critical reporting primarily benefits aggrieved citizens.

Second, orchestrated critical reports have a more predictable cycle of misbehavior correction. Typically, improvements or promises for correction are broadcast in the same or a follow-up report, because results tend to occur quickly, thanks to the direct support from the local leadership. In contrast, organic critical reports may or may not feature correction or have follow-up improvement reports, depending on the outcome of misbehavior correction. When follow-up reports do occur, the time elapsed between the initial critical report and the follow-up report varies. Sometimes it could be as long as two weeks before a follow-up report is broadcast. In rare instances, there may be a second or even a third follow-up report to document the developments in the case before reaching a final resolution. The varying gap time is a strong indication of the informal, varying, and difficult negotiation process between the local media and government officials. During this process, journalists strategize about potent but acceptable narratives to induce correction and to hold accountable misbehaving officials. Though organic critical reports usually have a broader scope in the selection and framing of stories, misbehavior correction and governance improvement may not result as easily, compared to orchestrated critical reports.

On March 19, 2017, *Zero Distance* covered a story about an alleged illegal parking fine. In Gaoxin district under Nanjing municipality, a Mr. Wang parked his forklift on February 23 on a street where parking was not allowed. Mr. Wang later learned that the city management bureau towed his forklift citing illegal parking, and he was fined 10,000 yuan (about US$1,400). This amount is unusually large for parking violations in China. After several inquiries, Mr. Wang was not given an explanation by the city management bureau of Gaoxin district. Without anywhere else to turn, Mr. Wang called *Zero Distance* on March 3, hoping that the journalists could help him. When a *Zero Distance* journalist showed up at the bureau to investigate the story, city management officers reluctantly provided an explanation, citing Article 42 of the Nanjing Urban Management Regulation, which stipulates that a fine for illegally occupying urban roads can be between 1,000 yuan and 10,000 yuan. Therefore, 10,000 yuan was not illegal, although it was a maximum penalty.

In helping Mr. Wang, the journalist reasoned with the officers that a forklift was not an 18-wheeler truck, and that it could not block an entire road. Mr. Wang also argued that his forklift was parked closely to the curb and thus did not block the traffic. When asked the reason why Mr. Wang was fined with the maximum amount, an officer said that he was in a stressed mood that day because his superiors were inspecting the bureau, thus he requested a maximum penalty. Otherwise, the fine would not be this heavy.

The journalist then helped Mr. Wang articulate the point that this was not an acceptable reason for a maximum penalty. While the regulation did not specify the criteria to judge how much fine is reasonable, the criteria cannot be an officer's mood. In the report, it was apparent that the journalist helped Mr. Wang, who was not versed in relevant laws and regulations, by feeding him words and phrases to reason with the officers.

In the next two weeks, Mr. Wang kept communicating with the city management bureau of Gaoxin district, hoping that the bureau would lower the fine. An officer told him in what appears to be a secret recording that if he wanted to lower the fine, he should "look for someone" (找人), a euphemism for bribery. Mr. Wang told the journalist that he was not a local resident and that he did not even know whom he should bribe. The report then interviewed a lawyer for consultation, who argued that the bureau should specify reasons for the maximum fine. This initial report ended without a resolution.

The next day, on March 20, *Zero Distance* aired a follow-up report, stating that more forklift drivers came forward and told *Zero Distance* about similar encounters with the bureau, after watching the initial report the day before. These forklift drivers were all fined 10,000 yuan. Some of the drivers bribed officers from the bureau to lower the fine, as instructed. A driver recounted that after he bribed the bureau officers, the fine was lowered to 5,000 yuan. Then an interesting twist in the story occurred. Some forklift drivers, through their own investigation, found out that the road on which they parked their forklifts was not even in the jurisdiction of the Gaoxin district government; it was part of a privately owned factory. The journalist then interviewed an official from the greening department of the city management bureau and confirmed that the road was indeed not in the district's jurisdiction. With all this evidence, a director from the city management bureau admitted on the record that the officer who was caught on camera asking for bribes violated party disciplines. This director further hinted that this officer might be fired. With regards to the fine, this director told the journalist that an investigation was underway. However, other forklift drivers who already paid the fine complained that they did not receive any explanation. Having learned from the journalist the rhetorical tactic to hold officials accountable, these forklift drivers reasoned that the lack of explanation violated the principle of transparency, which was posted on the wall in the bureau building and captured by the visuals of the television report. In the end, the follow-up report provided updates that this case was under investigation and that *Zero Distance* would continue to follow up so that the public can receive a satisfactory response.

On March 23, *Zero Distance* aired a second follow-up report that the Gaoxin district government had been involved in this case, due to the elevated public fallout after the previous two reports by *Zero Distance*. In this second follow-up report, the Gaoxin district government thanked *Zero Distance* for its supervision. The deputy chief of the environmental protection department in the city management bureau of Gaoxin district said that the fine would be lowered to below 200 yuan. In light of this result, while Mr. Wang received the justice he hoped for, other forklift drivers who already paid fines ranging from 3,000 to 5,000 yuan felt mistreated. On this, the deputy chief admitted wrongdoing, and said that explanations and corrections of the fines would be sent to those drivers. He further stated that the officer who was caught asking for bribes was already fired on March 20. Toward the end of the report, the deputy chief thanked *Zero Distance* again for supervision and expressed welcome for more media supervision in the future.

These dramatic developments spanned from February 23 to March 23. The journalistic investigation, negotiation, and following up with forklift drivers and city management officers clearly indicate the non-linear process of misbehavior correction following organic criticism. In addition to the factors outlined above in the regression analysis, the journalistic identity to advocate for the underprivileged, who tend to be poorly equipped with the legal knowledge and information to fight for their rights and dignity, played a critical role in achieving a successful resolution. Indeed, the reputation of livelihood news programs like *Zero Distance* is fundamentally defined by their compassion and concern for justice.

Conclusion

This chapter synthesizes earlier analysis and explains the variations in critical reporting by different livelihood news programs. Analyzing an original dataset, this chapter provides evidence supporting the expectations regarding how factors including local leaders' career interests, leadership style, the media market, and the governance context affect the outcomes of critical reporting. While existing studies already provide insights on the political and market logics that shape news reporting, less discussed is the role of local leaders. Statistical results from this chapter show that local leaders who are savvy about the media tend to recruit them as an informal instrument to improve local governance in a way that advances their careers.

The in-depth examination of select critical reports illustrates the formative role local leaders play in shaping orchestrated critical reporting. It also demonstrates how organic critical reports feature a nonlinear process of news production and a variable path of subsequent rectification, while orchestrated critical reports are marked by a bold critical tone referencing governance initiatives and leader speeches and a predictable cycle of swift correction. Local media have become an important actor in local politics and governance; they reflect citizen grievances, discipline misbehaving bureaucrats, facilitate governance improvement, and ultimately advance local leaders' career interests.

These findings reveal a dimension of the state-media relationship that is different from both deep antagonism and total subordination. The available space, albeit limited and varied, for journalists to push for critical reporting and the mutually beneficial outcomes of disciplinary correction and governance improvement indicate an emerging dynamic in the local state-media relationship. In the past three decades of media reforms, local leaders and local media evolved side by side within the rather broad contours of media control, discovering common ground between the supposedly opposite pulls of politics and market. Savvy leaders' recruitment of the media into the governance process forecasts the future evolvement of authoritarian media politics. When used as a governance tool, media criticism may advance short-term interests, but its long-term implications, which depend on many aspects of institutional and policy reforms, are far from clear. It is to the implications and the limits of convenient criticism that this book turns.

Conclusion

Recent political developments across the globe reveal that the evolution of media politics sometimes outpaces our grasp. Politicians relentlessly seek new ways to exploit the media for various political purposes. In authoritarian states, where the media are more subdued, their impact on politics still evolves with remarkable vigor. This book shows that in the state-dominated media landscape in China the ways in which media politics operates have expanded from propaganda and censorship to limited yet consequential media criticism that helps improve governance during rapid urbanization. In this process, political manipulation and journalistic agency have molded the media into a versatile instrument advancing the party-state's agenda at the local level by disciplining state agents and shaping the public mind.

Capturing and explaining this evolution in Chinese media politics from a ground-level perspective, this book addresses two main questions. First, it explains why media criticism exists at the local level. Motivated by career interests, local leaders with a media-savvy leadership style strategically use media criticism to discipline their subordinates and create governance results. In this process, critical reporting that addresses citizen grievances and governance issues also advances local media's commercial interests and journalistic aspirations. Aligning diverse interests in the rhetorical frame that blames and corrects street-level bureaucrats, the supervisory and disciplinary effects of media criticism transpire to be convenient to the key actors involved—local leaders' career interests are advanced, local media's profitability and reputation are enhanced, and citizen grievances are redressed.

Second, this book explains why the level of media criticism varies across time and region. Situating media criticism into local politics and governance, this book accounts for factors related to local leaders' career interests and leadership style, media competition, and the governance context. Ultimately, local media's supervisory and disciplinary power depends on local leaders' willingness to use it. These findings address the gaps in the literature regarding television news and local state-media relationship; they reveal the unlikely alliance between savvy leaders and keen journalists during a time of changing practices of bureaucratic control at the grassroots level.

This conclusion summarizes the key findings presented in the book, laying out the various conveniences that media criticism can afford to different actors. Then it discusses the limits of convenient criticism and the implications for the authoritarian rule.

Advancing Bureaucratic Control and Political Careers

Bureaucratic ineptitude is a common problem vexing local leaders in China. The formal institutions of cadre management, including performance evaluations, are not adequate to rein in street-level bureaucrats. Motivated by career ambitions, savvy leaders resort to informal politics to discipline subordinates in achieving their governance objectives. Leaders with a media-embracive style tend to use critical reporting, but only at the beginning of their tenure cycles, so as to create governance results in time for promotion. Furthermore, provincial leaders have stronger incentives to use media criticism as their ages approach the mid-60s, due to the pressure from the retirement age limits for national-level positions. Municipal leaders in the same age range have weaker incentives to use media criticism because of the slim chance for them to be further promoted as a result of the lower retirement age limits at their administrative rank. The tactic of media criticism, once mastered, proves to be especially handy when governance initiatives need to be accomplished timely and displayed for approval from the public and recognition from higher authorities. Some leaders take a step further to orchestrate critical reporting to achieve immediate governance outcomes, fulfilling their governance agendas and projecting an image of a competent leader. In comparison, organic criticism tends to reflect governance problems and citizen grievances more broadly, though it may be more constrained by political control. When allowed, organic criticism helps to redress citizen grievances and reduce local tension. Local leaders' strategic use of media criticism, therefore, reveals the evolving state-media relationship at the local level.

Addressing Citizen Grievances

Local leaders' use of media criticism, through tolerating or orchestrating critical reports, also lubricates the media channel of addressing citizen grievances. Local media's apt absorption of grievances and demands and their effective feedback for resolution smooth the rough edges of animosity formed between aggrieved citizens and local governments during a time of rapid urbanization and deeply problematic governance.

Compared to other informal channels that also vent citizen grievances, media criticism occupies a unique position where collaboration with the local government is frequent and effective, especially when it aligns citizen grievances with local leaders' governance agendas. Seasoned and compassionate journalists are empowered to check the ineptitude of street-level bureaucrats, in which process they broker between misbehaving bureaucrats and aggrieved citizens, mitigate miscommunication and conflicts, and facilitate resolutions. Other informal channels, such as protests on the more confrontational end and petitioning officials on the less confrontational end, may not be as effective as the media channel. Protests do not always elicit an effective response, and they risk antagonizing local officials who might otherwise be a willing partner in seeking resolutions. The more confrontational channels jeopardize local leaders' priority to maintain stability, thus undermining their prospect for career advancement. On the other hand, less confrontational channels, such as petitioning officials and lodging complaints using government websites, albeit low-risk, are not always effective because of potential distortion of information by the intermediate levels within the local bureaucracy. Furthermore, local officials in charge of answering citizen requests typically do not have the initiative, capability, or authority to maneuver and solve complex problems that implicate multiple government agencies. Many aggrieved citizens turn to the media for help precisely because these other channels are ineffective. Therefore, media criticism serves an important function to dilute local tension.

Enhancing Media Advocacy

Through immersive fieldwork, this book reveals the changing notions
and practices of television journalism in China. Despite the invariable
state control, the conventional categorization of journalism based on
political freedom has become inadequate to capture evolving television
journalism, which centers on the media's unique capability to help those
in need under the current socioeconomic conditions and governance
arrangements. Local media side with ordinary citizens while supporting
the government for effective resolution. Identifying common ground
between the supposedly opposite pull of the political logic and the
market logic of news production, television journalists practice their
conception of journalism as a bridge between the government and the
public. Exemplified by television livelihood news programs, this type of
populist-flavored advocacy journalism has created a powerful reputation
that sustains the media's capability to serve the interests of both local
governments and ordinary citizens.

The limited scope of this type of advocacy journalism is key to its
sustainability. The constrained focus on street-level bureaucrats differentiates livelihood news from the more critical and aspirational investigative
journalism practiced by well-known newspapers and magazines. Despite
its broader and deeper policy impact in the first decade of the new
century, investigative journalism, since then, faces existential challenges
of contracting reporting space and declining readership. Given the shifting politics in the reform era, critical journalism that is not hedged on
concrete political interests of leaders at central or local levels tends to
suffer from sudden change and demise. Without being nested in political
dynamics that generate political benefits, media criticism is often seen as
a grave threat by political leaders, which forecasts an inauspicious end.
In contrast, livelihood news programs benefit from their modest vision
for change and their learned ability to adapt to local leaders' evolving
media preferences. By serving local leaders' political interests, this type
of media criticism is convenient to and even desired by media-savvy
leaders. Somewhat counterintuitively, this type of media criticism benefits
from firm political control, because it allows local leaders to trust the
media as a tractable and keen partner capable of resolving issues in an
effective and acceptable way. These dynamics allow advocacy-minded
journalists to absorb and address citizen grievances that continue to

arise, advancing their commercial interests and enhancing their social impact. The party-state's expropriation of media criticism, however, also bodes its limits.

Limits of Convenient Criticism

The theory of convenient criticism captures the changing role of the media in local politics and governance. From a long-term perspective, however, local leaders' career interests, their leadership style, and the local governance context evolve constantly, which alters the strategic value of media criticism. Even for the critical reporting that did occur, its impact is limited by three problems: the lack of policy solutions, the lack of institutionalized bureaucratic control, and shortsighted leadership.

First, citizen grievances reflected in critical reporting may be resolved by correcting street-level bureaucrats' misbehavior, but this solution is transient. Media criticism is convenient because it can quickly turn critical reports into positive outcomes by deploying public shaming to solicit a quick response. This mechanism hinders thoughtful and long-term solutions, which require deep commitments and concerted efforts across the bureaucratic and political system. The issue of environmental pollution is an example. Repeated critical reports on the lax government oversight that allowed small businesses and large factories to violate environmental regulations have yet to fully resolve the problem of pollution. Hence critical reports on similar problems continued. Without a long-term solution, media criticism can only alleviate governance issues individually and temporarily. However, the preference for immediate results, shared among local leaders, local media, and aggrieved citizens, means that the transient impact of convenient criticism remains appealing. Local leaders need immediate governance results for career advancement; local media favor quick solutions to draw audience attention and increase social impact; aggrieved citizens are eager to redress their grievances. Therefore, convenient criticism does not incentivize policy change or other systemic reforms that would provide long-term solutions to governance problems.

Conditions do exist, however, that can facilitate long-term policy solutions. When governance problems afflict local politics so acutely that pressures from grassroots-level citizen demands or higher-level political orders disqualify perfunctory reactions, local leaders are incentivized or obliged to seek long-term solutions. In this scenario, media criticism can serve as a useful instrument to collect opinions and build broadly based support for policy change.

Second, convenient criticism does not fully tackle the principal-agent problem with bureaucratic control. Public shaming through media criticism does not equal an institutionalized solution for noncompliance. While the cadre management system seems to provide effective political selection, without transparency and the rule of law, insufficiency in commanding the party-state's vast crowd of local agents will not dissipate after periodic bursts of controlled critical reporting, which precludes independent and consistent supervision over street-level bureaucrats. As this book shows, critical reporting is closely monitored and adeptly controlled. Therefore, convenient criticism is not intended to systematically discipline street-level bureaucrats or to fully solve the principal-agent problem, but to selectively address this problem when it is convenient and necessary for local leaders to do so.

This brings us to the third limit of convenient criticism—local leadership. As the analysis in this book makes clear, individual characteristics of local leaders, such as their leadership styles, ages, tenures, and administrative ranks, play a critical role in shaping how they choose to strategically use media criticism. Media-savvy leaders tend to utilize critical reporting to help accomplish governance agendas; this process would also deposit reputation into their public profiles while elevating the social impact of the media. When local leaders do not perceive the utility of media criticism, due to personal characteristics or contextual factors, the space for critical reporting diminishes and the local state-media relationship becomes rigid and limiting, making it difficult for journalists to build a bridge connecting the government and the public and clogging the channel to address citizen grievances.

These limits have instigated some diverging opinions on how livelihood news should evolve in pursuit of broader social impact, and the competing visions in the television industry are far from settled. In the past decade or so, these diverging opinions suggest a gradual turn away from citizen-centered stories and toward government-centered policy interpretations and persuasion, as some media scholars and television executives started to propose the idea that livelihood news programs should pursue "big livelihood" (大民生), covering not only citizen grievances but also government policies to promote social development

(Han and Zhang 2018; Y. Liu 2009; B. Wang 2011). The argument is that by covering government policies, livelihood news programs can broaden their scope and break out of the trap of "trivialization" (琐碎化) that focuses excessively on individual grievances. In essence, the idea of "big livelihood" is to align livelihood news with official policies and discourse in search of larger impact, because many media practitioners have grown impatient with the continually limited scope and impact of their critical reporting. The political constraints and expropriation mean that the scope and impact of critical reporting are at the mercy of the local leadership, which is not always embracive toward the media. Thus, in moving away from citizen grievances in news production and toward government policies and official discourse, the hope is that more impact, authority, and standing can be drawn from a close alignment with the government. This proposal would recentralize the discursive power and strip away the conveniences afforded by media criticism to citizens and some local leaders.

These diverging opinions, however, have yet to be widely accepted or practiced. While some programs have seen increased coverage of government policies and official campaigns, other programs remain focused on stories of ordinary citizens. The descriptive statistics presented in chapter 1, for example, show that *Live Broadcast Nanjing* devoted more airtime than other programs on policy interpretation and persuasion. But, overall, the focus in livelihood news on ordinary citizens remains intact.

These limits are embedded in the mechanism of convenient criticism, and to a certain degree they ensure the continuity of media criticism. The persisting authoritarian rule, from which the limits of convenient criticism originate, sustains the media's bounded supervisory and disciplinary role in local governance. The institutional and governance problems that media criticism alleviates will not be fully resolved without democratic institutions and the rule of law, which are necessary to consistently reflect the public will and hold government officials accountable. However, had democratic institutions been put into place, the rule of law would replace convenient criticism to ensure transparent and institutionalized supervision over government officials. Therefore, the mechanism of convenient criticism is deeply dependent on the authoritarian rule. Although the degree to which convenient criticism takes effect varies under different local leadership, its utilities and boundaries compel continual relevance in the current authoritarian political system.

Implications for the Authoritarian Rule

Given its utility, elasticity, and embeddedness within the current political system, will convenient criticism help sustain the CCP rule, similar to the ways in which the following mechanisms bolster the regime: the people's congress at national and local levels (Manion 2015; Truex 2016; Wu 2015), social protests (X. Chen 2012), and social organizations (Hilde-brandt 2013; Teets 2014)? Or will convenient criticism foment challenge to the CCP rule, similar to the ways in which the following elements test the regime: labor politics (Friedman 2014), the legal system (Gallagher 2017), the local state (Juan Wang 2017), and the retreat from reform (Minzner 2018)? The long-term implications of convenient criticism for the authoritarian rule depend on the ability of the party-state at central and local levels to take seriously the institutional and policy challenges revealed through media criticism and to adapt through reforms.

The local government is capable of adaptation while seeking desired governance outcomes, as illustrated by examples like the "rotten tail buildings" discussed in chapter 5. However, the local government often prioritizes short-term results over long-term solutions, in part due to frequent leadership turnover. The preference for immediate results would make media criticism disguise the seriousness of certain problems, prolonging socioeconomic ills and exacerbating negative long-term con-sequences. For example, the crackdown on "illegal street vendors" does not solve the problem of congestion or untidy street appearance, because these street vendors resume their businesses once the inspection teams and journalists are gone. Crude crackdown that drives them away or confiscates their properties further alienates these marginalized groups, whose self-reliant efforts are met with spite and hostility. Critical reports that focus on street-level bureaucrats' failure to fully crack down on these street vendors indulge this simplistic and counterproductive approach.

At the central level, the long-term implications of convenient criticism rely on the central leadership's ability to overcome challenges emanating from the tension between an authoritarian political system and the need to represent and govern well. Without democratic insti-tutions, how free is the flow of information regarding local governance problems, and how willing and able is the central leadership to fully resolve governance problems, such as irresponsible policy-making and bureaucratic ineptitude? Under Xi Jinping's rule, the party's ability to control its local agents has evidently increased, not least demonstrated by the far-reaching anticorruption campaign. The recent overhaul of the central government bureaucracy spearheaded by Xi and approved by the National People's Congress in March 2018 suggests a major step to erase the institutional boundaries between the party and the state. However, the ability to control is not the ability to govern; bureaucratic control is a means not an end. The recent centralization of power has had ripple effects on local governance practices, disincentivizing local officials from engaging in governance innovation and policy experiments (Minzner 2015, 2018). The challenge in the party-state's ability to heed public feedback and to resolve governance issues intensifies in a time of domestic socioeconomic transformation and escalating international competition.

In this context, the grassroots quality and the public reputation of convenient criticism can serve as a powerful instrument to smooth the edges of mounting tension between local governments and the public. To amplify and sustain this role, there needs to be institutionalized protection over media criticism from the party-state. Based on current politics, however, the percipient national leadership required to ensure long-term, positive outcomes of media criticism is absent. As a veteran journalist at Xi'an television station told me, once the media-savvy leader is promoted elsewhere, the journalistic empowerment would likely be gone with him. Despite the cautionary foresight, this journalist remains hopeful that the succeeding leader would share a similar vision.

Appendix A

Ethnographic Observation and Interviews

Ethnographic observation was conducted at the municipal television station in a prefecture-level city in Jiangsu from June to July 2013 and in June 2015. The three-month fieldwork, spread over two different years, allowed me to be immersed in the television journalists' field while comparing differences and recognizing continuities. I shadowed journalists in their day-to-day work, sometimes carrying their microphone. My goal was twofold: observe and inquire. When journalists were busy with capturing and producing happening news stories, I observed the procedures and considerations in their work; when journalists were taking breaks, I asked them about different aspects of news reporting. The selection of interviewees was based on theoretical significance and convenience sampling. Table A.1 provides a list of the interviews.

Table A.1. Interview List

Code	Institution	Profession	Month and Year
01-DS	Municipal television station A	Producer	June 2012
02-DS	Municipal television station B	Reporter	June 2012
03-DS	Municipal television station B	Producer	July 2012
04-DS	Provincial television station C	Director	July 2012
05-DS*	Municipal television station A	Producer	May 2013
06-DS*	Municipal television station A	Reporter	June 2013
07-DS	Municipal television station D	Reporter	June 2013
08-WL	Nationally-circulated magazine A	Editor	June 2013
09-ZM*	Nationally-circulated newspaper A	Editor	June 2013

continued on next page

Table A.1. Continued.

Code	Institution	Profession	Month and Year
10-WL	Online news portal A	Editor	June 2013
11-DS	Provincial television station C	Reporter	July 2013
12-ZM	Nationally-circulated newspaper B	Editor	July 2013
13-DS	Provincial television station E	Reporter	July 2013
14-ZM	Nationally-circulated newspaper C	Editor	July 2013
15-XZ	Northwest University	Scholar	July 2013
16-XZ*	South China University of Technology	Scholar	July 2013
17-XZ*	Jilin University	Scholar	July 2013
18-ZM*	Nationally-circulated magazine B	Editor	July 2013
19-DS	Municipal television station B	Producer	July 2013
20-DS	Municipal television station B	Reporter	July 2013
21-DS*	Municipal television station A	Reporter	July 2013
22-DS	Municipal television station A	Reporter	July 2013
23-DS	Municipal television station A	Reporter	July 2013
24-DS	China Central Television Station	Producer	July 2013
25-XZ	Yangzhou University	Scholar	August 2013
26-XZ	Peking University	Scholar	August 2013
27-XZ	Communication University of China	Scholar	September 2013
28-DS	Municipal television station A	Producer	July 2015
29-DS	Municipal television station A	Reporter	July 2015
30-DS	Municipal television station A	Reporter	July 2015
31-DS	Municipal television station A	Reporter	July 2015
32-DS	Municipal television station A	Reporter	July 2015
33-DS	Municipal television station A	Reporter	July 2015
34-WL	Online news portal B	Editor	February 2017
35-ZM	Nationally-circulated magazine C	Editor	March 2017
36-DS	Municipal television station F	Producer	May 2017
37-WL	Online news portal C	Editor	June 2017
38-XZ	Sun Yat-sen University	Scholar	June 2017
39-XZ	Municipal television station G	Scholar	June 2017
40-DS	Municipal television station A	Producer	June 2017
41-DS	Municipal television station B	Producer	June 2017
42-DS	Municipal television station H	Producer	July 2017
43-DS*	Municipal television station H	Reporter	July 2017
44-DS	Municipal television station I	Reporter	August 2018
45-DS	Municipal television station I	Producer	August 2018
46-DS	Municipal television station J	Reporter	August 2018
47-DS	Provincial television station K	Reporter	September 2018

*indicates interviewees who I revisited during the course of this research.

Appendix B

Content Analysis and Variables

All five programs include sections of mini–talk shows, which are entertainment segments featuring television personalities discussing current issues. Because this book is interested in regular news reports, these entertainment segments are not included in the analysis.

To develop a codebook, I first conducted a preliminary analysis of a random sample of 100 reports from the five programs (20 reports each). This preliminary codebook was then revised during the training sessions with two student coders. Coders were trained to use the news report's narrative to make coding decisions, rather than bringing in their own evaluations of the issue covered in a news report. For example, considering a news report that criticizes jaywalking pedestrians for violating traffic rules, coders might think that, instead of pedestrians, the blame should be assigned to the traffic police who failed to monitor and correct pedestrians. In this scenario, coders are trained to code this news report as "policy violation" instead of "governance problem," because the narrative in the news report criticized the pedestrians instead of the traffic police. However, if this news report criticized the traffic police, instead of the pedestrians, then coders should label this report as "governance problem." The codebook consists of 21 categories of news reports, described below. Further information about the variables is provided in tables B.1–4.

Table B.1. The Codebook

Code	Category	Description
1	governance problem	Reports that criticize government bureaus or officials.
2	governance achievement	Reports that praise government bureaus, officials, or governance achievements.
3	governance improvement	A second-level category to label "governance problem" reports that feature misbehavior correction.
4	follow-up report	A second-level category to label follow-up reports after the initial critical reports.
5	new policy	Reports that announce, discuss, explain, or promote new policies.
6	learning experience	Reports that promote governance experience in other localities. This category largely applies to news programs in Shaanxi, where the local governments are keen on "learning advanced experience" (学习先进经验) especially from coastal, developed provinces and cities.
7	political meeting	Reports on the National Party Congress, National People's Congress, and Chinese People's Political Consultative Conference meetings at national, provincial, and municipal levels.
8	police	Reports on crimes and prosecution, often featuring police work in solving criminal cases; reports on how the police helps citizens in need.
9	policy violation	Reports that criticize citizens or businesses for violating laws, regulations, and government policies.
10	rumor rebuttal	Reports that clarify rumors from online social media. These rumors are mostly about government policies.
11	culture	Reports on celebration of festivals, promotion of tourist sites, and discussion of tradition and history.

Code	Category	Description
12	praising good people or businesses	Reports that praise citizens who exhibit desirable moral values, such as looking after ill parents or taking care of aging neighbors; reports that praise businesses for their innovation, profitability, or philanthropy.
13	dispute	Reports on conflicts or disputes between citizens or between citizens and businesses. For example, disputes between residential complex management companies (物业) and residents (业主) due to the latter's unwillingness to pay management fees are common reports labeled with "dispute."
14	accident	Reports of traffic accidents, fire, suicides, or other sensational stories.
15	public discussion	Reports that feature social media posts or interviews with citizens for their opinions on specific issues.
16	public education	Reports that offer everyday tips. Examples include reports reminding people to look out for thieves in crowded areas and reports educating people about seasonal diseases or food safety issues.
17	public interest	Reports that feature public interest projects. Examples include reports intended to raise money for people in need.
18	human interest	Reports on ordinary citizens' problems, concerns, or emotions. Examples include stories about how couples celebrate Valentine's Day.
19	news	Reports about information or international news. Examples include reports on the rising prices of eggs, vegetables, and pork.
20	weather	Reports about weather.
21	program promotion	Reports that promote the news program's own reporting or the television station's other programs and events.

Table B.2. Leadership Style towards the Media

Leader	Previous Position (tenure)	Party Newspaper (time range)	Articles with Name Mentions	Leadership Style Score
Li Qiang	Zhejiang governor (2012/12–2016/7)	Zhejiang Daily (January–March 2016)	75	9
Lou Qinjian	Shaanxi governor (2012/12–2016/3)	Shaanxi Daily (January–March 2015)	56	7
Hu Heping	Shaanxi governor (2016/4–2017/10)	Shaanxi Daily (January–March 2017)	55	6
All governors		January–March 2017	56 (mean)	
Wang Yongkang	Lishui party secretary (2013/3–2016/1)	Lishui Daily (January–March 2015)	59	9
Wei Minzhou	Shangluo party secretary (2005/6–2007/6)	Shangluo Daily (January–March 2007)	45	5
Wu Zhenglong	Taiyuan party secretary (2014/9–2016/9)	Taiyuan Daily (January–March 2016)	35	3
Zhang Jinghua	Zhenjiang party secretary (2012/4–2013/3)	Zhenjiang Daily (January–March 2013)	33	2
XYZ	Mayor (2010/1–2012/2)	X Daily (January–March 2011)	43	6
Selected municipal Party secretaries		January–March 2017	47 (mean)	
Selected mayors		January–March 2017	40 (mean)	

Source: CNKI.

Table B.3. Summary Statistics of All Variables

Variable	Min	Max	Mean	Std. Dev.
Critical reports (daily)	0	13	1.07	1.39
Positive reports (daily)	0	13	0.97	1.34
Improvement reports (daily)	0	9	0.61	0.94
Leadership style	2	9	6.41	2.38
Leader tenure (month)	1	71	19.97	23.39
Administrative level	1	3	2.2	0.75
Political events	0	3	0.40	0.91
Local initiatives	0	1	0.19	0.39
Media competition	3	6	4.21	1.19
Program age	6	16	12.86	3.20
GDP per capita (10,000 yuan)	4.8	11.8	8.31	2.40

Source: Author's dataset. n=2086. n indicates the number of days for all five programs included in the dataset.

Table B.4. News Reports by Leaders

Program	Leader	Daily Critical Reports	Mean Difference	t	Daily Positive Reports	Mean Difference	t
Zero Distance	Li Qiang	1.11	0.27	-1.36	0.38	0.01	-0.16
	Lou Qinjian	1.38			0.39		
Live Broadcast Nanjing	Wu Zhenglong	0.59	0.25	-3.27**	1.42	0.49	4.42***
	Zhang Jinghua	0.84			0.93		
Number One News	Lou Qinjian	0.98	0.40	2.13*	0.33	0.35	-2.79**
	Hu Heping	0.58			0.68		
Xi'an Zero Distance	Wei Minzhou	2.19	0.18	-0.57	2.58	0.94	-2.18*
	Wang Yongkang	2.37			3.52		

Notes: *p<0.05, **p<0.01, ***p<0.001

Source: Author's dataset.

Notes

Introduction

1. While Chinese scholars have agreed to use *minsheng xinwen* (民生新闻) to refer to this type of news programs, there has not been an agreed-upon English translation of this term. Translations seen in scholarly works include "livelihood news" (Yang 2010) and "citizen news" (Miao 2011). In this book, I adopt Guobin Yang's translation and use "livelihood news" to refer to *minsheng xinwen*.

2. The traditional news programs are typically titled with the location of the television station. For example, *Nanjing News* (南京新闻) is the traditional news program broadcast by Nanjing Television Station, which follows a similar style to *News Broadcast* (新闻联播), broadcast by China Central Television (CCTV) at the central level.

3. Notable early livelihood news programs include *Najing Zero Distance* (南京零距离), in Nanjing, *Attention* (关注), in Yangzhou, *First Report* (第一时间), in Hefei, and *Chengdu Full Contact* (成都全接触), in Chengdu.

4. According to a report from Sun Yat-sen University, cited by Freedom House, the number of investigative journalists has declined to only 175 as of 2017, a 58% decrease from 2011 (Cook and Henochowicz 2018). A recent report from the *New York Times* sheds further light on this professional decline, due to both political and business reasons (Hernández 2019). My interviews with former veteran investigative journalists corroborate this observation that the exodus is unprecedented.

5. Ya-Wen Lei's (2016) recent study is among the few that examine the varying, local-level dynamics in the state-media relationship.

6. Notable exceptions that do examine television news include Chan (2002), Miao (2011), and Y. Zhao (1998, 2008). The English literature on Chinese television largely focuses on the China Central Television (CCTV) (Chan 2002; Ying Zhu 2012; and Zhu and Berry 2009). According to Stockmann (2010, 124), a survey of the recent scholarship that systematically analyzes the content of Chinese media sources shows that about 65% of the articles published from

1981 to 2010 focused on newspapers and 23% focused on television programs. For those articles focusing on television, all programs were broadcast on CCTV.

7. The penetration rate of television was 98.77% in 2015, according to *China Statistical Yearbook 2016*, with very little rural-urban difference (rural penetration rate was 98.32%). The penetration for Internet was 50.3% in 2015, according to the *37th China Statistical Report on Internet Development* published by China Internet Network Information Center.

8. Zhou, Zhang, and Shen (2014) find that among the traditional and new media outlets, including newspapers, radio, magazines, websites, and online devices, television is the most trustworthy media outlet in China. According to the China portion of the third wave of Asian Barometer Survey (ABS), conducted in 2011, 76% of the Chinese respondents trust television, while 66% trust newspapers. The second wave of ABS, conducted in 2008, shows that 51% of the Chinese respondents trust television, while 43% trust newspapers. The first wave of ABS, conducted in 2002, shows that 86% of the Chinese respondents trust television, while 73% trust newspapers. Across the three waves of the survey, trust in television is consistently higher than trust in newspapers.

9. A similar argument is made in Jennifer Pan's (2017) study on how Chinese officials use the Internet to construct their public image. In this role, the Internet is used to influence not only "regime-society interactions" but also "dynamics among regime insiders." In the study of democracies, there is a recent call to examine how news media influence the behavior of elected representatives, in addition to members of the public (Arceneaux et al. 2016). Other examples of using the media to target the political elite, rather than the general public, in China involve higher-level officials from different political factions. See Tsai and Kao (2013) and Shih (2008).

10. According to *China Radio and Television Yearbook 2016*, the number of people working for radio and television stations was 900,700 as of 2015, an increase from 864,400 in 2014. According to *China Statistical Yearbook 2016*, the hours of television news programs produced increased from 918,296 hours in 2014 to 978,801 hours in 2015. In contrast, according to the *2016 Analysis Report of News and Publication Industry*, published by the State Administration of Press, Publication, Radio, Film, and Television, the number of people working for the newspaper industry was 224,000 in 2016, a decrease of 7.5% from 2015. Circulations of all newspapers decreased by 9.3% in 2016 from the previous year.

11. This is not to suggest that this group of journalists is monolithic. This book recognizes the diversity within the pragmatic journalists, as discussed in chapters 2 and 4.

12. For example, investigative journalism in China led to significant policy changes in the first decade of the new century (Tong 2011). However, investigative journalism has been severely limited since Xi Jinping took over power in late 2012 (H. Gao 2018). Furthermore, a recent report from Freedom

House shows that the reach of investigative and public interest stories by the elite print media is being challenged by censorship and financial woes (Cook and Henochowicz 2018). A recent *New York Times* report echoes this declining trend and the diagnosis that focuses on political and business reasons (Hernández 2019).

13. This is somewhat different from the conception of media capture in democracies where the press is relatively free; in this case, the government may capture the media and influence news content, which has negative consequences for political outcomes (Besley and Prat 2006).

14. After the media reforms in the 1990s, private ownership in the media sector is allowed up to a 49% stake, so the traditional media outlets in China (excluding Internet and social media companies) are still owned by the state.

15. One of the five programs, *Live Broadcast Nanjing*, also includes data from October 2016.

Chapter 1

1. As mentioned in Introduction, a notable exception is Lei (2016).

2. For an in-depth discussion on supervision by public opinion, please see Repnikova (2017a, ch. 3).

3. The first few cities that rolled out trial regulations on the bike-sharing services can be found in this report: http://www.xinhuanet.com/fortune/2017-03/24/c_1120684287.htm.

4. Some street-level bureaucrats may be able to lobby their superiors to censor critical reports about themselves, discussed in chapter 2, but their limited influence over the media is far from capturing the media completely, which is necessary to advance political careers.

5. The full text of the discussion section on *People's Daily* is available at http://politics.people.com.cn/n/2015/0525/c1001-27049133.html.

6. A recent reform recentralized the appointment power for township party secretaries from the municipal level to the provincial level, further discussed in chapter 3.

Chapter 2

1. The institutional setup that intends to differentiate the party from the state results in governmental institutions that have overlapping jurisdiction over television stations. On the party side, the propaganda department at each administrative level directs all work related to news, propaganda, and thought work. On the state side, the National Radio and Television Administration and

its counterparts at lower administrative levels manage the day-to-day operation, including drafting and implementing regulations and industry standards, supervising program content, coordinating national propaganda campaigns, and so on. Because the party controls the state, the Central Propaganda Department, representing the central leadership, has more say over media affairs than any other governmental institutions. Therefore, for analytical clarity, this chapter focuses on the propaganda departments to illustrate the crosshatching structure of the party-state and its implications at the local level. This analytical choice does not negate the role that other governmental institutions play in managing television news; rather, the focus on propaganda departments intends to make clearer the logic of other governmental institutions in managing media affairs.

2. Peter Lorentzen makes a similar argument that the logic of uncertainty keeping people in line is unclear, and that certainty of punishment should also deter unruly behavior and keep people in line (see Lorentzen 2017).

3. By the late 1990s, *Focus* had a daily audience of 300 million (Chan 2002).

4. According to the *Civil Servant Law* (公务员法), county chief level (县处级) is the seventh of the 13-level leadership positions from top down within the civil servant system.

5. According to a medical study, in 2015, smoking prevalence was 27.7% in China. Breaking this figure down by gender, smoking prevalence was 52.1% among men and 2.7% among women (Parascandola and Xiao 2019).

Chapter 3

1. The Forced TV Confessions Database compiled by RSDL Monitor (Residential Surveillance at a Designated Location) provides a useful list of televised confessions since 2015: "Forced TV Confessions Database," News, Safeguard Defenders, August 6, 2018, https://safeguarddefenders.com/en/blog/forced-tv-confessions-database.

2. The full text of the *People's Republic of China Open Government Information Regulations* (中华人民共和国政府信息公开条例) is available at http://www.gov.cn/zwgk/2007-04/24/content_592937.htm.

3. Exceptions include mayors and party secretaries of provincial-level municipalities and deputy provincial municipalities, who are appointed or approved by the Central Organization Department.

4. For a more detailed account of the policy origin of these cadre rotation rules, see Eaton and Kostka (2014).

5. The full text of *The Notice to Improve Local Party Leadership and Cadre Performance Evaluation Work* (关于改进地方党政领导班子和领导干部政绩考核工作的通知) is available at http://news.12371.cn/2013/12/09/ARTI1386590057904551.shtml.

6. The full text of *Regulations on Party Leadership and Cadre Promotion Work* (党政领导干部选拔任用工作条例) is available at http://news.12371.cn/2014/01/15/ARTI1389784871616867.shtml.

7. The full text of *Several Regulations to Further Leading Cadres' Ability to Fulfill Requirements* (推进领导干部能上能下若干规定) is available at http://syss.12371.cn/2015/07/28/ARTI1438087781582196.shtml.

8. A summary of Wang's political experience was published with his appointment as the Xi'an municipal party secretary on the official *China Daily* website: http://china.chinadaily.com.cn/2016-12/28/content_27803128.htm.

9. This article about Wang Yongkang, published by the Zhejiang television official website, is available at http://www.zjstv.com/news/zjnews/201612/329864.html.

10. All episodes of this program are available on Xi'an television official website: http://v.xiancity.cn/folder240/folder345/folder359/.

11. This quotation is obtained from the responsibility statement section in the 2016 budget report from the Jilin Provincial Propaganda Department that is publicly available on the Jilin Provincial Financial Department website: http://www.czt.jl.gov.cn/jlcz/5/41/2016/03/i2985.shtml.

12. This quotation is obtained from the section on the specific job responsibilities completed in 2015 in the final accounts of revenue report in August 2016 from the Sichuan Provincial Propaganda Department that is publicly available on the Sichuan People's Government website: http://www.sc.gov.cn/10462/10778/10876/2016/3/9/10372267.shtml.

Chapter 4

1. The data from the China Statistical Yearbooks do not differentiate staff working for television from those working for radio, due to their combined operation.

2. It is worth noting that the media's supervisory power can also corrupt journalists in China. Instances of news extortion and other forms of media corruption are well documented, as discussed in chapter 1 (Lin 2010; Wang, Cho, and Li 2018; Y. Zhao 1998; Zhou 2000).

3. Based on the curriculum for a journalism major published on the website of Renmin University, a top university in China, these courses are among the required courses.

4. For a more comprehensive and in-depth examination of China's urbanization and urban governance, see Eggleston, Oi, and Wang (2017).

5. The full text of the *Action Plan to Prevent and Cure Water Pollution* (水污染防治行动计划) is available at http://www.hcstzz.com/show.aspx?NewsID=94.

6. The magazine *Chinese Entrepreneur* published an article in January 2016 titled "Annual Keyword—Smog," available at http://www.iceo.com.cn/com2013/2016/0103/300696.shtml.

7. The full text of the *Action Plan to Prevent and Remedy Air Pollution* (大气污染防治行动计划) is available at http://www.gov.cn/zwgk/2013-09/12/content_2486773.htm.

8. For a more detailed account of the major policy changes regarding air pollution, see a report from the official Xinhua News Agency at http://www.xinhuanet.com/2016-12/18/c_1120139290.htm.

9. The full text of the revised Food Safety Law (食品安全法) is available at http://www.gov.cn/zhengce/2015-04/25/content_2853643.htm.

10. For more details, see the *Guangzhou Daily* report on the institutional reform in Shenzhen: http://news.sina.com.cn/c/2009-08-06/040618373631.shtml.

Chapter 5

1. A notable exception is a recent study of the political personalities of Chinese local officials by Hasmath, Teets, and Lewis (2019).

2. According to the *Administrative Measures for Official Documents of State Administrations* (国家行政机关公文处理办法), issued by the State Council in 2000, there are 13 types of official documents.

3. For an example of grid management applied to managing popular contention, see Chen and Kang (2016). For a systematic account of how grid management manifests itself in China's urban governance, see Tang (2020).

4. During a public appearance, Wang picked up a cigarette butt from a public square, prompting the media's adulatory portrayal of the municipal leader as someone who cared about the city's environment and was folksy enough to pick up trash himself. After that, removing all cigarette butts in public places became a key governance issue in Xi'an, dubbed by the media as "cigarette butt revolution" (烟头革命).

Works Cited

Andreas, Joel, and Yige Dong. 2017. "'Mass Supervision' and the Bureaucratization of Governance in China." In *To Govern China: Evolving Practices of Power*, edited by Vivienne Shue and Patricia M. Thornton, 123–52. Cambridge: Cambridge University Press.

Ang, Yuen Yuen. 2018. "Autocracy with Chinese Characteristics: Beijing's Behind-the-Scenes Reforms." *Foreign Affairs* 97 (3): 39–46.

Arceneaux, Kevin, Martin Johnson, René Lindstädt, Ryan J. Vander Wielen. 2016. "The Influence of News Media on Political Elites: Investigating Strategic Responsiveness in Congress." *American Journal of Political Science* 60 (1): 5–29.

Besley, Timothy, and Andrea Prat. 2006. "Handcuffs for the Grabbing Hand? Media Capture and Government Accountability." *American Economic Review* 96 (3): 720–36.

Birney, Mayling. 2014. "Decentralization and Veiled Corruption under China's 'Rule of Mandates.'" *World Development* 53:55–67.

Brady, Anne-Marie. 2008. *Marketing Dictatorship: Propaganda and Thought Work in Contemporary China*. Lanham, MD: Rowman and Littlefield.

Branigan, Tania. 2008. "Chinese Figures Show Fivefold Rise in Babies Sick from Contaminated Milk." *Guardian*, December 2. https://www.theguardian.com/world/2008/dec/02/china.

Brownlee, Jason. 2007. *Authoritarianism in an Age of Democratization*. Cambridge: Cambridge University Press.

Buckley, Chris, and Keith Bradsher. 2018. "When Xi Speaks, Chinese Officials Jump. Maybe Too High." *New York Times*, March 17.

Bueno de Mesquita, Bruce. 1981. *The War Trap*. New Haven, CT: Yale University Press.

———. 1985. "The War Trap Revisited: A Revised Expected Utility Model." *American Political Science Review* 79 (1): 156–73.

Burns, John P. 1989. *The Chinese Communist Party's Nomenklatura System: A Documentary Study of Party Control of Leadership Selection, 1979–1984*. Armonk, NY: M. E. Sharpe.

———. 1994. "Strengthening Central CCP Control of Leadership Selection: The 1990 Nomenklatura." *China Quarterly* 138:458–91.

———. 1999. "The People's Republic of China at Fifty: National Political Reform." *China Quarterly* 159:580–94.

Cai, Yongshun. 2004. "Irresponsible State: Local Cadres and Image-Building in China." *Journal of Communist Studies and Transition Politics* 20 (4): 20–41.

———. 2008. "Power Structure and Regime Resilience: Contentious Politics in China." *British Journal of Political Science* 38 (3): 411–32.

———. 2015. *State and Agents in China: Disciplining Government Officials*. Stanford, CA: Stanford University Press.

Cai, Yongshun, and Titi Zhou. 2019. "Online Political Participation in China: Local Government and Differentiated Response." *China Quarterly* 238: 331–52.

Chan, Alex. 2002. "From Propaganda to Hegemony: *Jiaodian Fangtan* and China's Media Policy." *Journal of Contemporary China* 11 (30): 35–51.

Chan, Joseph Man, and Jack Linchuan Qiu. 2002. "China: Media Liberalization under Authoritarianism." In *Media Reform: Democratizing the media, democratizing the state*, edited by Monroe E. Price, Beata Rozumilowicz, and Stefaan G. Verhulst, 27–46. London: Routledge.

Chen, Dan. 2016. "Review Essay: The Safety Valve Analogy in Chinese Politics." *Journal of East Asian Studies* 16 (2): 281–94.

———. 2017a. "Facilitating Public Service Provision: The Emerging Role of Municipal Television News in China." *China Quarterly* 229:130–49.

———. 2017b. "Local Distrust and Regime Support: Sources and Effects of Political Trust in China." *Political Research Quarterly* 70 (2): 314–26.

———. 2017c. " 'Supervision by Public Opinion' or by Government Officials? Media Criticism and Central-Local Government Relations in China." *Modern China* 43 (6): 620–45.

Chen, Fan. 2006. "The Study of Government-Media Relationship Enters Government Officials' Purview." *Chinadaily.com.cn*, November 13. http://www.chinadaily.com.cn/jjzg/2006-11/13/content_731270.htm.

Chen, Feng, and Yi Kang. 2016. "Disorganized Popular Contention and Local Institutional Building in China: A Case Study in Guangdong." *Journal of Contemporary China* 25 (100): 596–612.

Chen, Jidong, Jennifer Pan, and Yiqing Xu. 2016. "Sources of Authoritarian Responsiveness: A Field Experiment in China." *American Journal of Political Science* 60 (2): 383–400.

Chen, Long. 2004. "News Centered, Supervision by Public Opinion, Humanistic Care: Important Components of Credibility for Livelihood News" [新闻本位、舆论监督、人文关怀: 民生新闻的公信力要件]. *Chinese Television* [中国电视] 6:43–47.

Chen, Song. 2016. "Sichuan: Clearly Support Media's Public Opinion Supervision; Provide Convenience during Reporting" [四川: 旗帜鲜明支持媒体舆论监督, 为采访报道提供方便]. *Sichuan Daily* [四川日报], May 13. http://www.sc.gov.cn/10462/10464/10797/2016/5/13/10380145.shtml.

Chen, Xi. 2009. "Power of Troublemaking: Chinese Petitioners' Tactics and Their Efficacy." *Comparative Politics* 41 (4): 451–71.

———. 2012. *Social Protest and Contentious Authoritarianism in China*. New York: Cambridge University Press.

Chen, Yang. 2013. "Can People's Livelihood Journalism Transform into Public Journalism in China? The Observation from a Field Study" [民生新闻能否转型成为公共新闻？来自田野调查的思考]. *International News* [国际新闻界] 35 (5): 94–101.

Cheong, Pauline Hope, and Jie Gong. 2010. "Cyber Vigilantism, Transmedia Collective Intelligence, and Civic Participation." *Chinese Journal of Communication* 3 (4): 471–87.

"China Wants Eyes and Ears on Every Street." 2018. *Economist*, June 28. https://www.economist.com/china/2018/06/28/china-wants-eyes-and-ears-on-every-street.

Chung, Jae Ho. 2000. *Central Control and Local Discretion in China: Leadership and Implementation during Post-Mao Decollectivization*. New York: Oxford University Press.

Cook, Sarah, and Ann Henochowicz. 2018. "Investigative Journalism in China Is Struggling to Survive." *Freedom at Issue* (blog), Freedom House, February 8. https://freedomhouse.org/blog/investigative-journalism-china-struggling-survive.

Cook, Timothy E. 2005. *Governing with the News: The News Media as a Political Institution*. 2nd ed. Chicago: University of Chicago Press.

———. 2006. "The News Media as a Political Institution: Looking Backward and Looking Forward." *Political Communication* 23 (2): 159–71.

Cui, Haijiao. 2016. "Profoundly Grasping the Dialectical Unity of Positive Guidance and Public Opinion Supervision" [深刻把握正面引导与舆论监督的辩证统一]. *People's Daily* [人民日报], April 19. http://theory.people.com.cn/n1/2016/0419/c40531-28285585.html.

Dalton, Russell J., Doh C. Shin, and Willy Jou. 2007. "Understanding Democracy: Data from Unlikely Places." *Journal of Democracy* 18 (4): 142–56.

De Burgh, Hugo. 2003. *The Chinese Journalist: Mediating Information in the World's Most Populous Country*. London: RoutledgeCurzon.

Deng, Xiaoping. 1983. "The Important Party Tasks on Organizational and Thought Routes" [党在组织路线和思想路线上的重要任务]. A Report to the Twelfth National Party Congress. http://www.people.com.cn/GB/channel1/10/20000529/80786.html.

Diamond, Larry, and Marc F. Plattner. 2012. *Liberation Technology: Social Media and the Struggle for Democracy*. Baltimore: Johns Hopkins University Press.

Dimitrov, Martin K. 2013. "Vertical Accountability in Communist Regimes: The Role of Citizen Complaints in Bulgaria and China." In *Why Communism Did Not Collapse: Understanding Authoritarian Regime Resilience in Asia and Europe*, edited by Martin K. Dimitrov, 276–302. New York: Cambridge University Press.

———. 2015. "Internal Government Assessments of the Quality of Governance in China." *Studies in Comparative International Development* 50 (1): 50–72.

Distelhorst, Greg. 2017. "The Power of Empty Promises: Quasi-democratic Institutions and Activism in China." *Comparative Political Studies* 50 (4): 464–98.

Distelhorst, Greg, and Yue Hou. 2017. "Constituency Service under Nondemocratic Rule: Evidence from China." *Journal of Politics* 79 (3): 1024–40.

Eaton, Sarah, and Genia Kostka. 2014. "Authoritarian Environmentalism Undermined? Local Leaders' Time Horizons and Environmental Policy Implementation in China." *China Quarterly* 218:359–80.

Edin, Maria. 1998. "Why Do Chinese Local Cadres Promote Growth? Institutional Incentives and Constraints of Local Cadres." *Forum for Development Studies* 25 (1): 97–127.

———. 2003. "State Capacity and Local Agent Control in China: CCP Cadre Management from a Township Perspective." *China Quarterly* 173:35–52.

Eggleston, Karen, Jean C. Oi, and Yiming Wang, eds. 2017. *Challenges in the Process of China's Urbanization*. Washington, DC: Brookings Institution Press.

Esarey, Ashley. 2005. "Cornering the Market: State Strategies for Controlling China's Commercial Media." *Asian Perspective* 29 (4): 37–83.

Feng, Emily. 2018. "Chinese Developers Seek Piece of Booming Education Market." *Financial Times*, April 3. https://www.ft.com/content/0896df46-f6ba-11e7-88f7-5465a6ce1a00.

Foley, Kevin, Jeremy L. Wallace, and Jessica Chen Weiss. 2018. "The Political and Economic Consequences of Nationalist Protest in China: The 2012 Anti-Japanese Demonstrations." *China Quarterly* 236:1131–53.

Friedman, Eli. 2014. *Insurgency Trap: Labor Politics in Postsocialist China*. Ithaca, NY: Cornell University Press.

Frye, Timothy, and Ekaterina Borisova. 2019. "Elections, Protest, and Trust in Government: A Natural Experiment from Russia." *Journal of Politics* 81 (3): 820–32.

Fu, Zhengyuan. 1996. *China's Legalists: The Earliest Totalitarians and Their Art of Ruling*. New York: M. E. Sharpe.

Gallagher, Mary E. 2017. *Authoritarian Legality in China: Law, Workers, and the State*. New York: Cambridge University Press.

Gandhi, Jennifer. 2008. *Political Institutions under Dictatorship*. New York: Cambridge University Press.

Gao, Helen. 2018. "The Demise of Watchdog Journalism in China." *New York Times*, April 27. https://www.nytimes.com/2018/04/27/opinion/watchdog-journalism-china-oppression.html.

Gao, Jie. 2015. "Pernicious Manipulation of Performance Measures in China's Cadre Evaluation System." *China Quarterly* 223:618–37.

Gilley, Bruce. 2008. "Legitimacy and Institutional Change: The Case of China." *Comparative Political Studies* 41 (3): 259–84.

———. 2014. *The Nature of Asian Politics*. New York: Cambridge University Press.

Global Investigative Journalism Network. 2018. "Editor's Pick: The Best Investigative Stories from China 2017." *News and Analysis*, January 4. https://gijn.org/2018/01/04/the-best-investigative-stories-from-china-2017/.

Göbel, Christian. 2011. "Uneven Policy Implementation in Rural China." *China Journal* 65:53–76.

Göbel, Christian, and Thomas Heberer. 2017. "The Policy Innovation Imperative: Changing Techniques for Governing China's Local Governors." In *To Govern China: Evolving Practices of Power*, edited by Vivienne Shue and Patricia M. Thornton, 283–308. Cambridge: Cambridge University Press.

Gong, Pu, Hanzhi Yu, Tian Wu, and Xun Wu. 2015. "Policy Changes in Local Officials' Turnover, Tenure, and Expenditures: An Empirical Study Based on 1980–2011 Provincial Data." *China Public Administration Review* 18:17–31.

Gramsci, Antonio. (1926–37) 1971. *Selections from the Prison Notebooks of Antonio Gramsci*. Edited by Quintin Hoare and Geoffrey Nowell-Smith. London: Lawrence and Wishart.

Guan, Bing, Ying Xia, and Gong Cheng. 2017. "Power Structure and Media Autonomy in China: The Case of *Southern Weekend*." *Journal of Contemporary China* 26 (104): 233–48.

Guan, Tianru. 2019. "The 'Authoritarian Determinism' and Reductionisms in China-Focused Political Communication Studies." *Media, Culture and Society* 41 (5): 738–50.

Gueorguiev, Dimitar D., and Edmund J. Malesky. 2019. "Consultation and Selective Censorship in China." *Journal of Politics* 81 (4): 1539–45.

Han, Rongbin. 2018. *Contesting Cyberspace in China: Online Expression and Authoritarian Resilience*. New York: Columbia University Press.

Han, Wanchun, and Jun Zhang. 2018. "Municipal Television Stations: Make Livelihood News Programs More Competitive" [城市电视台: 让民生新闻栏目更具竞争力]. *Today's Mass Media* [今传媒], no. 6, 88–91.

Hao, Jiming. 2013. "Establishing a Sunshine Government in Nanjing" [南京市阳光政府建设]. In *Transparent Government* [透明政府], edited by Chengli Liu. Beijing: Central Compilation and Translation Press.

Hasmath, Reza, Jessica C. Teets, and Orion A. Lewis. 2019. "The Innovative Personality? Policymaking and Experimentation in an Authoritarian Bureaucracy." *Public Administration and Development* 39 (3): 154–62.

Hassid, Jonathan. 2008. "Controlling the Chinese Media: An Uncertain Business." *Asian Survey* 48 (3): 414–30.

———. 2015. *China's Unruly Journalists: How Committed Professionals are Changing the People's Republic.* London: Routledge.

He, Xin. 2013. "Judicial Innovation and Local Politics: Judicialization of Administrative Governance in East China." *China Journal* 69:20–42.

Heberer, Thomas, and Gunter Schubert. 2012. "County and Township Cadres as a Strategic Group: A New Approach to Political Agency in China's Local State." *Journal of Chinese Political Science* 17 (3): 221–49.

Heberer, Thomas, and René Trappel. 2013. "Evaluation Processes, Local Cadres' Behavior and Local Development Processes." *Journal of Contemporary China* 22 (84): 1048–66.

Heilmann, Sebastian, and Elizabeth J. Perry. 2011. "Embracing Uncertainty: Guerrilla Policy Style and Adaptive Governance in China." In *Mao's Invisible Hand: The Political Foundations of Adaptive Governance in China,* edited by Sebastian Heilmann and Elizabeth J. Perry, 1–29. Cambridge, MA: Harvard University Press.

Heilmann, Sebastian, Lea Shih, and Andreas Hofem. 2013. "National Planning and Local Technology Zones: Experimental Governance in China's Torch Programme." *China Quarterly* 216:896–919.

Hernández, Javier C. 2019. "'We're Almost Extinct': China's Investigative Journalists Are Silenced under Xi." *New York Times*, July 12. https://www.nytimes.com/2019/07/12/world/asia/china-journalists-crackdown.html.

Hildebrandt, Timothy. 2013. *Social Organizations and the Authoritarian State in China.* Cambridge: Cambridge University Press.

Holbig, Heike. 2013. "Ideology after the End of Ideology. China and the Quest for Autocratic Legitimation." *Democratization* 20 (1): 61–81.

Holbig, Heike, and Bruce Gilley. 2010. "Reclaiming Legitimacy in China." *Politics and Policy* 38 (3): 395–422.

Hong, Junhao, Yanmei Lü, and William Zou. 2009. "CCTV in the Reform Years: A New Model for China's Television?" In *TV China*, edited by Ying Zhu and Chris Berry, 40–55. Bloomington: Indiana University Press.

Howard, Philip N. 2010. *The Digital Origins of Dictatorship and Democracy: Information Technology and Political Islam.* Oxford: Oxford University Press.

Hu, Jieren, Tong Wu, and Jingyan Fei. 2018. "Flexible Governance in China: Affective Care, Petition Social Workers, and Multi-pronged Means of Dispute Resolution." *Asian Survey* 58 (4): 679–703.

Huang, Gengzhi, Desheng Xue, and Zhigang Li. 2014. "From Revanchism to Ambivalence: The Changing Politics of Street Vending in Guangzhou." *Antipode* 46 (1): 170–89.

Huang, Haifeng, Serra Boranbay-Akan, and Ling Huang. 2019. "Media, Protest Diffusion, and Authoritarian Resilience." *Political Science Research and Methods* 7 (1): 23–42.

Huang, Philip C. C. 2019. "Rethinking 'the Third Sphere': The Dualistic Unity of State and Society in China, Past and Present." *Modern China* 45 (4): 355–91.

Huang, Shengmin, and Yan Zhou. 2003. *The Big Change in the Chinese Media Market* [中国传媒市场大变局]. Beijing: Zhongxin Publisher.

Huang, Yasheng. 1995. "Administrative monitoring in China." *China Quarterly* 143:828–43.

Hwang, Yih-Jye, and Florian Schneider. 2011. "Performance, Meaning, and Ideology in the Making of Legitimacy: The Celebrations of the People's Republic of China's Sixty-Year Anniversary." *China Review* 11 (1): 27–56.

Iyengar, Shanto. 2015. *Media Politics: A Citizen's Guide*. 3rd ed. New York: W. W. Norton.

Jia, Ruixue, Masayuki Kudamatsu, and David Seim. 2015. "Political Selection in China: The Complementary Roles of Connections and Performance." *Journal of the European Economic Association* 13 (4): 631–68.

Jiang, Jie. 2011. "Institutional Reform to Cure the Persistent Disease of Private Use of Public Cars" [公车私用顽疾, 改革才能根治]. *People's Daily* [人民日报], November 8. http://data.people.com.cn/rmrb/20111108/17.

Jiang, Junyan. 2018. "Making Bureaucracy Work: Patronage Networks, Performance Incentives, and Economic Development in China." *American Journal of Political Science* 62 (4): 982–99.

Jiang, Zemin. 1997. *Report to the 15th Party Congress*. https://news.ifeng.com/mainland/special/zhonggong18da/content-4/detail_2012_11/04/18821363_1.shtml.

Kedrowski, Karen M. 1996. *Media Entrepreneurs and the Media Enterprise in the U.S. Congress*. Cresskill, NJ: Hampton Press.

Keller, Jonathan W. 2005. "Leadership Style, Regime Type, and Foreign Policy Crisis Behavior: A Contingent Monadic Peace?" *International Studies Quarterly* 49 (2): 205–31.

Keller, Jonathan W., and Dennis M. Foster. 2012. "Presidential Leadership Style and the Political Use of Force." *Political Psychology* 33 (5): 581–98.

Kernell, Samuel. 2007. *Going Public: New Strategies of Presidential Leadership*. 4th ed. Washington, DC: Congressional Quarterly Press.

Khor, Niny, and Jean C. Oi. 2017. "Institutional Challenges in Providing Affordable Housing in the People's Republic of China." In *Challenges in the Process of China's Urbanization*, edited by Karen Eggleston, Jean C. Oi, and Wang Yiming, 207–47. Washington, DC: Brookings Institution Press.

King, Gary, Jennifer Pan, and Margaret E. Roberts. 2013. "How Censorship in China Allows Government Criticism but Silences Collective Expression." *American Political Science Review* 107 (2): 326–43.

———. 2014. "Reverse-Engineering Censorship in China: Randomized Experimentation and Participant Observation." *Science*, August 22.

———. 2017. "How the Chinese Government Fabricates Social Media Posts for Strategic Distraction, Not Engaged Argument." *American Political Science Review* 111 (3): 484–501.

Kogan, Nathan, and Michael A. Wallach. 1964. *Risk Taking: A Study in Cognition and Personality*. New York: Holt, Rinehart and Winston.

Kostka, Genia. 2016. "Command without Control: The Case of China's Environmental Target System." *Regulation and Governance* 10 (1): 58–74.

Kostka, Genia, and Jonas Nahm. 2017. "Central-Local Relations: Recentralization and Environmental Governance in China." *China Quarterly* 231:567–82.

Kowert, Paul A., and Margaret G. Hermann. 1997. "Who Takes Risks? Daring and Caution in Foreign Policy Making." *Journal of Conflict Resolution* 41 (5): 611–37.

Kuhn, Anthony. 2017. "China's Few Investigative Journalists Face Increasing Challenges." *NPR*, August 6. https://www.npr.org/sections/parallels/2017/08/06/539720397/chinas-few-investigative-journalists-face-increasing-challenges.

Lampton, David M. 1987. *Policy Implementation in Post-Mao China*. Berkeley: University of California Press.

Lan, Jinlong. 2015. "A Comparative Study of Traditional Television and New Media in Their Integration Development Strategy" [从传统电视媒体和新媒体比较看融合发展对策]. *News Knowledge* [新闻知识], no. 2, 111–12.

Landry, Pierre F. 2008. *Decentralized Authoritarianism in China: The Communist Party's Control of Local Elites in the Post-Mao Era*. New York: Cambridge University Press.

Landry, Pierre F., Xiaobo Lü, and Haiyan Duan. 2018. "Does Performance Matter? Evaluating Political Selection along the Chinese Administrative Ladder." *Comparative Political Studies* 51 (8): 1074–1105.

Lawson, Chappell H. 2002. *Building the Fourth Estate: Democratization and the Rise of a Free Press in Mexico*. Berkeley: University of California Press.

Lee, Chin-Chuan, ed. 2000. *Power, Money, and Media: Communication Patterns and Bureaucratic Control in Cultural China*. Evanston, IL: Northwestern University Press.

Lee, Ching Kwan, and Yonghong Zhang. 2013. "The Power of Instability: Unraveling the Microfoundations of Bargained Authoritarianism in China." *American Journal of Sociology* 118 (6): 1475–1508.

Lee, Don S., and Paul Schuler. 2020. "Testing the 'China Model' of Meritocratic Promotions: Do Democracies Reward Less Competent Ministers than Autocracies?" *Comparative Political Studies* 53 (3–4): 531–66.

Lei, Qian. 2017. "Xi'an Municipal Government Issues '1+1+9' Plan to Cure Smog and Defend the Blue Sky" [西安市 "铁腕治霾保卫蓝天"1+1+9组合方案发布]. *China Business View* [华商报], March 10. http://news.hsw.cn/system/2017/0310/687325.shtml.

Lei, Ya-Wen. 2016. "Freeing the Press: How Field Environment Explains Critical News Reporting in China." *American Journal of Sociology* 122 (1): 1–49.

Lenin, Vladimir. 1963–70. *Collected Works*. 47 vols. Moscow: Foreign Language Publishing House.

Li, Cheng. 2001. *China's Leaders: The New Generation*. Lanham, MD: Rowman and Littlefield.

———. 2010. "China's Midterm Jockeying: Gearing Up for 2012 (Part 1: Provincial Chiefs)." *China Leadership Monitor*, no. 31 (Winter). https://www.hoover.org/sites/default/files/uploads/documents/CLM31CL.pdf.

———. 2012. "The Battle for China's Top Nine Leadership Posts." *Washington Quarterly* 35 (1): 131–45.

———. 2013. "A Biographical and Factional Analysis of the Post-2012 Politburo." *China Leadership Monitor*, no. 41 (Spring). https://www.hoover.org/sites/default/files/uploads/documents/CLM41CL.pdf.

Li, Hongbin, and Li-An Zhou. 2005. "Political Turnover and Economic Performance: The Incentive Role of Personnel Control in China." *Journal of Public Economics* 89 (9–10): 1743–62.

Li, Hui, and Lance L. P. Gore. 2018. "Merit-Based Patronage: Career Incentives of Local Leading Cadres in China." *Journal of Contemporary China* 27 (109): 85–102.

Li, Ke, and Colin Sparks. 2018. "Chinese Newspapers and Investigative Reporting in the New Media Age." *Journalism Studies* 19 (3): 415–31.

Li, Lianjiang. 2004. "Political Trust in Rural China." *Modern China* 30 (2): 228–58.

———. 2016. "Reassessing Trust in the Central Government: Evidence from Five National Surveys." *China Quarterly* 225:100–121.

Li, Yao. 2018. *Playing by the Informal Rules: Why the Chinese Regime Remains Stable despite Rising Protests*. Cambridge: Cambridge University Press.

Lieberthal, Kenneth G. 1992. "Introduction: The 'Fragmented Authoritarianism' Model and Its Limitations." In *Bureaucracy, Politics, and Decision Making in Post-Mao China*, edited by Kenneth G. Lieberthal and David M. Lampton, 1–31. Berkeley: University of California Press.

———. 2004. *Governing China: From Revolution Through Reform*. 2nd ed. New York: W. W. Norton.

Liebman, Benjamin L. 2011. "Changing Media, Changing Courts." In *Changing Media, Changing China*, edited by Susan L. Shirk, 150–74. Oxford: Oxford University Press.

Lin, Fen. 2010. "A Survey Report on Chinese Journalists in China." *China Quarterly* 202: 421–34.

Ling, Zhao. 2014. "China's First Report on Petitions Attracts High-Level Attention." *Contemporary Chinese Thought* 46, 1: 55–64.

Liu, Alan P. L. 1971. *Communications and National Integration in Communist China*. Berkeley: University of California Press.

Liu, Chengli. 2013. "Introduction: Build a More Transparent Government." In *Transparent Government* [透明政府], edited by Chengli Liu. Beijing: Central Compilation and Translation Press.

Liu, Derek Tai-wei. 2018. "The Effects of Institutionalization in China: A Difference-in-Differences Analysis of the Mandatory Retirement Age." *China Economic Review* 52:192–203.

Liu, Dongshu. 2019. "Punish the Dissidents: The Selective Implementation of Stability Preservation in China." *Journal of Contemporary China* 28 (119): 795–812.

Liu, Xuyi. 2017. "Use Well the Weapon of Criticism and Self-Criticism" [用好批评和自我批评的武器]. *China Discipline Inspection News* [中国纪检监察报], January 2. http://jjjcb.cn/content/2019-08/30/content_81288.htm.

Liu, Yanhui. 2009. "Thoughts on Livelihood News" [民生新闻的民生式思考]. *Today's Mass Media* [今传媒], no. 9, 81–82.

Lorentzen, Peter. 2014. "China's Strategic Censorship." *American Journal of Political Science* 58 (2): 402–14.

———. 2017. "Designing Contentious Politics in Post-1989 China." *Modern China* 43 (5): 459–93.

Lu, Jie, and Tianjian Shi. 2015. "The Battle of Ideas and Discourses before Democratic Transition: Different Democratic Conceptions in Authoritarian China." *International Political Science Review* 36 (1): 20–41.

Lucardi, Adrián. 2019. "Strength in Expectation: Elections, Economic Performance, and Authoritarian Breakdown." *Journal of Politics* 81 (2): 552–70.

Luehrmann, Laura M. 2003. "Facing Citizen Complaints in China, 1951–1996." *Asian Survey* 43 (5): 845–66.

Lukes, Steven. 2005. *Power: A Radical View*. 2nd ed. New York: Palgrave Macmillan.

Luo, Yadong. 2008. "The Changing Chinese Culture and Business Behavior: The Perspective of Intertwinement between Guanxi and Corruption." *International Business Review* 17 (2): 188–93.

Lust-Okar, Ellen. 2005. *Structuring Conflict in the Arab World: Incumbents, Opponents, and Institutions*. Cambridge: Cambridge University Press.

Magaloni, Beatriz. 2006. *Voting for Autocracy: Hegemonic Party Survival and Its Demise in Mexico*. Cambridge: Cambridge University Press.

Malecha, Gary Lee, and Daniel J. Reagan. 2012. *The Public Congress: Congressional Deliberation in a New Media Age*. New York: Routledge.

Manion, Melanie. 1985. "The Cadre Management System, Post-Mao: The Appointment, Promotion, Transfer and Removal of Party and State Leaders." *China Quarterly* 102:203–33.

———. 2015. *Information for Autocrats: Representation in Chinese Local Congresses*. Cambridge: Cambridge University Press.

Mao, Zedong. 1944. "Serving the People" [为人民服务]. *The Liberation Daily* [解放日报], September 21.

———. (1929) 1951. "On Correcting Wrong Thoughts within the Party" [关于纠正党内的错误思想]. In *Selected Works of Mao Zedong*. Vol. 1 [毛泽东选集], 85–96. Beijing: People's Publisher.

———. (1959) 1968. "Politicians Should Create Newspapers" [要政治家办报]. In *Long Live Mao Zedong Thought* [毛泽东思想万岁]. Wuhan: Wuhan University Publisher.

McCubbins, Mathew D., and Thomas Schwartz. 1984. "Congressional Oversight Overlooked: Police Patrols versus Fire Alarms." *American Journal of Political Science* 28 (1): 165–179.

Meng, Tianguang, Jennifer Pan, and Ping Yang. 2017. "Conditional Receptivity to Citizen Participation: Evidence from a Survey Experiment in China." *Comparative Political Studies* 50 (4): 399–433.

Mertha, Andrew C. 2006. "Policy Enforcement Markets: How Bureaucratic Redundancy Contributes to Effective Intellectual Property Implementation in China." *Comparative Politics* 38 (3): 295–316.

———. 2009. "'Fragmented Authoritarianism 2.0': Political Pluralization in the Chinese Policy Process." *China Quarterly* 200:995–1012.

Meyer, David, Victor C. Shih, and Jonghyuk Lee. 2016. "Factions of Different Stripes: Gauging the Recruitment Logics of Factions in the Reform Period." *Journal of East Asian Studies* 16 (1): 43–60.

Miao, Di. 2011. "Between Propaganda and Commercials: Chinese Television Today." In *Changing Media, Changing China*, edited by Susan L. Shirk, 91–114. Oxford: Oxford University Press.

Michelson, Ethan. 2007. "Climbing the Dispute Pagoda: Grievances and Appeals to the Official Justice System in Rural China." *American Sociological Review* 72 (3): 459–85.

Miller, Alice L. 2016. "Projecting the Next Politburo Standing Committee." *China Leadership Monitor*, no. 49 (Winter). https://www.hoover.org/sites/default/files/research/docs/clm49am.pdf.

Minzner, Carl. 2015. "Legal Reform in the Xi Jinping Era." *Asia Policy*, no. 20, 4–9.

———. 2018. *End of an Era: How China's Authoritarian Revival is Undermining Its Rise*. Oxford: Oxford University Press.

Mudde, Cas, and Cristóbal Rovira Kaltwassver. 2017. *Populism: A Very Short Introduction*. Oxford: Oxford University Press.

Nadeau, Richard, Vincent Arel-Bundock and Jean-François Daoust. 2019. "Satisfaction with Democracy and the American Dream." *Journal of Politics* 81 (3): 1080–84.

Nathan, Andrew J. 2003. "Authoritarian Resilience." *Journal of Democracy* 14 (1): 6–17.

———. 2009. "Authoritarian Impermanence." *Journal of Democracy* 20 (3): 37–40.

Newland, Sara A. 2018. "Innovators and Implementers: The Multilevel Politics of Civil Society Governance in Rural China." *China Quarterly* 233:22–42.

O'Brien, Kevin J., and Lianjiang Li. 1995. "The Politics of Lodging Complaints in Rural China." *China Quarterly* 143:756–83.

———. 1999. "Selective Policy Implementation in Rural China." *Comparative Politics* 31 (2): 167–86.

———. 2006. *Rightful Resistance in Rural China*. Cambridge: Cambridge University Press.

Ong, Lynette H. 2012. "Between Developmental and Clientelist States: Local State-Business Relationships in China." *Comparative Politics* 44 (2): 191–209.

Pan, Jennifer. 2019. "How Chinese Officials Use the Internet to Construct Their Public Image." *Political Science Research and Methods* 7 (2): 197–213.

Pan, Jennifer, and Kaiping Chen. 2018. "Concealing Corruption: How Chinese Officials Distort Upward Reporting of Online Grievances." *American Political Science Review* 112 (3): 602–20.

Pan, Zhongdang, and Joseph M. Chan. 2003. "Shifting Journalistic Paradigms: How China's Journalists Assess 'Media Exemplars.'" *Communication Research* 30 (6): 649–82.

Pang, Baoqing, Shu Keng, and Lingna Zhong. 2018. "Sprinting with Small Steps: China's Cadre Management and Authoritarian Resilience." *China Journal* 80:68–93.

Parascandola, Mark, and Lin Xiao. 2019. "Tobacco and the Lung Cancer Epidemic in China." *Translational Lung Cancer Research* 8 (S1): S21–S30.

Perry, Elizaebeth J. 2008. "Chinese Conceptions of 'Rights': From Mencius to Mao—and Now." *Perspectives on Politics* 6 (1): 37–50.

Przeworski, Adam. 1985. *Capitalism and Social Democracy*. Cambridge: Cambridge University Press.

Qian, Gang, and David Bandurski. 2011. "China's Emerging Public Sphere: The Impact of Media Commercialization, Professionalism, and the Internet in an Era of Transition." In *Changing Media, Changing China*, edited by Susan L. Shirk, 38–76. Oxford: Oxford University Press.

Qiu, Weirong. 2011. "Guangzhou Will Install GPS on Public Cars; Non-public Use Will Be Charged Based on Kilometers" [广州公车将装GPS跟踪管理, 非公务用车按公里收费]. *Guangzhou Daily* [广州日报], February 23. http://www.chinanews.com/gn/2011/02-23/2861172.shtml.

Orwell, George. (1949) 1961. *1984*. New York: New American Library.

Ramzy, Austin. 2014. "Assault by City Management Officers Triggers Clash." *New York Times*, April 21. https://sinosphere.blogs.nytimes.com/2014/04/21/assault-by-city-management-officers-triggers-clash/.

Randall, Vicky. 1993. "The Media and Democratisation in the Third World." *Third World Quarterly* 14 (3): 625–46.

Remington, Thomas F. 2018. "Bureaucratic Politics and Labour Policy in China." *China: An International Journal* 16 (3): 97–119.

Regulations on Intraparty Supervision of the Chinese Communist Party (Trial). 2004. http://cpc.people.com.cn/GB/33838/2539945.html.

Repnikova, Maria. 2017a. *Media Politics in China: Improvising Power under Authoritarianism*. Cambridge: Cambridge University Press.

———. 2017b. "Thought Work Contested: Ideology and Journalism Education in China." *China Quarterly* 230:399–419.

Roberts, Margaret E. 2018. *Censored: Distraction and Diversion inside China's Great Firewall*. Princeton, NJ: Princeton University Press.

Rocca, Jean-Louis. 2017. "Governing from the Middle? Understanding the Making of China's Middle Classes." In *To Govern China: Evolving Practices of Power*, edited by Vivienne Shue and Patricia M. Thornton, 231–55. Cambridge: Cambridge University Press.

Rozenas, Arturas, and Denis Stukal. 2019. "How Autocrats Manipulate Economic News: Evidence from Russia's State-Controlled Television." *Journal of Politics* 81 (3): 982–96.

Schudson, Michael. 2002. "The News Media as Political Institutions." *Annual Review of Political Science* 5:249–69.

Shao, Li. 2018. "The Dilemma of Criticism: Disentangling the Determinants of Media Censorship in China." *Journal of East Asian Studies* 18 (3): 279–97.

Shi, Tianjian, and Jie Lu. 2010. "The Shadow of Confucianism." *Journal of Democracy* 21 (4): 123–30.

Shi, Yaojiang, and John James Kennedy. 2016. "Delayed Registration and Identifying the 'Missing Girls' in China." *China Quarterly* 228:1018–38.

Shih, Victor. 2008. "'Nauseating' Displays of Loyalty: Monitoring the Factional Bargain through Ideological Campaigns in China." *Journal of Politics* 70 (4): 1177–92.

Shih, Victor, Christopher Adolph, and Mingxing Liu. 2012. "Getting Ahead in the Communist Party: Explaining the Advancement of Central Committee Members in China." *American Political Science Review* 106 (1): 166–87.

Shirk, Susan L. 2011. "Changing Media, Changing China." In *Changing Media, Changing China*, edited by Susan L. Shirk, 1–37. Oxford: Oxford University Press.

Shue, Vivienne, and Patricia M. Thornton. 2017. "Introduction: Beyond Implicit Political Dichotomies and Linear Models of Change in China." In *To Govern China: Evolving Practices of Power*, edited by Vivienne Shue and Patricia M. Thornton, 1–26. Cambridge: Cambridge University Press.

Skidmore, Thomas E., ed. 1993. *Television, Politics, and the Transition to Democracy in Latin America*. Baltimore: Johns Hopkins University Press.

Sorace, Christian. 2016. "Party Spirit Made Flesh: The Production of Legitimacy in the Aftermath of the 2008 Sichuan Earthquake." *China Journal* 76:41–62.

Sparrow, Bartholomew H. 1999. *Uncertain Guardians: The News Media as a Political Institution*. Baltimore: Johns Hopkins University Press.

Stern, Rachel E., and Jonathan Hassid. 2012. "Amplifying Silence: Uncertainty and Control Parables in Contemporary China." *Comparative Political Studies* 45 (10): 1230–54.

Stern, Rachel E., and Kevin J. O'Brien. 2012. "Politics at the Boundary: Mixed Signals and the Chinese State." *Modern China* 38 (2): 174–98.

Stockmann, Daniela. 2010. "Information Overload? Collecting, Managing, and Analyzing Chinese Media Content." In *Contemporary Chinese Politics: New Sources, Methods, and Field Strategies*, edited by Allen Carlson, Mary E. Gallagher, Kenneth Lieberthal, and Melanie Manion, 107–25. New York: Cambridge University Press.

———. 2013. *Media Commercialization and Authoritarian Rule in China*. Cambridge: Cambridge University Press.

Stockmann, Daniela, and Mary E. Gallagher. 2011. "Remote Control: How the Media Sustain Authoritarian Rule in China." *Comparative Political Studies* 44 (4): 436–67.

Sun, Yüsheng. 2003. *Ten Years: From changing television language*. [十年: 从改变电视的语态开始] Beijing: Sanlian Books.

Svensson, Marina. 2017. "The Rise and Fall of Investigative Journalism in China: Digital Opportunities and Political Challenges." *Media, Culture and Society* 39 (3): 440–45.

Swider, Sarah. 2015. "Reshaping China's Urban Citizenship: Street Vendors, *Chengguan* and Struggles over the Right to the City." *Critical Sociology* 41 (4–5): 701–16.

Tang, Beibei. 2020. "Grid Governance in China's Urban Middle-Class Neighbourhoods." *China Quarterly* 241:43–61.

Teets, Jessica C. 2014. *Civil Society under Authoritarianism: The China Model*. Cambridge: Cambridge University Press.

Teets, Jessica C., Reza Hasmath, and Orion A. Lewis. 2017. "The Incentive to Innovate? The Behavior of Local Policymakers in China." *Journal of Chinese Political Science* 22:505–17.

Teets, Jessica C., and William Hurst. 2014. *Local Governance Innovation in China: Experimentation, Diffusion, and Defiance*. London: Routledge.

Thornton, Patricia M. 2017. "A New Urban Underclass? Making and Managing 'Vulnerable Groups' in Contemporary China." In *To Govern China: Evolving Practices of Power*, edited by Vivienne Shue and Patricia M. Thornton, 257–81. Cambridge: Cambridge University Press.

Tomba, Luigi. 2014. *The Government Next Door: Neighborhood Politics in Urban China*. Ithaca, NY: Cornell University Press.

———. 2017. "Finding China's Urban: Bargained Land Conversions, Local Assemblages, and Fragmented Urbanization." In *To Govern China: Evolving Practices of Power*, edited by Vivienne Shue and Patricia M. Thornton, 203–27. Cambridge: Cambridge University Press.

Tong, Jingrong. 2010. "The Crisis of the Centralized Media Control Theory: How Local Power Controls Media in China." *Media, Culture and Society* 32 (6): 925–42.

———. 2011. *Investigative Journalism in China: Journalism, Power, and Society.* London: Continuum.

Tong, Jingrong, and Colin Sparks. 2009. "Investigative Journalism in China Today." *Journalism Studies* 10 (3): 337–52.

Truex, Rory. 2016. *Making Autocracy Work: Representation and Responsiveness in Modern China.* Cambridge: Cambridge University Press.

Tsai, Kellee S. 2006. "Adaptive Informal Institutions and Endogenous Institutional Change in China." *World Politics* 59 (1): 116–41.

Tsai, Lily L. 2007. *Accountability without Democracy: Solidary Groups and Public Goods Provision in Rural China.* New York: Cambridge University Press.

Tsai, Wen-Hsuan, and Peng-Hsiang Kao. 2013. "Secret Codes of Political Propaganda: The Unknown System of Writing Teams." *China Quarterly* 214:394–410.

Van Aelst, Peter, and Stefaan Walgrave, eds. 2017. *How Political Actors Use the Media: A Functional Analysis of the Media's Role in Politics.* New York: Palgrave Macmillan.

Van Aken, Tucker, and Orion A. Lewis. 2015. "The Political Economy of Noncompliance in China: The Case of Industrial Energy Policy." *Journal of Contemporary China* 24 (95): 798–822.

Vinson, C. Danielle. 2017. *Congress and the Media: Beyond Institutional Power.* New York: Oxford University Press.

Volland, Nicolai. 2012. "From Control to Management: The CCP's 'Reforms of the Cultural Structure.'" In *China's Thought Management*, edited by Anne-Marie Brady, 107–21. London: Routledge.

Wang, Bing. 2011. "Observations on Guangzhou Livelihood News" [广州本地民生新闻的生存观察]. *Media Digest* [传媒透视], no. 6, 8–10.

Wang, Haiyan, and Colin Sparks. 2019. "Chinese Newspaper Groups in the Digital Era: The Resurgence of the Party Press." *Journal of Communication* 69 (1): 94–119.

Wang, Jiamin. 2009. "Central Government Promotes Direct Provincial Management of Counties; Counties Party Secretaries to Be Appointed by Provincial Party Committees" [中央力推省直管县，县委书记将由省委直接任命]. *China News Weekly* [中国新闻周刊], July 23. http://politics.people.com.cn/GB/1026/9707456.html.

Wang, Juan. 2017. *The Sinews of State Power: The Rise and Demise of the Cohesive Local State in Rural China.* New York: Oxford University Press.

Wang, Peng, Li-Fung Cho, and Ren Li. 2018. "An Institutional Explanation of Media Corruption in China." *Journal of Contemporary China* 27 (113): 748–62.

Wang, Ruosi. 2011. "On the Current State of 'Life News' and Its Future Development" [民生新闻现状与出路的思考]. *Today's Mass Media* [今传媒], no. 8, 127–28.

Wang, Shaojun, and Fuxing Zhang. 2009. *Anticorruption Storm: The First Anti-corruption Battle after the Founding of the Republic* [反腐风暴: 开过肃贪第一战]. Beijing: Party History Publisher.

Wang, Shaolei. 2006. "The Meaning and the Road Ahead for New Livelihood News" ["新民生新闻"的意义和出路]. *News Research* [新闻研究], no. 6, 67–69.

Wang, Shichuan. 2011. "Public Cars with GPS Monitor: This Is Good!" [公车用GPS监控, 这个可以有!]. *People's Daily* [人民日报], January 30. http://opinion.people.com.cn/GB/13845042.html.

Wang, Yiming. 2017. "Urbanization in China since Reform and Opening-Up." In *Challenges in the Process of China's Urbanization*, edited by Karen Eggleston, Jean C. Oi, and Wang Yiming, 15–29. Washington, DC: Brookings Institution Press.

Wang, Yuhua. 2014. *Tying the Autocrats' Hands: The Rise of the Rule of Law in China*. New York: Cambridge University Press.

Wang, Yuhua, and Carl Minzner. 2015. "The Rise of the Chinese Security State." *China Quarterly* 222:339–59.

Weller, Robert P. 2017. "Shared Fictions and Informal Politics in China." In *To Govern China: Evolving Practices of Power*, edited by Vivienne Shue and Patricia M. Thornton, 154–73. Cambridge: Cambridge University Press.

White, Stephen, Sarah Oates, and Ian McAllister. 2005. "Media Effects and Russian Elections, 1999–2000." *British Journal of Political Science* 35 (2): 191–208.

Whiting, Susan H. 1996. "Contract Incentives and Market Discipline in China's Rural Industrial Sector." In *Reforming Asian Socialism: The Growth of Market Institutions*, edited by John McMillan and Barry Naughton, 63–110. Ann Arbor: University of Michigan Press.

———. 2004. "The Cadre Evaluation System at the Grass Roots: The Paradox of Party Rule." In *Holding China Together: Diversity and National Integration in the Post-Deng Era*, edited by Barry J. Naughton and Dali L. Yang, 101–19. New York: Cambridge University Press.

———. 2011. *Power and Wealth in Rural China: The Political Economy of Institutional Change*. New York: Cambridge University Press.

Wong, Edward. 2016. "Chinese Leader's News Flash: Journalists Must Serve Party." *New York Times*, February 23.

Wu, Guoguang. 2015. *China's Party Congress: Power, Legitimacy, and Institutional Manipulation*. Cambridge: Cambridge University Press.

Xi, Jinping. 2016. *Selected Works by Xi Jinping on Comprehensively and Strictly Ruling the Party* [习近平关于全面从严治党论述摘编]. Beijing: Central Literature Publisher.

Xie, Yungeng, and Hongfeng Zhou. 2005. "Report on Competitions of Chinese TV News Programs" [中国电视新闻竞争报告]. *World of Sight and Sound* [视听界], no. 1, 4–14.

Xu, Bin. 2012. "Grandpa Wen: Scene and Political Performance." *Sociological Theory* 30 (2): 114–29.Xu, Juan, and Ge Ni. 2018. "Why Is Illegal Construction So Prevalent" [私搭乱建为何如此任性]. *People's Daily* [人民日报], January 17. http://data.people.com.cn/rmrb/20180117/17.

Xu, Xin. 2009. "The Current State of the Chinese Television Program Evaluation System and Thoughts on Its Reform" [中国电机节目评估机制的现状及改革设想]. *Today's Mass Media* [今传媒], no. 8, 43–45.

Yang, Guobin. 2010. "Brokering Environment and Health in China: Issue Entrepreneurs of the Public Sphere." *Journal of Contemporary China* 19 (63): 101–18.

Yang, Guobin, and Craig Calhoun. 2007. "Media, Civil Society, and the Rise of a Green Public Sphere in China." *China Information* 21 (2): 211–36.

Yang, Hongxing, and Dingxin Zhao. 2015. "Performance Legitimacy, State Autonomy and China's Economic Miracle." *Journal of Contemporary China* 24 (91): 64–82.

Yang, Yuan, Min Tang, Wang Zhou, and Narisong Huhe. 2014. "The Effect of Media Use on Institutional Trust in China." *Problems of Post-Communism* 61 (3): 45–56.

Ye, Hao. 2008. "On Learning from the Mechanism in Which the American Government Deals with the Media" [美国政府的媒体应对机制及其启示]. *Jianghai Journal* [江海学刊], no. 8. http://gb.oversea.cnki.net/KCMS/detail/detail.aspx?filename=JHXK200803019&dbcode=CJFD&dbname=CJFD2008.

Yin, Yungong. 2017. "Adhere to and Advance the Integration of Intraparty Supervision and Public Opinion Supervision" [坚持和推进党内监督与舆论监督相结合]. *Party Literature* [党的文献], no. 3. https://www.wxyjs.org.cn/ddwxzzs/wzjx/20170706/201707/t20170706_224587.htm.

Zand, Dale E. 1997. *The Leadership Triad: Knowledge, Trust, and Power.* New York: Oxford University Press.

Zang, Xiaowei, and John Pratt. 2019. "Are Street-Level Bureaucrats in China Hardnosed Cops or Consultants? An Institutional Account of Policing Behavior in Autocracy." *Journal of Contemporary China* 28 (116): 232–44.

Zeng, Wenna, Colin Sparks. 2019. "Production and Politics in Chinese Television." *Media, Culture and Society* 41 (1): 54–69.

Zhan, Xueyong, Carlos Wing-Hung Lo, and Shui-Yan Tang. 2014. "Contextual Changes and Environmental Policy Implementation: A Longitudinal Study of Street-Level Bureaucrats in Guangzhou, China." *Journal of Public Administration Research and Theory* 24 (4): 1005–35.

Zhang, Bo, and Cong Cao. 2015. "Four Gaps in China's New Environmental Law." *Nature* 517 (7535): 433–435.

Zhang, Jiangeng, and Jia Wang. 2012. *Manufactured by Zero Distance* (零距离制造). Nanjing: Nanjing Publisher.

Zhang, Junchang, and Jiangeng Zhang. 2012. *21 Century Trends in Chinese Radio and Television* [21世纪中国广播电视大趋势]. Beijing: China Radio and Television Publishing House [中国广播电视出版社].

Zhang, Lei. 2016. "Profoundly Understanding the Important Exposition of Comrade Xi Jinping on News Public Opinion Work." *Chinese Journalists*, no. 3. http://www.xinhuanet.com/zgjx/2016-03/14/c_135185092.htm.

Zhang, Xiaoling. 2007. "Breaking News, Media Coverage and 'Citizen's Right to Know' in China." *Journal of Contemporary China* 16 (53): 535–45.

Zhang, Zhi'an, and Fei Shen. 2012. "Investigative Reporters' Job Satisfaction and Its Antecedents." [调查记者的职业满意度及影响因素研究] *Journalism and Communication Research* [新闻与传播研究] 19 (4): 64–75.

Zhao, Dingxin. 2009. "The Mandate of Heaven and Performance Legitimation in Historical and Contemporary China." *American Behavioral Scientist* 53 (3): 416–33.

Zhao, Gang. 2017. "Accurately Demolish Illegal Construction; Create a More Beautiful Urban Environment for the People—an Interview with the Deputy Head of Shijingshan District Government of Beijing Li Jinke" [精细拆违, 为民打造更加优美的城市环境——访北京市石景山区人民政府副区长李金克]. *Urban Management and Technology* [城市管理与科技], no. 5, 64–67.

Zhao, Yuezhi. 1998. *Media, Market, and Democracy in China: Between the Party Line and the Bottom Line.* Urbana: University of Illinois Press.

———. 2004. "The State, the Market, and Media Control in China." In *Who Owns the Media: Global Trends and Local Resistance*, edited by Pradip N. Thomas and Zaharom Nain, 179–212. London: Zed Books.

———. 2008. *Communication in China: Political Economy, Power, and Conflict.* Lanham, MD: Rowman and Littlefield.

———. 2011. "Sustaining and Contesting Revolutionary Legacies in Media and Ideology." In *Mao's Invisible Hand: The Political Foundations of Adaptive Governance in China*, Sebastian Heilmann and Elizabeth J. Perry, 201–36. Cambridge, MA: Harvard University Press.

Zhao, Yuezhi, and Wusan Sun. 2007. "Public Opinion Supervision: Possibilities and Limits of the Media in Constraining Local Officials." In *Grassroots Political Reform in Contemporary China*, edited by Elizabeth J. Perry and Merle Goldman, 300–24. Cambridge, MA: Harvard University Press.

Zhao, Ziyang. 1987. "Report to the 13th Chinese Communist Party Congress" [赵紫阳在中国共产党第十三次全国代表大会上的报告]. October 25. http://cpc.people.com.cn/GB/64162/64168/64566/65447/4526368.html.

Zheng, Siqi, Matthew E. Kahn, Weizeng Sun, and Danglun Luo. 2014. "Incentives for China's Urban Mayors to Mitigate Pollution Externalities: The Role of the Central Government and Public Environmentalism." *Regional Science and Urban Economics* 47:61–71.

Zhou, Shuhua, Hongzhong Zhang, and Bin Shen. 2014. "Comparison and Magnitude Credibility: Whom to Trust When Reports Are Conflicting?" *Open Communication Journal* 8:1–8.

Zhou, Titi, and Judy Xinyu Cai. 2020. "How Are the Exposed Disciplined? Media and Political Accountability in China." *Journal of Contemporary China* 29 (122): 286–303.

Zhou, Yuezhi. 2000. "Watchdogs on Party Leashes? Contexts and Implications of Investigative Journalism in Post-Deng China." *Journalism Studies* 1 (4): 577–97.

Zhu, Hong. 2008. "Chinese Television in Transition: Commemorating the 50th Anniversary of Chinese Television" [中国电视在转折中——纪念中国电视诞生50周年]. *China Radio and TV Academic Journal* [中国广播电视学刊], no. 9, 18–19.

Zhu, Ying. 2012. *Tow Billion Eyes: The Story of China Central Television*. New York: New Press.

Zhu, Ying, and Chris Berry, eds. 2009. *TV China*. Bloomington: Indiana University Press.

Zhu, Yuchao. 2011. "'Performance Legitimacy' and China's Political Adaptation Strategy." *Journal of Chinese Political Science* 16:123–40.

Index